The Crescent and the Pen

The Crescent and the Pen

The Strange Journey of
Taslima Nasreen

Hanifa Deen

Westport, Connecticut
London

Library of Congress Cataloging-in-Publication Data

Deen, Hanifa.
    The crescent and the pen : the strange journey of Taslima Nasreen / Hanifa Deen.
      p.   cm.
    Includes bibliographical references and index.
    ISBN 0–275–99167–9 (alk. paper)
    1. Nāsarina, Tasalimā—Censorship.   2. Nāsarina, Tasalimā—Exile.   3. Nāsarina,
    Tasalimā—Political and social views.   4. Women authors, Bengali—Bangladesh—
    Biography.   5. Islamic fundamentalism.   6. Politics and literature.   I. Title.
    PK1730.3.A65Z66   2006
    891′.4417—dc22   2006021039
    [B]

British Library Cataloguing in Publication Data is available.

Library of Congress Catalog Card Number: 2006021039
ISBN: 0–275–99167–9

First published in 2006

Praeger Publishers, 88 Post Road West, Westport, CT 06881
An imprint of Greenwood Publishing Group, Inc.
www.praeger.com

Printed in the United States of America

The paper used in this book complies with the
Permanent Paper Standard issued by the National
Information Standards Organization (Z39.48–1984).

10 9 8 7 6 5 4 3 2 1

Copyright Acknowledgments:
Grateful acknowledgment is made to the following for permission to reprint previously
published material:
Professor Kabir Chowdhury: *100 Poems of Taslima Nasreen*, Dhaka 1997.
Meredith Tax: 'For the People Hear Us Singing, "Bread and Roses! Bread and Roses!" ' in
The Feminist Memoir Project, ed. Rachel Blau DuPleiss and Ann Snitow, New York, Crown,
1998; 'Women and Her Mind: The Story of Daily Life', New England Press, 1970.

There are also the poems, speeches and essays written by Taslima Nasreen. Although much
of her earlier writing has not yet been translated from her mother tongue Bengali, in 1997
Taslima kindly gave me access to some English translations, which, at the time, were
unpublished.

Every attempt has been made to gain copyright permission for additional quotations used.

For Franz Oswald, in gratitude for
never tiring of me or Taslima

Contents

Acknowledgments

I am always amazed at how people are willing to help a stranger who disrupts their work and then, having stolen pieces of their lives, moves on. I thank the many people who have helped me for the information and insights they shared so unselfishly. Most of them are mentioned in the book, so I will only list those who are not named. My apologies to anyone I have overlooked.

I am indebted to Liz Wane for her invaluable research assistance during my first trip to Bangladesh. Liz did more than assist; her experience of working with Dhaka journalists opened doors and was invaluable. I also thank my partner Dr Franz Oswald for translating German and French materials.

Further away from home, I thank Arne Ruth, Azar Nahloujian, Elisabeth Zila, Monica Nagler, Morten Haahr, Ursula Setzer, Barbara Frank, Thorvald Steen, Angelika Pathal; Sandra Kabir, Syed Mahmoud Ali and Mirza Hassan. In Calcutta, Dr Indira Chowdhury, and her colleagues from Jadavpur University, as well as Soumitra Mitra and S. Dasgupta; in Sydney thanks to Dr Devleena Ghosh.

I regret that I can only name a few of the people who helped me in Dhaka: my good friend, journalist Saiful Amin, never failed to come to my rescue. I am especially grateful to the many other journalists in Dhaka and Mymensingh who helped me and never turned down the opportunity for a good argument. Thanks also to Hasarul Huq Inu, Anis Alamgir, Tasmima Hossain, Faustina Pereira, Dr Sonia Amin, Dr Islam Chowdhury, Dr Firdous Azim, Shireen Huq, Dr Shameen Chowdhury.

I am grateful for the funding provided by the Australia Council for the Arts, the Australian government's arts funding and advisory body.

The State of Western Australia has made an investment in this project through ArtsWA.

Sources

Nearly two hundred hours of taped interviews from more than one hundred interviewees form the foundation of this book. These 'conversations' took place between December 1995 and March 2000. To piece together the story of what happened to Taslima Nasreen in 1994, I visited Bangladesh five times in all, for a total of six months. Other cities I traveled to because they were part of the Taslima story include Calcutta, London, Stockholm, Copenhagen, Helsinki, Paris, Berlin, Cologne, New York, Atlanta and Sydney.

Numerous articles and press clippings in English, French, German and US newspapers appearing in the text were valuable sources, which provided not only facts, but also prevailing media attitudes coloured by the Salman Rushdie experience and global politics. This also applies to the articles I read from the Indian media published in 1993–1994. When juxtaposed against Bangladeshi print media sources, in English and Bengali—which I was able to have translated—they reveal just how complex the story was and the role played by mythmakers of all persuasions in many different parts of the world.

My work has also been vastly informed by access to archival materials held by Burkhard Mueller-Ullrich in Berlin, Niels Barfoed in Copenhagen, Meredith Tax of Women's WORLD New York, Christian John from the German Humanists' Organisation, and the Berlin office of the German Academic Exchange Service.

There were a number of books that I found most useful:

Ali Riaz, *Voice and Silence: Contextualizing Taslima Nasreen*, Ankur Prakashani, Dhaka, 1995;

Briefe an Taslima Nasrin, Kore Verlag, 1995, with Reporters sans frontièrs and the *taz*;

Fiction, Fact and the Fatwa 2000 Days of Censorship, compiled by Carmel Bedford, Article 19, London, 1994;

Burkhard Mueller-Ullrich, *Medienmarchen: Gesinnungstaeter im Journalismus* (Media Fairy Tales: Perpetrators out of Conviction), Goldmann Verlag, Munich, 1998.

Author's Note

In the eyes of most of the world, the writer Taslima Nasreen stands as a symbol of resistance against Islamist fanatics, male oppression and those who would curtail freedom of expression in one form or the other. She is widely admired and acclaimed by an international coalition of people passionately engaged in the politics of freedom of expression who at first lauded her as 'the female Rushdie'. This has given rise to a mythology in the West which eulogises her past exploits and makes little attempt to understand the political drama in which she became embroiled after a warrant for her arrest was issued by the Bangladesh Government charging her with injuring religious sentiment. This charge led to anti Taslima riots which, in turn, forced her into hiding and eventually to leave the country surrounded by secrecy and ill will.

In the eyes of many of her fellow countrymen in Bangladesh, however, she is a reckless, self-willed and ambitious woman of no particular literary worth who played into the hands of two different groups of extremists: firstly the religious fanatics and Islamic-based political parties, large and small, inside Bangladesh; and secondly, just across the border—their mirror image—the Hindu supremacists who, at the time of the 'Taslima crisis' in 1994, were growing in strength and within two years would form a national coalition government in India. In her own country this has given rise to a mythology which, by and large, rejects her and in some quarters demonises her.

But when I first came across the Taslima story, these contradictions were hidden from me for I was watching her case from a distance. My only information came from Western media sources, leaving me blinded by my own imagination, yet free to embellish what I was seeing on television screens and reading in the papers—like everyone else at the time. The newspaper accounts of huge crowds rallying against the author in Dhaka, urging the Bangladesh Government to place her on trial and punish her for anti-Islamic comments caught, and held, my interest.

At the time I had decided to write a book about Muslim women. I remember feeling guilty that I was able to write about Muslims and female discrimination—be as critical and as searching as I chose—without running the gauntlet of censorship, let alone the threat of physical danger, like the Bangladeshi author.

But there came a time when I began to sense that the relatively simple tale of a persecuted writer threatened by Muslim fanatics was acquiring a complicated life of its own and evolving into a narrative with huge emotive power for two sides facing each other across the barricades: those using Islam for political purposes, labelled Religious Fundamentalists, versus Post-Enlightenment Fundamentalists who regard freedom of speech as an absolute and see a uniformly threatening world of demons and dragons in what they like to call 'The Islamic World'.

The picture of Bangladesh being constructed by Western media sources was a Bangladesh I found hard to recognise. The anti-Taslima rallies and the demonstrations the media saw through the eyes of their camera lens made for a 'Grand *Tamasha*', a wonderful show. Bangladeshis saw the demonstrations through different eyes and gradually, so did I.

I started to look beyond the shouting and noticed the silences. The only female voices defending Nasreen publicly were voices from the West. Where were the voices of Bangladeshi feminists? Bangladesh had a seasoned women's movement, why were they silent? Could it be jealousy? Were they being gagged by the Government? Surely Bangladeshi women supported her? And where were all the male secularists and intellectuals hiding?

There must be more to the Taslima Nasreen story, I told myself, than I was reading in print and watching on my television screen. At first it was only a faint suspicion, but the seed started to grow after I went to Bangladesh in December 1995 and began talking to local journalists and women activists. These voices the Western media had ignored. When we first met they were recovering from the events of 1994; they'd had their fill of foreigners asking questions about Taslima Nasreen and felt their country was being maligned in the eyes of the world, and while they supported the principle of free speech, they held Nasreen largely responsible for her own fall from grace. I knew there were other voices and other stories. For the first time I began thinking in terms of a Taslima mythology and asked myself whose needs it served.

For the moment I turned away; my focus became fixed on stories connected to the women's movement, which eventually became a book on Bangladesh and Pakistani women, although I wrote a chapter on Taslima in *Broken Bangles* that asked more questions than it answered. Yet somehow I always knew that I would return to the Taslima story one day if only to discover why the author was cast in a different mould to everyone around her. The medical doctor–turned writer was a woman far ahead of her times and there was a sense of dark secrets and unhappy stories about her early years.

When I finally came face to face with Taslima Nasreen in late 1997, in Stockholm, I know there were times when she thought it contrary of me to pursue stories about her early life in Dhaka, but as I tried to explain to her—without great success—I wanted to discover the woman behind the poems and essays, to rouse the mythology and locate the source of her anger which has driven her for most of her life. I did not want to be fobbed off with partly invented anecdotes which she has shared in the past with fans and journalists beating a path to her door.

My journey on the trail of Taslima gained momentum in 1998 and I became immersed in a larger narrative of international literary politics. I returned to London, which became my headquarters for the three months I shifted between Stockholm, Copenhagen, Helsinki, Berlin, Cologne, Paris, New York and Atlanta, where I met leading activists from a number of freedom of expression organisations like Amnesty International, PEN, Article 19, Reporters sans frontièr, Human Rights Watch, Women's WORLD and their fellow travellers. I was impressed by their passion, their commitment and their honesty.

The book began to take on another dimension as I found myself drawn towards the politics of the human rights groups involved in 'rescuing' Taslima and the role played by the Indian and Western media—the Dragon Slayers as I began to think of them, for the most part fondly, in my mind.

But there were still missing pieces to the narrative that troubled me and so I found myself returning to Dhaka, five times in all, to assemble the final pieces of the Taslima puzzle. With the passage of time, people were willing to discuss what they had only hinted at in earlier visits and so I was able to learn more about the political tensions of 1994 and the role played by the judiciary of Bangladesh.

There were occasions when I felt trapped between two warring mythologies. On the one hand, many of the myths belonging to the official version, constructed by the West, with the help of India, were a weird and wonderful concoction of truths, half-truths and fabrications. Strong emotions were in play, based on a desire to compensate for what, at the time, appeared to be a lowering of the flag, or at the very least a stalemate in the long-drawn-out Rushdie–Iran confrontation, which lasted almost a decade, where the forces of Post-Enlightenment took on the forces of Religious

Obscurantism. On the other hand, the myths brewed by Taslima's enemies and critics were an incongruous mix of Islamic outrage—often genuine, sometimes assumed—scurrilous rumours, and a feeling of betrayal felt by many genuine progressive men and women in Bangladesh.

The Crescent and the Pen is not the story that freedom of expression activists around the world may want to see written; I can understand their feelings and even sympathise with their point of view—up to a point. Then again, Bangladeshi activists, who support secular politics and continue to confront religious militancy at home, may wish to read a narrative less critical of certain aspects of Bangladeshi cultural and political traditions.

Perhaps my version of the truth will please no one in the end: nobody, that is, except myself. And I won't quarrel with that for what kept me going as I moved from one Taslima city to the next was always my own need to know: to discover for myself the international cast of diverse characters, most of whom jostled each other in the wings of this writer's imagination as they waited their turn to appear on stage. As often happens in any production, the supporting cast contributed so much and received so little applause. As for the extras marching shoulder to shoulder in their street rallies threatening violence and eternal damnation to Taslima and other apostates, perhaps they received more attention from the television cameras than they deserved. For there were times when the leading character, Taslima Nasreen, crouched in the middle of all this turbulence, almost disappeared off stage to become an afterthought in her own personal drama.

The hidden story I discovered explains why Taslima Nasreen remains unwelcome in her own country and for eleven years has lived abroad, with the legal cases against her pending and her life on hold.

The Snake's Fangs—A Prologue

I have seen death. I have seen fire.
I have seen the snake's fangs

Taslima Nasreen, *Selected Columns*, 1989

The djinns escaped from the bottle that year, as djinns have a habit of doing in Dhaka, city of mosques and mega capital of Bangladesh. Of course the Sorcerers were working overtime in 1994 and summoning the demons of Lawlessness and Disorder was all in a day's work for the Greybeards. Heat, dust and pollution hovered over the crowded streets and narrow alleyways of the city, as did the long dark shadow of the Magicians. This time their target was a woman, an evil-doer, they said, who must be punished.

But as we know, not everyone was deceived by the Magicians' sleight of hand and political deftness. Madness did not go unchallenged in the traffic-choked streets of Dhaka, for the Secular Tribe was not slow to rally its supporters. Men and women in their thousands grappled with the djinns using incantations from their own holy books, the Law and the Constitution, to keep the Bearded Ones at bay.

Sixty days passed while Magic and the Law wrestled each other for control of the streets and the courtrooms. Violence begets violence in Bangladesh. It rushes in and then recedes like the floodwaters that cover the land.

In the collision of forces that took place in Bangladesh in 1994, there were no victors: in spite of the gamesmanship, neither side won in the end. The story I discovered was far more complex than the outside world ever imagined and in reality the woman was never the centre of everything as the foreign media led us to think at the time. For in June and July of that year, as we turned the pages and scanned the headlines, it was easy to believe that

1

another version of the Salman Rushdie saga was unfolding—this time with a female in the lead role. Once again the eyes of the world became focused on mad mullahs and mad mobs. But was the woman a second Rushdie, and was Bangladesh another Iran?

Taslima Nasreen's life went out of control on 4 June 1994, after the Bangladesh Government issued a warrant for her arrest under Section 295-A of the Bangladesh Penal Code. In this case, which is still pending, the State of Bangladesh is the complainant and Taslima Nasreen stands accused of deliberately hurting religious sentiment. There is a full measure of irony in the official indictment, for Bangladeshi parliaments have thus far resisted periodic calls for a blasphemy act, and the law the author is charged with breaking is secular—not religious. Enacted under British colonial rule, in 1860, at the time of an undivided India, the legislation was meant as a way of preventing Hindus and Muslims from vilifying and attacking each other: as history shows, it failed miserably at Partition. The law remains a relic of British colonial criminal law.

Taslima went underground before the warrant for her arrest was served and, in the eyes of the government, was officially a fugitive from justice. The comments she was alleged to have made took place during an interview she gave in India on 9 May 1994, later published in *The Statesman*, a Calcutta newspaper. She publicly denied that she had told the Indian reporter that the Qur'an should be thoroughly revised. Islam's central article of faith is the belief that the Qur'an is the literal word of God and thus above revision. In Medieval times dissenters have been put to death for publicly doubting this.

Taslima had founded her writing career by defying and ridiculing religious and social norms. Until now she had led a charmed life and escaped government censure. However, careless words, spoken to a journalist in neighbouring India, were about to land her in the Supreme Court. Oddly enough, it was the spoken word and not Taslima's poetry, novels and newspaper columns that provided the catalyst—more than a quirk of fate as I discovered. There were political games afoot and the unpopular feminist author—whom everybody read but few admired—became a pawn used by both the Government and the Islamist parties.

An outsider will most likely make a film about the 'Taslima Affair' one day; perhaps it will be an Indian production; there is a certain irony in that which makes me smile, for the Indian media worked hard at promoting her cause to the outside world and were the first to evoke the Rushdie analogy. But it will be an unworkable script and the facts will contort themselves into yet another version of the truth. The giant screen will have difficulty reflecting what really happened with the Taslima Nasreen story: its complex origins and its circulation and passage across time. But all the excitement and drama that signifies a 'Grand *Tamasha*' or 'Great Theatre' will be met. 'Bangladesh is so fascinating!' say the foreigners, and the Bangladeshis smile and say nothing.

The tabloid version offers up a technicolour melodrama: a lone woman writer doing daily battle with 'barbaric' Muslim fanatics; a variation of India's famous Bandit Queen-cum-politician, rescued just in time by the cavalry (read international forces); a woman escaping the country of her birth with a howling mob at her heels as she makes for the airport disguised in a long black veil. In this rendition Bangladesh and Iran are seen as one. This version refuses to go away and has spawned an entire legend, even though it parodies, even misconstrues, what really took place.

It really is a shame to embellish the facts. There is no need for fiction: the real story is fascinating enough.

Nevertheless, should they ever decide to turn the 'Taslima Affair' into a film, what a fine location the Supreme Court Building in Abdul Gani Road, Dhaka, would make. What better opening scene than Court Room Six on the morning of 4 August 1994 at 11:30. A long driveway leads up to a white stucco, three-storey building with broad verandahs and large court rooms, originally built in the days of the British Raj, but stylishly extended since then; the cast is ready and we watch as black-robed lawyers hurry along the tiled verandahs—a real courtroom drama is about to begin.

Today it was whispered, Taslima Nasreen, the writer, would come out of hiding at last and present herself to the High Court Division of the Supreme Court of Bangladesh. Sixty days had passed since she had 'disappeared' from sight, on 4 June 1994, to avoid being arrested for having injured religious [Islamic] sentiment.

Hiding with carefully selected strangers and moving from one location to the next, always at night, always hidden on the floor of the car, thirty-two-year-old Taslima stayed underground but remained alive in the headlines abroad. Journalists covering 'the Taslima crisis' were unaware, however, of another story hidden in the shadows. Since late June, negotiations had been going on behind the scenes between Taslima's lawyers, the Bangladesh Government, under the Bangladesh National Party (BNP), and certain countries of the international community with diplomatic missions in Dhaka. It would all come to fruition today. Those working behind the scenes acted quickly, knowing that the arrangements must be kept secret as long as possible from mullah-led extremists demanding her punishment.

Sara Hossain, a member of the Taslima Nasreen legal team, is the daughter of two of Bangladesh's most prominent human rights activists. She has her father's astute legal mind and her mother's patience and understanding of social change. The Hossain family willingly threw in their lot with the Taslima cause of civil liberties and freedom of expression. Some admirers said it was in their genes.

Sara has a foot in two worlds and spends half her time in London, where she works on matters of civil liberties: you might say she specialises in 'Blasphemy Laws'. We finally met face to face in London in 1998. The young lawyer emphasised that the constant pressure and lobbying from human rights groups, the back-room diplomatic exercises and the bonfire created by a zealous Western media, were all vitally important, but none of this, she argued—none of this—would have been enough to cut the Gordian knot without Bangladeshi law intervening.

Her arguments were persuasive, her insider's knowledge undeniable and she stopped me in my tracks, for, until my meeting with Sara, I'd given little thought to any domestic legal response. There was scant mention by Western media sources to the law having played any role at all in the Taslima drama.

'This was the key,' Sara kept insisting, 'to transforming a very fraught political situation into a legal problem which could be resolved through the law. In the end it became a simple matter about bail.'

To a legal mind, that sums up the situation neatly. But the law doesn't operate in a vacuum. I knew there were complicated manoeuvres going on behind the scenes that Sara could only hint at, involving senior ministers and bureaucrats, lawyers and diplomats. Although this never became public knowledge, we must rely on circumstantial evidence and the odd giveaway sign that the law and politics were not strangers. It was well disguised in 1994, as I later discovered.

What happened between June 4 when the Government's warrant went out for the author's arrest and the moment of her court appearance sixty days later? This is the fascinating story, but onlookers have always been distracted by the story Taslima likes to call 'My Sixty Days of Darkness'. This tabloid adventure is full of truths, half-truths and untruths, but it makes a damned good story. It also creates a smoke screen for which her lawyers and the handful of decent, courageous people who hid her must be grateful.

In reality, the main players knew that the Taslima crisis required a solution which would not compromise Bangladesh's sovereignty, remained within the law and took into account the human rights sensibilities of all the freedom of expression lobbyists around the world who had mounted an unrelenting campaign, dragging their respective governments into the fight. There were times when Taslima Nasreen, the person, became lost in the middle of all this 'diplomacy'.

✦

Taslima's legal team received half an hour's notice that their petition would be heard that morning and rushed their client to the court from her latest hiding place. A plea for bail was to be entered and couldn't be done in her absence. Speed, secrecy and a police escort added to the drama; at all costs they must avoid tipping the hand of certain mullah leaders who could summon a noisy mob of demonstrators in the wink of an eye.

'She's coming!' The word spread like ink on blotting paper. Along the corridors, from one floor to the next, lawyers and legal clerks told each other that Taslima 'was on'. Advocates rushed to the court room, hundreds filling a room meant to hold fifty, even spilling out onto the wide verandahs on this uncomfortably humid monsoon month. Everyone wanted to witness the outcome of this high profile case. Everyone wanted to show their support for freedom of speech and to stand shoulder-to-shoulder with the author and her highly respected legal team. Some human rights lawyers had shied away from this controversial case, but Taslima's defense team consisted of eight committed lawyers, people from different chambers, including young Sara Hossain. The case had been taken on a pro bono basis and was led by two of the country's most eminent barristers: Dr Kamal Hossain and Amrul Islam, both well-connected, politically astute men.

Sara and her girlfriend pushed their way to the front of the court through a throng of grumbling men who muttered loudly about the rude young women of today, but in the end made way. The women wanted to hear, word for word, the submissions by Sara's father, Kamal Hossain, and his colleague, the velvet-toned Amrul Islam.

After listening to the submission, the bench, consisting of two judges, promptly granted Taslima Nasreen bail under a Bangladeshi law which says that women, children and the infirm should be granted bail. Justice Sadeque (now retired) found it to be a bailable case—there was no question of that in his mind—he told me over lunch at the Bar Council in Dhaka five years later, and the Attorney General, Aminul Huq, a highly respected barrister with an outstanding human rights record, moved no objections.

A week before, Huq had urged lawyers, at a law seminar, to resist any attempts to introduce a blasphemy law, labeling it 'an attempt to send everybody back to the dark ages.' It contradicted the basic rights ensured in the Constitution and contradicted the teachings of Islam. 'Those who have the least idea about true Islam, democracy and human rights have devised the law.' For the defense team he was the ideal Prosecutor and the decision to have him lead the Government side was well thought out.

Eminent justices of the bench like to have their little laugh, and Justice Sadeque insisted that Taslima's defense counsel act as their client's guardians, meaning they must at all times know her whereabouts. Taslima didn't take kindly to male control and this was a hard thing for any man to enforce. Justice Sadeque enjoyed his joke, and in spite of Amirul Islam's pleading in his private chambers, later that day, refused to change his ruling. No, they were not to be rid of their charge so easily, he told him.

The author was permitted to travel overseas, although the Attorney General and his team initially voiced objections, insisting that it be a condition of bail that she must remain in the country and surrender her passport. The court on the other hand accepted arguments that as a writer she received invitations to attend conferences and the like, and must travel abroad.

There is every reason to believe that the Prosecution must have been aware of what was afoot: that the arrangements for her to leave the country were all in place. Perhaps the Attorney General's objections were part of the political charade which had to be played out to the end: perhaps he was just going through the motions so that the Government could handle any later criticism from the anti-Taslima brigade waiting to accuse them of giving in to Western demands.

After the decision was handed down, Sara tried to stay near Taslima, who was caught in a crush of people. Everyone else had the same idea— protect the young author by surrounding her—for reasons that at the time seemed necessary, but on hindsight were an obvious overreaction. Sara found herself caught up in the melee, she is a woman who does not scare easily, but when she spotted a suspicious-looking man next to her client, she became alarmed. Thinking that he might be an assassin, tiny Sara and her friend kept blocking his way until he finally snapped, 'Madam, I am a Special Branch Officer, I'm here to protect her. Will you please stop pushing me away!'

Although no stranger to packed courtrooms, Sara was stunned. People were jammed in corridors and stairwells. Taslima could see nothing but a wall of bodies. Her own lawyer, Amirul Islam, struggled to stay by her side and at times lost sight of his client.

Wearing a sari and a black-and-white headscarf and dark sunglasses, Taslima seemed drained of emotion and unable to make sense of what was happening around her; it was the first time she'd been in a public place in sixty days and was her first experience in a courtroom. Alarmed by the crowd of men pressing around her as she made her way to the car, Taslima mistook them for her enemies about to attack her, not realising that they were lawyers, trying to form a guard of honor.

There were rumours that day that the religious extremists were waiting for the outcome, and gathering in large numbers at the city centre, ready to run riot if the Court decision failed to please them. Like many rumours in Dhaka, this was unfounded. Curious onlookers, who lived nearby, rushed to see for themselves. But not a single untoward event broke out that day. The following day, on August 5, a small procession, tiny by local standards, made the traditional protest against the Government, which they accused of having a secret entente with Taslima and providing her with sanctuary. Truckloads of policemen trailed the several hundred protesters, but nothing out of the ordinary happened. The country's strongest religiously based political party put out a press release, vowing never to give up their fight to have Taslima the apostate and blasphemer punished, but that was all. It was quiet in Dhaka. The Grand *Tamasha*—or great spectacle—was over, almost as suddenly as it had begun. The Religious Sorcerers and their apprentices were quiet, waiting in the wings for the next opportunity to perform.

However, there was still another page of the story waiting to be read. Local journalists, all wanting to be the first to break the news and make a name for themselves, sensed something was in the air. Taslima would have to leave the country, it was only a question of time, but where would she go?

The news officially broke on 8 August. Quietly, but perfectly legally, with her passport in her hand and the Government aware of her destination, Taslima Nasreen left Bangladesh for Sweden. She arrived in Stockholm on 9 August 1994 thinking that she would return to her own country 'after things have quietened down,' she said.

❈

How had it come to pass that an unknown Bangladeshi author had made world headlines, including a lead article in *Time* magazine? I was amazed that a writer whose work had not been translated into Western languages and was therefore not read outside the Indian subcontinent had turned into a cause célèbre almost overnight.

As events later showed, her fate became embroiled with Bangladeshi politics that coincided with her 'discovery' by the West in late 1993. The real story, however, never reached the outside world, which became totally fixated on establishing and refining the myth of a female Salman Rushdie trapped inside a fundamentalist nation, similar in all respects to Iran, it was said.

Bangladesh has a strong secular tradition and the popular Islam of rural Bangladesh represents the more syncretic culture of Bengal. This local tradition is based on a blend of Sufism, yogism and different animist and Hindu cults: a world of spirits, of trees, of birds and snakes. Buddhist, Hindu and mystical Sufi elements all merged and came together with the more legalistic Sunni Islam of the nineteenth century. It is stretching a very long bow indeed to compare Bangladesh with Iran. Certainly it is not the religiously fundamentalist country it was portrayed as by the international media during the Taslima crisis. The country's constitution defines Islam as the state religion; however, it also guarantees the right to practise the religion of one's choice. Bangladeshi intelligentsia regards Islamist extremism as a political movement rather than a religious or spiritual one. The progressive movement has always kept at bay the extremist Wahabbi modes of Islam that have been 'imported' over the last decades. Human rights activists watch carefully, never giving an inch.

In Bangladesh there is always another demonstration or procession around the corner in a land of ongoing political confrontation—it's embedded in the young nation's political culture. Politics take on a surrealistic edge and, to an outsider, it often seems that the same groups appear, disappear and re-emerge, like a crowd of Bollywood extras hired for the occasion to trudge round and round in circles, waving their placards in the air. The banners are different but, on closer scrutiny, the cast is the same, only the organisations' names have changed: the organised Islamist militants in one guise or the other, versus the liberal, secular forces in their costume de jour.

The choruses of hate—simulated and real—can change their focus from one person to the next in the twinkling of an eye. The cries of 'Hang Taslima!' will die and someone else will offer up a new symbol of vilification proving 'Islam is in danger!' The age-old rallying cry still works, especially on Fridays after prayers when the young *madrassah* (religious school) students, with too much time on their hands and too little money to spend, gather to hear the latest demagogue work up the crowd with a brilliant show of oratorical skills. Entertainment for everyone and it's free! When called on, they're ready to march around for half an hour with loudspeakers, sometimes for nothing if they're bored, or owe someone a favor.

Year in, year out, the processions and counter processions clash; the *hartals* or general strikes wreak havoc on the economy, and opposition politics carry the day. Around election time, of course, deals are struck and yesterday's enemy becomes today's brand-new accomplice.

Not everyone is as cynical as politicians, fortunately, and millions of ordinary people look back to the Liberation Struggle of 1971 to give meaning to their lives. After bloody fighting, and great loss of life, East Pakistan threw off the domination of West Pakistan to become the independent nation of Bangladesh. There has never been a process of reconciliation inside Bangladesh and with the older generation, the wounds have never healed: people are still labeled either 'Anti-liberation' or 'Pro-liberation'; lists of 'traitors' who wanted to remain with Pakistan are still in circulation. Today they continue to face one another across the barricades: the religiously based political parties, better known to the outside world as the 'fundamentalists' or—in the language of the twenty-first century—'Islamists' versus the progressives or secularists, hardly known to anyone outside their own borders.

As I held the Taslima story up to the light, I couldn't help but notice how it changed shape and how the colours intensified. Along the way memory and myth merged and the tale acquired a life of its own, a universal story with a hundred different authors. Somewhere along the way, I suspected, the real story had got lost. In its place a mythology emerged that various players fed and Taslima 'the writer' acted out as part of her public persona. I stood in the wings watching the performance of a lifetime.

Part I

The Grand Tamasha

Myth is a genre between fairy tale and a detective story.

Nadine Gordimer

Chapter 1

On the Trail of Taslima

Why should Eve always control her desire,
always check her step?

Throttle her thirst. . . .
Eve, wherever you find forbidden fruit
make sure that you taste it.
 Taslima Nasreen. Translated from the Bengali by Prof Kabir Chowdhury

In a strange way I was as wary of Taslima as I imagined she was of me. And there were long intervals, when I became fixated on shadows, whispered allusions and minor characters, allowing myself to become caught up in the hullabaloo of the chase. Distracted by the mythology and the politics surrounding Taslima, I paused instead of moving on to discover the woman behind the fiction.

The circumstances of her exile meant that so far our paths had never crossed. Yet by following the trail of Taslima to Sweden, there was every chance that this stalemate would end, and the book would take on a new energy. Yet instead of moving forward, I toyed with the idea of how the narrative might be affected if Taslima refused to take part. I was sure she would resist a stranger's attempts to probe behind the recent events in her life and I wanted more of her time and more of her real self than she was used to granting any of the hundreds of journalists beating a path to her door.

Would she allow me to look behind her public persona—would she agree to see me at all? Like most celebrities, there must be parts of her story she needed to control: certain improvisations which might give way under closer scrutiny.

13

Taslima's life is replete with stories which over time have become distorted or lost. She is a woman who has always made more enemies than friends and her critics extend well beyond right wing, religious factions. Petty jealousies, gossip and a history of snubbing people have helped build a wall of resentment, while the remoteness between the author and organised progressive–secular opinion, in Bangladesh, has created an impasse.

The nearer I edged to Taslima, the stronger the feeling grew that the trail leading to her door would be messy. There were too many conflicting versions about the life and times of Taslima Nasreen and they all had the ring of truth, but with Taslima perched high up on a literary pedestal somewhere in the northern hemisphere, and me in Australia, we were safe from each other for the moment.

In the end, curiosity stamped out any flickers of hesitancy. Her friends and enemies—even those who claimed to be indifferent to the Taslima mythology—had buried me in an edifice of claims and counterclaims. I needed to move beyond the artifice to try and discover her true self, the damaged self I sensed in her poetry and column writing.

The thought of walking through the ruins of Taslima's life, without her knowing, had seemed ghoulish in 1996 when I first went to Bangladesh. To avoid this, I'd left letters with her lawyer and relatives in Dhaka, asking that they be forwarded to her wherever she might be. Because of concerns for her safety, Taslima's address was kept secret, although it was widely believed that she resided somewhere in Sweden or maybe even Germany.

Dear Taslima,
I hope this letter will reach you by whatever route necessary, for I am not exactly sure where you reside these days. I will enlist the help of your friends in Dhaka to locate you in Sweden or Germany or wherever you have made your headquarters as a writer-in-exile. . . .

Written in November 1996, the letter explained my commitment to telling her story in all its complexity and outlined my visits to Dhaka and my plans to visit Calcutta the following year. The letter expressed my admiration for her poetry and her nonconformist stand. I hoped that she would agree to see me or to communicate with me in some way and I emphasised that understanding what lay behind the events in Bangladesh was important and should be shared by others.

For reasons unknown, Taslima received this letter only a year later in Sweden, just before we met. Unaware of this, I kept myself busy and waited nervously in Australia for an answer. Like an old bureaucrat, I put my faith in the process I'd elected to follow. This was a mistake. Six months went by. I decided to try again; this time I would bypass intermediaries. Taslima's brother Noman had once given me an old unlisted Swedish telephone number, which I now tried half-heartedly, not really expecting an answer. Seconds later I was stunned to hear Taslima's voice (which I recognised from television and radio) on the other end. Afterwards I could recall only a few details of our conversation—I think I was overcome at hearing her voice and babbled.

Taslima had never received my original letter but sounded flattered to hear that someone wanted to write a book about her. Armed with her fax address I sent a second letter of introduction in July 1997, asking whether she would agree to see me in four months' time, in Stockholm, Berlin, New York, wherever she chose. Included in the letter was a list of twenty names or more of people I'd already spoken to in Dhaka and Calcutta: it seemed important that she knew, right from the start, that I had come face-to-face with both anti- and pro-Taslima 'forces'.

Finally everything was set for what I hoped would be a series of discussions stretched over a week. This would be squeezed into her busy schedule after her return from Cape Town, Dublin and Edinburgh, where she was to be a guest speaker at various congresses dealing with human rights. The plan was to meet in Stockholm later that year.

Sweden in November is cold and grey; winter is calling and the streets are dark and half deserted by early afternoon. Matrons in fur hats and fur-trimmed coats, feet encased in shiny leather boots, with soft-gloved hands clutching designer leather bags, sail along the boulevards peering at window displays which, like themselves, are too perfect to be disturbed. Now and then young mothers march by rugged up in warm practical trousers, caps and anoraks, pushing smart baby chariots with gleaming wheels. A fat baby, red-cheeked, bonneted and buried under an avalanche of doonas peeps out waving a tiny red-mittened hand. Even the children are chic, blonde and expensive and I look foreign and out of place, much like Taslima, I imagine, and I wonder—not for the first time—what else we have in common.

Twenty thousand kilometres away it is summer in Australia and people of all ages oil and BBQ themselves on the beaches in a country with the highest rate of skin carcinoma in the world. A tribe of young people wait to catch a wave before tumbling head over heels in the surf, mouths full of sand and salt water. The uniform is shorts, T-shirts, and informality.

People are obsessed, in a curiously indolent way, with water shortages and keeping their gardens alive during the hot season. This is my birthplace, although there are days when a look in someone's eye or a polite, but banal, question reminds me that I am still a curiosity, standing out against the human landscape around me. Memories of the summer I am missing fail to keep me warm as I walk along the dark streets of Stockholm, hunting for food, thankful for my thermal underwear, which does its best to keep out the cold and almost succeeds.

Inside Swedish apartments, everything is bright and *gemütlich*, as the neighbouring Germans say: glassware sparkles against the glow of table lamps and flickering candles; fat tasselled cushions cry out to be leaned on. The furniture has that 'Ikea' look that the rest of the world associates with Swedish design: clean, simple lines and quality materials constructed into a unified piece—the rooms are harmonious, icons of good taste; but perhaps they are too functional, too predictable, like background sets from 'Home Beautiful'—or is it my own sense of style which is awry?

My landlady's sense of style was intimidating. Her name was Ingrid, a tall blonde woman with a lined unhappy face. Over the years, she had adopted a regime where the daily minutiae of her life was regulated: breakfast at such and such an hour; lunch in the office canteen one to one-thirty; aerobics twice a week; a regular mid-week visit from a smug middle-aged boy friend with thinning hair and a worn-out marriage.

No matter what hour of the day or night, Ingrid always remained perfectly groomed. Under a brusque demeanour she was friendly enough to her less-than-perfect lodger, who found Swedish hotel prices beyond her reach. As if I were a child, she instructed me in the Swedish custom of removing one's shoes immediately on stepping through the front door; light hued carpets and cream-coloured, birch wooden floors were popular floor coverings. In Bangladesh also, people remove their footwear, in a swift and graceful transition from sandals to bare feet: no hopping on one foot trying to wrench off a stubborn boot. Australians, always less fastidious in observing protocols from the outside world, trudge the country dust and urban sand in and out of their houses with good humour and a disregard for rituals of purity and hygiene.

I spent a lot of time boiling water in Ingrid's little kitchen, a monument to sterility and modern design. Not a crumb nor a fingerprint could be detected on any surface, at any time of the day. The toaster looked unused and hid beneath a knitted cover, a facsimile of a cottage complete with red roof and green shutters. Although welcome in Ingrid's kitchen, I wasn't permitted to do any cooking; I refused to take this personally—a slight against my weakness for spices, onions, ginger and garlic. Ingrid never seemed to cook, existed on sherry and exotic smorgasbord morsels and was as thin as a pencil. This left me roaming the supermarkets, trying to buy food that was warm and not bland to my taste.

⊞

The first time I met Taslima I knew immediately that she was not pleased with me, not pleased at all. She'd been kept waiting and made no attempt to hide her annoyance—needless to say this was not the beginning I'd hoped for. She and her friend Gunnar Svensson had been ringing my apartment bell downstairs, but the wiring must have fused for I heard nothing. Fortunately I saw them from an upstairs window, just as they were about to leave. Arrangements had been made for this first visit, that they would drive me to the house they shared together on the outskirts of Stockholm. On the way they would show me the train and bus stops I would have to negotiate each day as I set off to visit Taslima, a round trip of about four hours; we would get to know one another and work out a schedule for the next week. I was invited for lunch—good Bangladeshi food I hoped, the spicier the better!

After a cool beginning, Taslima mellowed and pointed out the local landmarks as we drove along the dark grey streets lined with leafless trees. All I could see of her was the back of her head and the side of her face. She giggled through a cloud of cigarette smoke when I asked aloud where all the people were hiding. Not like Dhaka, she answered, and changed mercurially from an impatient child into a charming woman. Gunnar immediately brightened and so did I.

Taslima and Gunnar's house, from the outside, looked like a typical Swedish design but once over the threshold the imprint of Taslima was everywhere. The hallway where I removed my shoes was cluttered with a pile of footwear; the coat rack draped with scarves, coats, and hats, listed to one side like a pirate's mast ready to topple. Inside the kitchen, half-opened cupboards revealed jars of spices and pickles and shelves loaded with chillies, fresh ginger, and the devil's favourite additive—garlic! Counter tops cluttered with utensils, and chopping boards demonstrated that this was a serious working kitchen. Food mattered, and its preparation was a gregarious, and probably long-drawn-out, ritual. The house design, inside and out, might be Swedish, but Taslima's kitchen and eating areas were Bangladeshi. Her mother was visiting her from Dhaka, and this reinforced old traditions of a dreamtime where a nurturing mother prepared her daughter's favourite dishes. Food and family, love and language mixed like the spices in a *garam masala*: memories that expatriates hunger for, where food becomes the metaphor for the life that has slipped through their fingers.

Many of Taslima's poems-in-exile talk of food: the smell, touch, taste and texture of dishes; her verses record a deep sense of loss. She remembers '. . . puffed rice, hot peanuts, steaming tea . . . and a whole house reeking with the pungent smells of kedgeree and baked hilsa [fish].'

> I'll sit on the courtyard of my village home,
> eat with relish rice soaked in water
> mixing chilli and salt,
> and the meal over, chew a betel leaf
> wrapped in a fragrant foil
> > (extracts from the poem 'On A Rainy Day', circa 1995)

She writes of standing ovations and city keys, red-carpet receptions in the great cities of Europe, of meeting kings and cabinet ministers, receiving gold medals and bouquets, yet she longs for home and her mother.

Waiting inside to greet me with her eyes cast down, but a sweet smile on her face, was Taslima's mother. Mother and daughter stood side by side and I realised just how tall Taslima was for a Bangladeshi woman, much taller than her parent whose delicate build made her seem doll-like in contrast to her daughter's full face and sturdy round body.

'In Bangladesh they call me tall but here in Sweden they think I'm a small woman,' Taslima said.

For the first time that day, I was able to see my author properly. She was dressed in a black leather jacket and cord trousers; perched at a cheeky angle, on a head of thick black curls, she wore a brown western-style hat. As far as the eye could tell, there was no make-up except for a bright lipstick. She looked younger than thirty-five and seemed cheerful and in good spirits. Smooth unblemished skin showed no lines or furrows indicating any traumas from her immediate past. Taslima must have learnt to mask her passion and hide her pain very early in life, I decided, but there were still traces of the sweet-faced young student, with the dimpled chin and large serious eyes I'd glimpsed in family photographs: the girl from Mymensingh District, population four million, which used to be famous for its agriculture, its educational centres, its poetry and folk songs, and is now famous for its connection with the most reviled woman in Bangladesh.

'She is not like other Bangladeshi women,' was my first thought. There was something about her. . . . Even if we'd met in Dhaka, in a room full of sari-clad female activists, this woman would have stood out. She was not like the Bangladeshi women I counted as personal friends; Taslima and her 'sisters' had not drunk from the same well.

Nasreen and the women's movement have never understood each other. It was the silences which first drew me to the Taslima Nasreen story in 1994, a year before I visited Dhaka for the first time. As I followed events through newspaper stories I noticed that the only female voices supporting Taslima in her confrontation with Muslim fundamentalists were Western feminists. If Taslima was the foremost feminist in her country, as the media was telling me, where were the voices belonging to the local women's movement?

Bangladesh had a seasoned women's movement, alive and well—yet it was silent. Was it jealousy? Were they being gagged? Surely they supported her? This was the beginning of my quest.

I looked, but never found evidence that feminist leaders were overly jealous—these were prominent women from academic, political and legal backgrounds, no strangers to international forums. I found them resentful yes, and often angry, but it was always men—or Taslima herself—who introduced the word 'jealousy'. So if they weren't jealous and they weren't being censored, why were they so quiet?

'After 1993 it was impossible to support her and impossible not to support her,' said a member of the radical women's group Naripokkho.

Several prominent women who admired her courage and liked her writing assisted Taslima in the first stage of her career in 1991, by introducing her to well-placed people, even though she was notorious for her rude behaviour. At social gatherings she behaved badly to other women guests, even snubbing young fans, as she headed straight for the men, especially men of influence.

Women leaders had long felt uneasy with aspects of her work that mocked Islam and held men up to ridicule. Personally, they liked what she wrote, but were worried by its impact on the hardline religious elements and other conservatives with whom they were locked in daily battle. The lines had been drawn many years earlier. Certain privileged groups opposed their activities: money lenders, landlords, conservative mullahs and rich farmers tucked away in remote areas harboured strong feelings of resentment, as they saw their power, influence and even wealth being eroded by micro credit loans, employment projects, and—worst of all in their eyes—non-religious education and legal education for impoverished men and women. These projects formed the backbone of the foreign-funded non-governmental organisations (NGOs) working in the rural areas, mainly staffed by women. NGO schools competed with the *madrassah* seminaries, new health clinics robbed the local mullahs of clients needing their holy water and holy verses to ward off infection and the evil eye—there was less money in their pockets and they were angry and resentful that social change was menacing their interests.

Women activists were practised at negotiating their way through the minefield of conservative attitudes and hierarchies in remote villages and towns, where if they grew careless, or overconfident, they would soon find themselves targeted in noisy marches led by religious die-hards threatening to burn down their clinics or schools and send them packing. But Taslima had never been part of the women's movement and never gave a moment's thought to the strategic concerns they lived by: at that stage of her career, repercussions never bothered her.

The women's movement in Bangladesh has been at work for more than forty years and in spite of ideological and political party differences, on most key issues, like violence towards women, they work together. They are like members of a choir who submerge their personalities, in stark contrast to their Pakistani counterparts who soar like operatic divas, just like Taslima Nasreen.

'Everything was always happening to her; there was never any looking out to others,' said an academic friend. 'Read her and it's like nobody but herself exists. And I can only read about someone's ego for so long before it starts to lose appeal.'

'You have to work in a way that is changing, but not destructive,' another NGO worker explained.

'Taslima Nasreen brought out the worst attacks that face women in our society: the gossip, the ridicule—she clearly relished the gossip and loved being the martyred woman. We don't want to be martyred women—we want to be successful women,' yet another feminist said, trying to explain her frustration over Taslima's behaviour.

'She was used against us!' cried another. 'Used against us by the Grey-beards and by the so-called progressive men as well. Even men who were not praying Muslims seized the opportunity to strike back. "Oh, so you want to be another Taslima Nasreen?" they would throw at us.'

In the eyes of many veteran campaigners, Taslima Nasreen was a liability.

In one sense, Taslima and the women's movement were opposite sides of the coin: the insider-activists working from within society, facing Taslima, the supreme outsider who, in the years ahead and in other circumstances, might one day have become the movement's conscience, if either side had ever wanted this.

These women should have welcomed the rebellious author with open arms, and there was a time, before the 1994 crisis, when some of them tried—but Taslima, who saw herself as an anarchist, always refused to join. 'Why would I do that? I'm me,' she said to a friend at the time.

Six years later she explained her reasoning to an Indian interviewer who questioned her about the role of writers and their relationship with social movements. 'I intentionally abstained from membership of any woman's organisation because I believed that as an individual I had the right to say what I wanted, a right that would get qualified if I became part of any women's organisation. Women's organisations compromise so much. I did not want that for myself. . . . I am actually not very good at street marches. All my anger and protest is through my writing.'

Years later, standing back from it all, it was easy for me to see how Taslima Nasreen and the women's movement could have used one another. Women knew what she meant when she cried out, 'The whore is always a woman, never a man!' Taslima possessed a natural ability to communicate in a language that everyone understood—she was fearless and had grown indifferent to personal slander. The women's movement could have adopted her, while she in turn could have called on their support later, when enemies began to crowd in as they were bound to do if she kept on writing with abandon. Why didn't this happen?

The answer lay in the totally disparate views they held of the women's movement and how to go about introducing change. In 1993 the differences intensified when many women and men began to feel that Taslima Nasreen was not truly 'progressive', but a self-interested ambitious woman who lacked real commitment to the causes they had spent decades fighting for collectively.

The girl from Mymensingh baffled them: they were unable to define her politically and she had never joined in any of the popular protest movements of the day, that are a part of living and breathing in Bangladeshi student circles. In Bangladesh society, dissent is collective: petitions, marches and rallies, letters to the editor, concerts, huge coalitions, student movements. Protest is always public and individual dissent is strange and Western. Taslima believed traditional forms of protest were too slow and achieved little; she never hesitated in letting people know what she thought of their life's work. Her blunt refusal to join any women's organisation or any writers' coalition increased her isolation.

'Let blind angry fire burn down all the bricks of the temples, mosques, *gurudwaras* and churches,' said Nasreen in a poem. She wanted the rubble transformed into schools, libraries, and flower gardens.

In another poem, 'Liberation', she talked metaphorically about women throwing a lighted match on petrol to burn the laws imprisoning them and the myth of 'the chaste self-sacrificing pure woman, and the Heaven that is polluted'.

Outside Bangladesh her feminist views might be considered outdated and belonging to the sixties, but she shocked her own people. Feelings intensified within feminist circles that Taslima had no idea of the need to 'manage' social transformation.

The women's movement wanted change; they also wanted women to come out onto the streets, but not to be stoned. They hated the restrictions on their lives but understood the nature of social change, strategically by-passing some of the issues Taslima confronted head on, especially the subject of female sexuality. Taslima, they believed, was destructive and never provided strategies to combat poverty and illiteracy—only anarchistic solutions clothed in angry words and verses. In the face of an overwhelmingly traditional society they were prepared to compromise, but, to Taslima, compromise meant surrender.

Bangladeshi feminists looked to employment, health and legal education; they wanted more micro credit projects, family planning programs and an end to violence in the home. Unlike their angry author they did not want to stamp out Islam—although they certainly wanted the human rights, promised them in the Qur'an and the Hadith (teachings derived from the Prophet's life), delivered.

'She is a woman who used shock tactics and sensationalism, but these simply do not introduce lasting change in a patriarchal society like ours—they only alienate,' said Sigma Huda, a leading female lawyer and human rights activist. 'Smoking a cigarette on TV while you are reading the Qur'an only alienates people. You are not helping the cause. You are definitely not with the movement. Taslima's activities rendered everyone's work invisible. We lost a lot of ground.'

Maleeka Begum, political activist and feminist leader, was a woman who knew her own mind and spoke plainly—everyone seemed in awe of this remarkable woman. Like a veteran woman warrior she knew how to galvanise her troops and advance into the mullah heartlands—she also knew when to retreat and live to fight another day. When we first met in 1995 her views on Taslima were severe and in line with the views of Sigma Huda and other women leaders, but in later years I noticed a mellowing, as if time was healing the wound.

'In fifty years Taslima will be judged differently,' claimed Maleeka. 'Her greatest impact was not on the progressives in Dhaka. She was listened to by women who had no voice, "This is me. This is my pain," they said when they read her newspaper columns and novellas.'

Taslima's provocative style caused many ordinary women to think for the first time. But then, almost in an obligatory aside, the same women would lower their voices and tell me that some of her writings were 'vulgar', a Bangladeshi euphemism for sexually explicit, as if they must publicly repudiate her. I asked every young woman I met the same question. 'Who is the woman you most admire?' expecting some mention of the current prime minister, Khaleda Zia, or opposition leader Sheikh Hasina, or Taslima Nasreen. From the twenty or more young women I polled, the answer was always the same: Begum Sufia Kamal and Begum Rokeya Hossain. The former was their beloved feminist leader and poet (now deceased), while the marvellous Rokeya was the first Bengali-Muslim female protest writer whose utopian vision of a society controlled by women, *Sultana's Dream*, was written in 1905, long before Charlotte Perkins Gilman's *Herland*.

Taslima, and many of her readers, stood outside the clique of city feminists and middle-class NGO careerists that I knew. They were different to the caste of well-educated, well-travelled female activists who looked for reforms and had the patience of Job, the women who had taken me into their circles. I discovered that while Taslima's name often closed doors, mentioning Begum Rokeya's name opened doors wherever I went. Women became animated when they learnt that we had more in common than South Asian and Muslim ancestry, that I had read Rokeya. For a short while I found a place in a corner of their lives as they shared their experiences with me and accepted me as a sister.

The generation of leadership Maleeka came from was both radical and traditional: it was a political movement, an economic movement, either pro- or anti-government, but it did not publicly discuss sexuality or power relations. Taslima stubbornly refused to join with them, but never stopped criticising their life's work in her writing and in the interviews she gave to Indian and Western papers.

'I can't join your traditional movement,' she told Maleeka. 'I am an individual. I think about my feelings and I touch the individual woman.'

'And that is why,' said Maleeka, 'writers and men folk don't like her—because when she touched the women, she struck a blow at men!'

'Scratch a progressive male in Bangladesh, and you soon find a traditional husband, son or brother,' I muttered to myself in what became my favourite mantra, as I made the rounds of Dhaka city talking to enlightened-sounding men. Their politics might differ from their Islamist opponents, but an overblown sense of honour was something common to men on both sides. The clothes they wore gave nothing away: men in western suits or jeans and T shirts often behaved no differently towards women than their brothers wearing turbans and baggy pyjama trousers.

In Maleeka's eyes, being 'progressive' in Bangladesh was often a narrow political definition. 'These men,' she said, 'are progressive with their secularism, their human rights and their politics, but when it comes to family matters like dowry and giving their sisters their inheritance rights from their father's property, they are very conservative—just as conservative as their political opponents. Taslima wrote about what we in the movement don't touch—the power relations between husband and wife, brother and sister, mother-in-law and daughter-in-law.'

The women's movement was fighting on two fronts: a political front and a home front. In their private lives, while they struggled to break with tradition, in the main, they played by the unwritten laws, and that meant remaining silent over their own sexuality.

So on that very first day when I met Taslima, and in the days to follow, I came to realise that it wasn't the Western clothes she favoured, or her medical qualifications, which made her stand out from the crowd. There were other reasons, all to do with her inner self and how she perceived herself as a writer. Outwardly, others had given in to the demands of social conformity while Taslima had stayed true to her instinctive energies including her sexuality, although the tension between the two forces often showed itself in a deep antagonism to what she saw around her, especially the behaviour of men.

Whenever I look at the photographs I took that day, in Stockholm, of Taslima and her mother working in the kitchen together, I am reminded of the strong sense of self she projected: the way she moved and held herself, her complete naturalness—a funny mixture of artlessness and intensity. Perfectly at ease with her own body, she knew that she was at the peak of her sexuality; she was, after all, a doctor and the human body held no secrets for her.

In real life she was nothing like her photos on magazine covers and in newspapers, and this helped me understand her impact on Bangladeshi men, something which had long puzzled me in the abstract, for Bangladesh is a land replete with classically beautiful women, fine-boned and exquisite. While not beautiful according to Bangladeshi standards, Taslima was striking and threw off an energy, a kind of magnetism, which the male libido quickly translated as 'sexy'. The kind of allure men detected, had escaped me until now, because it was missing in her photographs, where she often looked like a wide-eyed schoolgirl. To the cameras, she gave nothing away. Years before, I had examined her likeness looking for some signs of the passion I read in her verses, but the face I saw was impassive. You had to see Taslima with your own eyes, and hear her voice to understand her mystique.

Men always mentioned her voice. Perhaps it was the combination of a soft contralto—low and sweet, as a decent woman's voice should be, in the company of men—and the faintest suggestion of something unorthodox, even dangerous. The contradictions seemed to excite them. The TV interviews I'd seen, where she appeared either nervous, or struggling with her new vocabulary, gave only a hint. Her voice had never been professionally trained but it was steady and controlled, like someone used to reading aloud to themselves. I think she knew the effect of her voice on men.

When I first went to Dhaka, I struggled to understand why men persisted in drawing near in spite of all the danger signs emanating from a woman who may have liked them personally, but held their sex in contempt and seemed to enjoy making fools of them. I think this habit was so deeply ingrained that she couldn't stop herself-: it was stamped all over her writing

>If you see a pack of mad dogs
>Run
>Remember rabies
>If you see a pack of men
>Run
>Remember syphilis

Her second husband Naim had been happy—even eager—to relive with me the pain and the pleasure of being married to 'Nasreen', as all of her friends used to call her. Years later he was still trying to make sense of their time together.

'I remember the first time I saw Nasreen,' he said. 'She was jumping down from a rickshaw in her red blouse and jeans. The physical movement attracted me, because it was so different to girls who step down very carefully in their saris or *salwar kumeez* outfits and take small conscious steps. She walked so freely, just like you see in Europe where boys and girls walk the same way. Today you see more of this,' he added 'but not in the mid-eighties, when we first met.'

Other men, who knew her in their student days, were also enraptured and always mentioned her red blouse, knotted high at the waist, her black jeans and short hair; it was something they still remembered years later when I quizzed them. Although they made her sound like the local femme fatale, they always shied away from discussing the effect she had on their sexual libido. I knew they were censoring their answers out of respect.

The only man prepared to do some straight talking was Nasreen's reporter friend and Associated Press correspondent Farid Hossain, the journalist who wrote the first *Time Magazine* article about her in 1994 that introduced her to American readers. He had invited me to the Dhaka Press Club for lunch one day, where he showed no embarrassment in discussing sexual politics with a woman.

'There are many Taslimas in India,' Farid told me. 'Lots of women who have her mystique, her sense of glamour,' he added, 'but I'd never before seen anything like her in Dhaka. Other Bangladeshi women are elegant and beautiful, but there is a stillness to their beauty, while she displays her sexuality and spontaneity in an unusual style.'

Dhaka and Calcutta looked at Taslima with different eyes. Farid was right: in Calcutta there were thousands of girls who cut their hair, wore jeans and smoked cigarettes, drank with the boys and spoke out cheekily; but in Dhaka she was a rare specimen.

'Men do not have platonic relationships with women, in Dhaka society,' Farid reminded me.

He sat back in his chair, legs elegantly crossed, drawing on his cigarette and watching as the rest of the world ran around in circles. There was a touch of ennui about him, almost, but not quite, the cynic. At our last meeting in 1997, three years had passed since Taslima had 'fled' and during all this time he'd kept his cards close to his chest, never vouchsafing any information that wasn't already in circulation. Now at last he was prepared to discuss Nasreen and the morass of Dhaka morality with me. It was never clear to me why he changed his mind. He may have accepted that I would return, year after year, until he broke which he finally did on our fourth interview in so many years.

'People think because this is a Muslim country that married men don't have a girlfriend or a mistress. They're wrong! Other men look up to some of our big womanisers in admiration, it's macho, they think, a sign of your status that you can afford this kind of wild life-style and, in many cases, wives know about it but don't protest because divorce is still a stigma.'

In Dhaka society, sexuality is always repressed and opportunities for boys and girls to meet are curtailed. That explained why marriages between cousins were so popular. 'Who are the only girls a boy is allowed to mix with at celebrations and weddings? These are the girls you meet first and so you fall in love immediately,' Farid said.

According to Farid, even the girls at university were shy young women, ignorant and afraid of their own sexuality. 'So when you find a girl like Taslima, outspoken and beautiful who gossips with men, laughs and drinks, you really are beguiled. You'll only find one or two girls like this in all of

Dhaka, girls who enjoy this kind of "popularity". And people readily label them *noshta* "spoilt" or "fallen".'

✤

Nasreen's reputation was always under scrutiny, even in her teens. She graduated from writing poetry in her diary when she was thirteen and, a few years later, in high school, developed a reputation by writing letters to a film magazine *Chittrali* on anything that struck her fancy in the fantasy world of Indian films; she loved corresponding, but, most of all, she loved seeing her name in print.

When she was sixteen, she discovered another ruse and the stories grew wilder after Taslima began placing personal ads in the weekly *Bichittra* magazine, which was all the rage among a clique of young people. Soon her name was appearing regularly and Nasreen and her other personas received a flood of answers, to her daring literary 'poses', printed in the next week's edition. For the small sum of two taka (5 cents) you could place a small ad—perhaps some lines of your favourite poem—with your name underneath, asking like-minded people to reply.

In a country where social segregation, especially amongst adolescents, is the norm, this was a fun way of young people communicating—it was legal and inexpensive and you could attract members of the opposite sex. Apparently, most parents were kept in the dark: a magazine would be circulated amongst a group of students, and, now and then, smuggled inside the house. Taslima, and her sister Yasmeen, even had their own secret language, as sisters sometimes do.

Fayez, now a well-known journalist in Dhaka, remembered the Taslima of old. In fact many grown men I met along the way, respectable husbands and fathers, laughed or sighed as they recalled reading her ads in their youth. Her rejoinder to someone called Zia, a prig of the first order, who labelled girls who advertised on these pages as 'characterless' enhanced her reputation for boldness.

Taslima replied: 'Mr Zia, at long last you have given away your true identity. You were perhaps born from a characterless mother.' She knew instinctively how to attract attention; it was a style she would carry with her when she started writing newspaper columns years later.

'The world exists, because I exist!' she trumpeted in another famous line ad, expressing a brilliant summary of philosophical solipsism. And her cry, 'I couldn't care less about anything!' hinted to her male readers that here was a young girl different to everyone else.

How Taslima loved to boast. 'I am at the acme of success!' 'I am incomparable!' Her writing enabled her to take on another identity far removed

from the shy young girl she seemed to be. Indeed there are many people who insist to this day that the 'Taslima' who writes the sensational
books and verses is using an assumed voice. But isn't this what every writer
does?

'Give me love,' called the voice of Taslima, 'I shall offer you *Puja* (worship). Perhaps a line of someone else's poetry but it drew the bees to the
honey. Responses like 'Taslima, your whole body is aching, where should
I apply medicine?' was pretty racy stuff for young people to 'say' to one
another in a society as cloistered as Bangladesh.

Now that I'd seen Taslima with my own eyes, I could finally understand why
men were so attracted to this 'dangerous woman'. Pushing these thoughts
aside, for the moment, I took out the presents I'd brought with me from
London in the time-honoured tradition of gift giving. I presented a box of
gift-wrapped chocolates to her mother.

'My mother is diabetic,' Taslima informed me.

I flinched at my faux pas, apologised and moved on to the next gift
and so I handed Taslima a small package containing a pair of delicate silver
earrings meant for her. 'I don't wear earrings,' was her only comment after
she finished opening her present.

Never one to give up without a fight, I decided to brazen my way through
this second gaffe. 'I'm not doing too well, am I?' I laughed. Once again
her mood changed and she smiled at me. Later that same night, back in the
safety of my room, I worked hard at trying not to feel foolish and managed
to do this by blaming Taslima for my present fiasco. Hadn't I offered to
bring her a bottle of Scotch whisky as a gift, on my way through duty-
free shopping? She had demurred, implying that she didn't drink Scotch,
curious to learn how I'd thought of such an idea. At the time I'd smiled to
myself, for everyone's drinking habits are fairly open knowledge in Dhaka
and in certain circles nothing to be frowned at; but if this was something
she preferred to keep hidden from me as part of some game, then I would
not spoil her day, I decided, and hence the earrings which Naim—husband
number two—had told me she wore!

Meanwhile Gunnar discovered that we both shared a weakness for American writer James Ellroy's dark novels. The Swede seemed content to bask
in Taslima's shadow. He worked as a computer programmer, Taslima said,
adding in an aside that they only shared the house, implying that they were
not 'involved', which I thought a nonsense. Gunnar treated Taslima like
a child to be indulged. She watched him like a hawk whenever we were
together, and even when we were alone for a few minutes looking at his

books, we weren't really alone. There was always the presence of Taslima nearby, straining her ears to hear our conversation. When I mentioned how it would help my research to have a few words with Gunnar, Taslima gave a lazy laugh and called out to him in a slow teasing voice, 'Eh Gunnar, do you want to be interviewed?' We all laughed at what seemed a joke, but her voice held the hint of a threat and Gunnar and I both knew that we would never talk to each other alone.

Dinner was magnificent: chicken and fish curries, pilau, dhal, vegetables; Taslima was an excellent hostess and served me herself, according to custom. We ate with our hands and this gave me an opportunity to see Taslima at her most natural, filling everyone's plate, passing her mother's home-made pickles and enjoying her own food with great gusto. She was no timid, delicate eater, but then neither was I!

What would I like to drink, Taslima asked me. Much as I would have liked 'a drink' I could not bring myself to do something *haraam* (religiously forbidden) in front of her mother whom I knew to be a devout, praying Muslim who of course abstained from drinking alcohol. Taslima, who was no hypocrite, drank her beer openly at the table while I drank water and felt like a fool.

I admired her honesty but could not follow her lead. Even if it meant she thought less of me, I couldn't bring myself to drink in front of her mother. While a born Muslim, I abstained from following ritual—but for one curious exception; I could never bring myself to eat pork—the very idea made me feel sick, such is the power of taboos learnt from childhood.

Muslims are a strange lot. They will openly admit to not praying, or not fasting, even admit this in the presence of devout Muslims, but are loathe to admit they drink alcohol. I tried not to offend practising Muslims by throwing my unorthodoxy in their faces. Respect for elders had been drummed into me as a child and for me there was no escape. It's a game some Muslims play, where deception is given the status of respect, and honesty labelled as disrespect. This tedious tug of war colours the lives of most liberally disposed Muslims.

Later that night I sat alone thinking about the day that had ended and the thrill of finally meeting 'my author'. In the future I suspected that I'd be dealing with another Taslima, a woman who'd decide for herself what she'd share with me and what she'd conceal. Once she'd made up her mind, I doubted that she could be shifted. Taslima, the writer, I expected to be difficult, especially now that the opening ceremonies of 'the games' were over. There were already signs: I'd asked Taslima, before leaving that night, for the names of any Swedish PEN members she thought I should meet. I knew no one. All I carried in my head was the name Gabi Gleichmann, an unusual name I thought at the time, a name with a definite rhythm to it, a certain panache.

'Why do you want to meet Gabi?' she had asked, laughing lightly. The laugh, and the look she gave me made me curious; I remember thinking it a strange question.

I told her what I knew: that his name had appeared in press clippings; that I'd once seen a press photo of the man. . . . I'd read of her welcome in Sweden and thought that I'd learn a great deal by talking to the PEN president, who'd been a part of it all; it seemed only logical. As if she'd never heard me, she gave me instead, the name and telephone number of a man, a member of a Swedish humanist organisation. I was on my own and would receive no further help from her—I dropped the subject. I felt quarantined. I never ever asked her again.

I entered just five words in my journal that night, all beginning with the prefix 'self', which I wrote down without a moment's thought, so strong were the traces Taslima had left behind. As an afterthought I sent off a post card to my agent. 'Complications have arisen. Damned if I don't like the woman!'

⊕

Taslima's new life in Europe was far removed from the fairy-tale ending her friends in the West had predicted. The twists and turns in her life continued—only the political scenery had changed.

'This is not how I expected my life to turn out; this is not the life I wanted.' Quiet words; no hint of passion, no trace of bitterness. 'I did not plan to be here in a foreign country being made a fuss of; publishers telephoning constantly, bidding for my books, offering me sums of money beyond my dreams.' She paid too high a price, she told me, for the kind of reception many authors only dreamt about.

Sitting back in her office chair, she drew deeply on her cigarette and flicked the ash into the glass ashtray on her desk next to her computer. The cigarette habit she'd started during her underground time in Dhaka, and by now she chain-smoked as a way of handling stress and, most of all, to ease the pain caused by a sense of displacement, which never seemed to leave her.

On August 10, 1994, Taslima arrived in Stockholm exhausted and emotionally battered after two months of hiding amid the hysteria and uncertainty surrounding her case. Her legal advisers, her family and friends urged her to take what, to them, seemed the best course.

The time had come to leave Bangladesh. During this hectic period Taslima was in a highly emotional state. Anxiety played games with her memory and her natural predilection towards exaggeration has been well documented. 'Taslima Nasreen must always embellish,' writer Shamsur Rahman told me with a laugh; at the time he was one of her strongest supporters. 'It's not enough that she's in hiding—she has to make it bigger!'

Taslima tells everyone that in the early hours of the morning, thousands of screaming fundamentalists surrounded Zia International Airport in Dhaka, determined to prevent her from leaving, but there have never been any witnesses verifying this—and the local journalists I have spoken to emphatically deny any such thing ever took place. Her legal team is also reticent over this 'incident'. A mass demonstration of the kind she still refers to in many of her speeches and interviews, almost as an obligatory reference, is most unlikely at three in the morning in Dhaka; like many airports in the region, only passengers are allowed to set foot inside the terminal. There are, however, always throngs of people—taxi drivers, touts, and the like—with time on their hands who stand and stare from behind railings, but they're kept at a good distance by guards.

At three in the morning, even fanatics melt away. It's hard for photojournalists to take pictures in the dark and TV crews have long gone to bed. Processions always march through the main streets of Dhaka in broad daylight; the Pied Pipers know how to play the game. The most that can be said about this story is that news of her impending departure was certainly kept a secret as long as possible to avoid any escalation of the anti-government demonstrations, but ever since the international community had moved in to aid Taslima, the Islamists had lost the upper hand; they no longer had the power to stop her from leaving. Only Taslima and her family, it seems, believed the mullahs' threats.

The image of screaming religious zealots surrounding the airport at midnight to prevent her from leaving is something which Western audiences need to believe if they are to accept the story of Taslima, as a martyr on the altar of free speech. Taslima literally 'fleeing' Bangladesh remains a sturdy foundation plank in the parts of her mythology which eulogise her personal qualities, exaggerate her persecution and is served up on each occasion that a new article about her is released. At the time Taslima was resigned to disguising herself in traditional clothes, which she wore most of the time anyway, but not the tent-like *burqua*, covering her from head to toe, which is also part of the story. She merely added a long shawl to frame her bare face, pretending to be the most traditional of women—which she was not, and must have hated, unless she was so distraught that it no longer mattered.

The most forbearing one can be about Taslima's version is to say that she was mistaken, and put it down to her state of mind at the time. Yes,

Taslima must have been mistaken but has, with a story teller's eye and ear, incorporated this exciting scene, with a few dramatic touches, into the pages of the Taslima folklore, adopting this as part of her 'fleeing Dhaka extract'. Now it's stored in her memory as fact.

She arrived in Stockholm, a silent figure accompanied by a small entourage from the Swedish Foreign Ministry. The Swedes had boarded her plane in Bangkok. Until then she had been accompanied by a respected Bangladeshi man of senior years who, as part of the negotiations, was accompanying her. Bravado is second nature to Taslima, but she had never travelled alone before. While she knew her destination, she'd had no say in the matter.

But before she even arrived in Stockholm, the word was out in Dhaka that 'the bird has flown'. Sitting in the VIP lounge in Amsterdam, on the last leg of her flight, she saw pictures of herself on the television monitor. CNN was breaking the news that she was on her way to Sweden.

'They were so scared,' she said, speaking of the Foreign Ministry men who'd travelled with her. 'They were very scared,' she recalled, drawing out each word softly for effect, with a note of contempt in her voice.

On her arrival at Arlanda Airport she was met by the Swedish Foreign Minister and the president of Swedish PEN, Gabi Gleichmann. Policemen were everywhere.

Everyone involved with Taslima's case was euphoric: it was a time of celebration, which allowed them to momentarily forget Salman Rushdie's case, which was dragging on and on, with no end in sight. The European activists breathed a collective sigh of relief; finally they were moving ahead in their ideological war. Freedom-of-expression organisations around the world saw her case as a great victory in their fight against censorship and blasphemy laws. They thought that the Taslima campaign was over: for once the good people had won and she would live happily ever after.

They were being naive. Taslima is not a fairy tale princess; these delicate creatures belong to an alien tradition where princes awaken them with a kiss and they are expected to be grateful-ever-after. Their heroine had been rescued but, from the start, was never 'beholden' enough. I think the Swedes and their associates were disappointed, although they didn't completely understand her situation at the time. But of course, this is not the stuff of legends. Taslima had been rescued from the fire-breathing dragon of Islamic fundamentalism. The Dragon Slayers expected a happy ending and a happy ending they would have!

Unexpectedly, within a short time of her arrival in Stockholm, things took a turn for the worse and everything began to go wrong for Taslima. The play had ended; after a certain amount of celebrating everyone could get on with their lives as usual: Taslima, they thought, only needed peace and quiet and she could put her troubles behind her and get back to writing. But of course she needed much more than 'peace and quiet and a place to write'. This misunderstanding soured Taslima's relationship with Sweden almost from the beginning.

The life she was leading was far from normal; she found herself estranged from everything around her, although to many this would seem like indifference on her part. She was a terribly lonely and unhappy woman: nothing had ever prepared her for this new life. Now for the first time in her life, she was by herself, communicating with strangers in far-from-fluent English. As the months passed, Taslima became depressed, although at the time she withdrew into herself and only one or two people understood.

Even for a woman as outwardly independent as Taslima, there is no substitute for the family. Being part of a family in Bangladesh, Pakistan or India gives you a sense of belonging that nothing else does: loosening these bonds is agonising for many women and men. Longing to increase their own personal freedom and space, they find themselves emotionally paralysed when they try to negotiate a way out. As hard as they try, the time never comes for their own fulfilment.

Families may be loving or tyrannical—sometimes both—homes may be full of dark secrets or laughter, but the extended family still walls in its sons and daughters, and the mortar used is an age-old litany of duties and obligations where individualism is seen as selfish and Western. Taslima's background was no different. I knew because I'd visited her hometown of Mymensingh eight months before we came face-to-face in Sweden.

Mymensingh is a small scruffy district town with an amazing number of educational institutions and a smaller number of ruins going back hundreds of years ago to the time of the local rajahs and Hindu *zamindars* who collected revenue for the British and for themselves. The great Brahmaputra River, on whose banks Taslima played as a small child flows through the district and on the day I walked along the banks, young people were out on the water in boats enjoying themselves.

I talked for hours with her father and elder brother; who guarded the family secrets well, but everyone else I spoke to in her hometown told the same stories, and the anecdotal evidence was overwhelming.

Secrets have a way of spilling out in small towns and villages. Wagging tongues sift through every small sign looking for nuggets to trade. Other countries have the tabloids to spread their culture of gossip; Bangladesh uses other means.

A culture of gossip acts as a weapon of social coercion; its claws are sharp and it stands ready to attack the nonconformists, the prosperous, the failures; those who commit the sin of being beautiful or being too happy, or straying from approved ways. Like ripe mangoes, people fall from grace and waiting underneath to catch them are any number of celebrants with grasping hands stretched out waiting . . . Rich man, poor man, beggar man, thief, they are all on equal terms, and almost anyone can join in.

Unwritten laws, buried in customs and traditions, often conflict with the secular laws of the land and the constitution. There are times when they even override what is written in the Qur'an. These ways are entrenched in the nation's psyche and stretch back through history. Men control and, in most cases, protect women under their guardianship: sisters, wives, mothers and daughters, and, in return, women are expected to be chaste and obedient, and above all, self-sacrificing.

People have long memories and much of the ill will shown towards Taslima has its origins in the northern district town of Mymensingh where she grew up, the eldest daughter and third child amongst four children. Her family had a certain reputation which made life difficult for a sensitive young girl. The root of the trouble was her father.

According to Bangladeshi middle-class standards, Taslima did not come from 'a good family'. The family clan had no political ties, nor any recorded links of having fought alongside the freedom fighters in the 1971 Liberation War. They stood outside the magic circle of the district Establishment, for her father, although a doctor, was only the first generation in his family to be educated. Coming from a good family also meant there having no scandal attached to your name, a certain moral standing and a reputation for integrity. These were important values; you did not have to be rich, but people must respect you.

Dr Rajab Ali was an unpopular man, especially in the early part of his career as a forensic doctor. This was generally the lot of most forensic doctors at the time in Bangladesh. More recently the profession has emerged from under a dark cloud, but even today, in remote towns, they are viewed with muted hostility by their communities. Twenty or thirty years ago, unless they had overseas qualifications, forensic specialists were usually disliked in spite of their title and often found themselves friendless for two reasons: the post mortems they performed were regarded as ritually unclean, contravening Islamic law; but the main reason was because they often profited from their forensic trade. A bribe from an influential family could sway them to alter their autopsy reports and falsify death certificates; they were also seen as being in cahoots with the police. The further you are from Dhaka, the more likely it is that the police make their demands, and some doctors under their control become accomplices.

Strange stories circulated amongst the people of Mymensingh. During the day Dr Ali moved around the town normally, but at night he drank (religiously forbidden, but not uncommon in Bangladesh) and beat his wife and children. Taslima's father was obsessive about protecting the virtue of the females in his family: even in a society concerned about such matters, he stood out as a man of excessive behaviour. There were times when he locked the door of his house, allowing no visitors inside and refusing to let his wife and daughters out. Unusual behaviour, townspeople thought, for a man who was proud of his modern outlook; a man who was Muslim but not a devout believer and who revelled in his scientific background.

When I finally met Dr Ali and his son Faizul Kabir Noman, it was plain to see that age had caught up with Taslima's father, who was by then in his late sixties. The years had changed him; the anger, the passion, the control he had once exercised were gone. His eldest son practiced a benign authority over his father and now spoke for the family. Bengali sons serve many years before they inherit any authority of their own, and Noman, an educated man with exquisite manners, couldn't quite disguise how much he enjoyed his new role.

Noman made no secret of how proud he was of his sister and I sensed that he had always been protective; that it wasn't something he'd assumed because she was suddenly famous. He was the collector in the family and kept all of her clippings, video documentaries and other memorabilia.

Turning the pages of a program, he held it out for me to inspect as he pointed out all the important conferences his sister attended now that she lived in Europe. 'You see, at the University of Michigan, Taslima is the opening speaker.' He noticed details like that. He showed me the long list of events where his sister had been the state guest of presidents and chancellors, of ministers and mayors all over Europe.

Taslima's family home was simple and unsophisticated. When I looked around the small sitting room there were no expensive curtains or sofas, no rich carpets nor displays of brassware. It looked like a typical home from someone of the lower middle class, with all the giveaway signs of people not long removed from a village background and reminded me of my ancestral village home in Pakistan—the same displays of kitsch, the same calendars hanging on the green painted walls, the same rustic toilet arrangements. . . .

The brother was intent on creating a shrine to his famous sister. On one side of the room, sat a bust of Tagore, the grand master of Bengali culture, winner of the Nobel Prize for Literature in 1913. On the adjacent side of the room, on top of the sideboard containing her books, was another shrine, a large black-and-white portrait of Taslima. Noman was confident that one day his sister would receive the Nobel Prize for Literature just like her beloved Tagore. Most sisters would be happy to have a brother like Noman.

Noman's stories of family life were bathed in a golden light and he guarded the family secrets just as he watched over his sister's 'shrine'. But after three days in his hometown, I knew that his parents' union had been very unhappy and there was constant talk about his sisters and his younger brother—nothing they did escaped scrutiny.

❄

In accounts of her childhood Taslima does not hide the regular beatings her father gave his four children, for not learning their lessons properly, she tells us. Studying was all they were permitted to do. 'For a student, study should be all-absorbing, a manner of worship,' her father would regularly intone using an ancient Sanskrit injunction. Parents of today are still authoritarian but, in his day, Dr Ali was seen as harsher and stricter than even his contemporaries.

Taslima's parents were an unlikely match. Dr Ali's origins were humble and he was only a generation away from the plough. The man who helped him finance his studies and employed him at his own small *madrassah* as a tutor, in return for board, became his father-in-law, when it was arranged that he would marry his patron's daughter, Edul Wara Begum. Relatives on Taslima's mother's side were said to have links with a few small rural hotels, very modest establishments in Bangladesh. Taslima's parents married when her mother was thirteen and her father twenty-six.

Dr Rajab Ali was an ambitious man who raised himself in the world through his own efforts. He was determined that he would father a family of high achievers and increase the family's social worth. By contrast his wife was an uneducated woman who sought some kind of solace, for her suffering on earth, through folk Islam, sometimes falling under the influence of religious *pirs*—revered, saint-like figures—some of them holy men but others nothing more than charlatans and perverts. The unhappier women are, the more desperate they often become, moving from one *pir* to the next. The young Taslima grew up in a house divided; on one side hemmed in by her father's explosive anger, on the other side witness to her mother's mute resentment; a battle raged: education versus superstition, and science against religion.

Early on in life, Taslima began learning the wrong lessons. She witnessed terrible things: she learnt that men—even men you loved, like your father— were callous and violent. She witnessed her father 'doing something' with their maid in the kitchen, something the little girl could not understand at the time. She later recorded how a young uncle sexually assaulted her. You were not safe if you were female: men preyed on women—in her world women were powerless

When she was about twelve her father created a stir in the town by taking another wife (although there is some ambivalence as to the legality of the marriage), a former patient, it was said, with children of her own. The two wives were not kept under the same roof, and during these years Taslima's mother and the children lived with her parents while his second wife lodged with her children in a rented home. These were very bad years for Taslima. This marriage, or liaison, created tremendous ill feeling between her father's and her mother's family, which later abated when the second wife died prematurely.

Except for her father's drive and scientific outlook, there was nothing else for Taslima to admire, nothing she would want to imitate. There were only fragments of behaviour that she could learn from and they were full of contradictions: a scientific father, who beat them and left them for another family, a mother whose religiosity imposed a kind of tyranny on the household; she loved her mother as little girls do, but witnessed the way her father treated his uneducated wife, like a non-person. 'My mother was treated like a slave,' she has said many times.

'I think I've been angry all my life,' she told American journalist Mary Anne Weaver, in an article published in *The Washington Post* in 1994 'It began as a child. From the moment I entered puberty, I couldn't leave the house.'

Weaver's article is ambiguous about whether Taslima was ever sexually abused as a child, although she quotes verses from the poem 'The Kings' House' and Taslima's own words in conversation with her that seem to imply this. Three years later in Sweden, when I asked Taslima about the Weaver interview, she could not recall ever discussing this with the American journalist and rejected the idea that she may have given the impression that she was the abused child in the poem. The poem had nothing to do with her at all, she told me. She used the first person only to give the poem authenticity. If this was her purpose, then she succeeded beyond her wildest dreams. A year later, in her published memoir about her childhood, she again referred to being sexually assaulted by a young uncle.

When she entered puberty at the age of twelve she found her movements restricted, her earlier freedom was gone. A *chowkhidar* or guard—escorted her to and from high school, nothing unusual in Bangladesh, although Taslima enjoys telling this story as proof of her suffering. She hated the restrictions at home and at school, where a guard sat by the heavy metal gate preventing girls from going outside or boys edging near to talk to them. Her teachers told her she was a brilliant girl, but warned her against breaking the rules. If you broke the rules, they said, you were a bad girl; if you were obedient, you were a good girl.

So little Taslima grew up learning to hide her real self and to pretend. For eight years she lived as part of a large extended family of six to eight households all living in the same compound. A child with a soft sweet voice who carefully avoided eye contact, as becomes a young girl, she silently watched the goings on, how husbands treated wives, how mothers-in-law terrorised their daughters-in-law, drawing inside her the inequalities in treatment she observed between boys and girls, knowing that this was wrong and that there must be another way. She developed the habit of using silence as a way of punishing others, a habit observed from watching her mother.

She became the perfect student to please her father, and by her teens had discovered the emptiness of religion. Like many children she began to tell lies at a pre-adolescent age, falling into the only recourse for unhappy children surrounded by deceit, mistrust and suffocating restrictions. She soon discovered that in order to negotiate a bearable existence, young girls must learn how to manipulate and tell lies. In spite of warnings from her father and brothers that she keep away from boys, once Taslima went to college she broke the rules. 'I defied them, I used to talk to boys,' she says.

Over the years, I've met numerous young women in Dhaka, who become distressed as they describe the chicanery they employ just to stay out till five in the afternoon to attend a girl friend's birthday party—only females present of course—or some such innocent excursion. Parents and brothers watch them like hawks—and it's not just for the sake of being tyrannical or being obsessive about family honour. Acid attacks on young women are increasing; the stories are there in the papers for everyone to read next to horrific photos of disfigured young women.

Young Taslima learnt to steal her freedom and often slipped out of the house. Townspeople questioned her morals from about the age of fourteen for the string of boyfriends she was said to have, which added to her reputation as a 'spoilt' girl. This description dogged her even after she left Mymensingh, until the day in 1992, when she decided to embrace the pejorative term *noshta* by throwing it back in her critics' faces and writing a newspaper column translated into English as 'The Fallen Prose of a Fallen Woman'. In that one Bengali word the attitude of a whole society is revealed. *Noshto* (male) or *noshta* (female) has several complicated meanings, ranging from loss of virginity to the more general usage of someone whose honour is lost, whose sense of decency is awry—in society's eyes, they are 'spoilt', like fruit that has turned rotten.

But Taslima's first career, before she reinvented herself as a writer, was as a medical doctor. Determined to have another doctor in the family, her father turned his attention to his eldest daughter, who showed early signs of being much cleverer than her brothers. Other fathers thought education wasted on girls who eventually marry and leave their fathers' households to live under the guardianship of other men—Dr Ali wanted something different for his girls. Taslima's mother was not allowed to teach her daughters cooking and sewing. 'My father wouldn't permit it because he didn't want them to become housewives,' said her brother Noman. Dr Ali's belief in education redeemed himself in his daughter's eyes. 'If you have an education,' he told his children, 'then you can wash all your sorrows away.'

Slowly her father's dream became Taslima's dream, although at first she wanted to be an architect. But he would have none of that. 'My father wanted a doctor and he got one,' she told me in Sweden. Her sardonic smile and hard voice revealed everything I needed to know about this period of her adolescence.

The story of Taslima's adolescence is the story of a young girl whose natural instincts were smothered; this created an antagonism which later turned into a terrible rage against men. She knew she wanted more than was being offered and so she began to make herself the subject of her own life. To do this she had to turn her back on certain social values and Islamic traditions; this she was able to do without much inner conflict, but there were ties that held and they were all to do with her family—a close-knit, secretive group of people regarded askance by their local community. These scars Taslima carried with her when she moved to the capital city of Dhaka, where a much larger Establishment would view her as an outcaste.

An anarchist spirit like Taslima still needed relatives around her even if they caused her pain. Living alone in Europe would become a depressing experience for a woman used to an extended family, who for practically all of her adult life had at least one relative living with her. Other than a few days in Paris, she had never lived outside the Subcontinent before. These fears were not in keeping with her defiant heroine image and so she kept them hidden.

Originally Taslima thought her stay in Sweden would be temporary. Her writer's stipendium was only for one year. Nobody ever said as much, but she thought that sooner or later the situation must improve and she would go home—not spend years waiting for her case to be heard, waiting for the fundamentalists' anger to cool, maybe even a change of government?

As time passed, so hope died. Slowly it registered that there would be no return in the immediate future. Her lawyers advised against this until they'd received assurance from the government of the day that Taslima would obtain police protection and that those who had threatened her life would be prosecuted, according to the law.

Eleven years later they are still waiting for that assurance.

Back home, people thought Taslima had everything she'd ever wanted: fame, fortune, travel—heady champagne days. 'She loves playing the martyr and now she's the darling of the West.'

Yet despite all the media attention in the world, publication offers from everywhere, people wanting film rights, agents lining up to represent her, she remained unhappy and unsure of what was expected of her. For the moment she had lost her way. The evidence is overwhelming on this point. All she could do was hide her grief and carry off with dignity her role of 'the Woman from the East'. The supreme self-confidence she pretended, especially the bravado she acted out before the international media was at first a sham and it seems that she fooled most people, for a long while. Taslima Nasreen is a proud woman; if she cries, she cries in private. But clearly she didn't know how to behave on this new stage; she lacked the skills, while her new friends, of course, were expecting a female Salman Rushdie, or at the very least a Western-educated member of the literary elite who knew the rules and how to play the game of literary politics.

Lacking Rushdie's scholarly background and sophistication, in order to survive in this new world, Taslima had to focus on keeping her rescuers interested and working on her behalf. At first this wasn't difficult: they were joined in a symbiotic relationship and she became very adept at telling them what they wanted to hear. These tales were readily added to by the myths that had been created even before she landed on Swedish soil, myths which painted a picture of Taslima as her country's foremost feminist and the only voice in Bangladesh to speak out against Muslim extremists, stories which transformed Bangladesh into another Iran.

Competing with Rushdie as to which writer was the most endangered species became a subconscious habit to which her status was linked; she had to outdo him and so she allowed herself to become a professional victim. One thrilling story followed the other . . . Sheherazade needed 1001 tales to survive.

Taslima refers frequently to her '60 Days of Darkness' whenever she relives the last two months of her life in Dhaka. The tale of her living underground has the sound of a tale told once too often, but it's almost true, with only a few grandiose touches. It's a good story, one guaranteed to wring sympathy from her audience, and she tells it well in a low, almost monotonal voice, so that her audience hangs on her every word, reliving the experience with her, day by day. She feeds their appetites for the tabloid-like details they want to hear. No matter whether she is talking to an audience of atheists or humanists, ecofeminists or human rights activists, campaign journalists or politicians, there's something for every taste, a tailor-made soap opera, where the complex is reduced to a simplistic formula and everyone goes home satisfied . . . well worth the price of the ticket.

The real story of how she came to feel like a prisoner in Sweden after her arrival is something she shares with only a few friends. Perhaps she thinks people will label her ungrateful, and after all the Swedes have been, and continue to be, sympathetic towards Taslima, in spite of the fallout.

From the very beginning, Sweden seemed like another prison to Taslima. The tight security arrangements turned her into a captive all over again. In Dhaka she had hidden to avoid being served with a warrant for her arrest. Who was she hiding from in Sweden? The Iranian death squads endangering the life of Rushdie were real; with Taslima the notion that Bangladeshi extremists were linked to overseas terrorists was imagined.

'I was not a free person,' she said. 'The authorities made all the decisions for me. Twenty to thirty guards in the house all the time.' Stringent security arrangements hemmed her in, and wherever she went there was always a car in front of her vehicle and another behind.

She found herself trapped in a land with no rainy season, with no Monsoon.

> they have no thunder storm
> no gathering mangoes blown off the trees . . .
> All the white sallow skins always eagerly pray
> for the sun.

The life she was leading was claustrophobic, with few opportunities to make friends; her visitors were restricted. At one stage, except for her guards, she lived alone on a small island outside of Stockholm. This continued until even the Swedes realised that their author wasn't in danger from any death squads hot on her trail.

The Chairman of the Islamic Council in Sweden, Mahmood Aldebe, assured Taslima and the Swedish Government, in a press statement, that she was safe from any death threats. 'To punish those who blaspheme Islam is for God to do, not us,' he said. This message, he promised, would be conveyed to Muslims at all mosques in Sweden, but he warned that there was always the chance that someone might not pay heed. 'Taslima Nasreen should refrain from being provocative while she is here,' he said. But Taslima would not change her song for anyone.

Her lawyers' warnings, their threats that they would walk away, kept her in check for a while, but then the old reckless Taslima would re-emerge, and now that she was in Sweden and they were far away in Dhaka it was becoming increasingly difficult to restrain her.

In 1994 Sweden's Muslim community numbered about 200,000 in a population of eight million, mainly immigrants from Bosnia, Iran and Turkey. When the Swedish version of her banned book *Lajja* came out, there were no organised cries denouncing either the book or its author. The Bangladeshi Islamist groups hounding Taslima in 1994 were well outside those international networks which Rushdie had reason to fear.

Since mid-1995 therefore, she has been able to live without extra security surrounding her wherever she goes, although tight controls still spring into place when she gives lectures in public places, no matter which country she is visiting. France still seems to go overboard with security arrangements, but Taslima is a Francophile and the French left-wing intellectuals love her in return. The standing ovation she received from an audience gathered in the Hall of Versailles in their thousands demonstrated this.

When talking about her homesickness Taslima says simply, 'I suffered a lot.' Her phone bills to her family in Bangladesh were astronomical, although later she laughed as she related how most of her prize money went to pay them. Because of the time difference between Sweden and Dhaka, her sleep was broken. The simple words 'I suffered a lot' reveal little. Only when she plunges into herself do we have any indication: the sleepless nights, the incessant ringing of the phone, the sobbing of her relatives. What she was hearing from those near to her, fed her vivid imagination. The only calming influence she could trust was her team of lawyers.

Midnight phone, do not ring.
I give you a pillow, blanket, sleeping pills.
Come fall asleep.

The whole city is sleeping like the dead. . . .
When you ring lumps of ice slide down my spine
and turn me into stone,
and my whole body begins to tremble
like the leaves of a date-palm . . .

Here I lie all alone in
a distant land of snow
with no kin or friend
From time to time news come that
brainless dunces are running crazily
in the slush of politics. . . .

Slums grow and villages fill
with whores, preachers and beggars . . .
I hear that the pain in my father's chest
has become more intense,
that his sight is failing,
and as to my friends they have begun
to run away, one by one,
who knows where.

Midnight phone, do not ring.
No one is awake so late.
You too go to sleep.
    'Midnight Phone', Taslima Nasreen. Translated
    by Prof Kabir Chowdhury.

'I was dying,' she gasped, re-enacting her feelings for me, making it sound like her last breath of air. 'Here in this prison-like place, an isolated island in dark winter. There were times I wanted to commit suicide,' she said. 'Never to see my family again or go back to my country. I thought my life was totally destroyed.'

The reality of exile, with its heartbreaking sense of displacement crushes many individuals; it takes on the intensity of a physical pain. Strong men and women who have survived years in prison, or endured physical torture can find themselves broken by the never-ending day-after-day experience of exile. Writers are especially vulnerable because they are cut off from owning a sense of place.

Exile destroys many writers by cutting them into a hundred small pieces, which are thrown to the wind so that they never come together again. A piece here, a piece there, tearing them out of their context and whirling them away. More than a loss of identity, it implies the loss of a world, leaving you hanging in space; you are lost in the worst kind of existential loneliness imaginable—a dark alienation.

To many it's the wound from which they never recover. Only the strongest, or those who find a new meaning to cling to, continue to write. Many who lose their way are deeply affected when they discover that they've lost their relevance: their raison d'etre. Some break down. The society which spawned their writing, even societies whose mores they protest, connect them to their writing. Who listens to them now? Who will publish them now? How can they write in a foreign language?

Chapter 2

A Cold Red Carpet

You start forgetting everything. Even the impression of what an African forest is like, the smells, the colours. Your poetry becomes drier and you compensate by becoming more combative. . . .

Vincent Macombe, exiled Ugandan writer.

W hen Carola Hansson saw Taslima for the first time, she looked at her with a writer's eye. Down the red-carpeted aisle glided the woman they had all waited so long to see, making the perfect entrance at the annual Kurt Tucholsky presentation at Government House. Dressed in a red and yellow sari, Taslima was the centre of attention: people strained their heads to get a better look and a murmur of admiration swept through the hall. Sweden's newest human rights acquisition was on show and everyone rose to the occasion.

Carola remembered thinking at the time, that the woman seemed so calm and regal, as if she had an intuitive feeling for the part she was playing on this grand night. 'She behaved just like a queen. Yet underneath it all, I sensed she was not so sure of herself.' Carola writes fiction and had just had her seventh novel published, which is all about exile.

I had travelled by train to Uppsala, the famous medieval university town, to meet Swedish writer Carola Hansson, who, in 1994, was Swedish PEN's International Secretary. Taslima had ignored my request for the names of people who might help me develop a feel for her Swedish experience, so I'd been thrown back on my own resources. I turned for help to the Swedish Writers' Union and here my fortunes took a turn for the better, for the union gave me the names of two well-known local authors who were also members of PEN. Up till now, I had looked at the Taslima camp only through Bangladeshi eyes, but now I would have the chance to hear the story of Sweden's involvement and, with luck, meet some of the leading players.

Carola Hansson finally agreed to see me, if I was prepared to travel to Uppsala, about an hour's train journey from Stockholm.

She was a reflective woman in her forties, a generous woman I guessed, with short straight blond hair and a precise way of speaking. She helped me put together the first pieces of the Swedish narrative by telling me how Swedish PEN had originally come to hear of Taslima.

Information about Taslima's plight came from two sources as she recalled. London PEN, which houses the international secretariat, is headquarters for the International Committee of Writers in Prison and acts as PEN's nerve centre. Intelligence briefings are transmitted to its hundred or more sister centres around the world. Rapid Action Memos as they are called (RAMS for short) solicit immediate action: each PEN centre, from Kathmandu in the Himalayas to Perth, Australia, in the Indian Ocean, from Moscow to Mexico, begins its intensive lobbying campaign; letters, faxes, petitions, e-mails, an avalanche of paper, target governments and embassies, ministers and prime ministers. PEN members and their allies are committed to the cause of freedom of expression; their networks are impressive, and Taslima could not have found a stronger alliance. She was lucky and they have served her well—or better said, they serve each other well.

In my musings, PEN veterans and their cohorts behaved like the Dragon Slayers of ancient mythology, ready to slay the dragon, rescue the princess and carry her away to the cheers of the local peasantry. I kept these irreverent fantasies to myself, for Dragon Slayers take their work seriously, but, as I told myself, with only a trace of smugness, the Slayers fought for freedom of expression for writers the world over, and that included me.

The Swedish campaign to save Taslima began in late March, early April 1994. But as Carola remembers, the action this time was even more intense than usual, for the information on the Bengali author was coming simultaneously from two sources: out of London HQ as expected, but also from PEN's International Women's Committee in New York, where an American woman, Meredith Tax, organised what amounted to an additional campaign on Taslima's behalf.

Swedish PEN joined in the campaign and was finally able to head off rival offers from other countries, by offering Taslima the 1994 Kurt Tucholsky (KT) Prize, an annual award given to a writer in exile. The prize was a memorial to the anti-fascist German writer who had lived in exile in Sweden in the nineteen thirties. During the Second World War, Sweden was a neutral country, but not all Swedes were as welcoming as they are today; many were pro-German. Tucholsky was German, but anti-Fascist, which did not endear him to all Swedes. His experiences were unhappy, and he committed suicide in 1935.

The KT prize in 1993 was presented to Salman Rushdie. Although Rushdie was not actually placed in physical exile, as Carola explained, he nevertheless languished in a state of inner exile, a marked man hiding in fear of his life in London.

The PEN Board had made the decision to give Taslima the prize in May 1994, nearly three months before she 'fled' from Bangladesh. The timing of this decision is interesting because it occurred just before the controversial interview with *The Calcutta Statesman*. Carola said it was a unanimous decision. It was becoming clearer that even before matters had escalated in Bangladesh, months before the warrant for her arrest, Taslima and her foreign friends had made plans for her to leave Bangladesh, at least for one year, well before her desperate spate of midnight faxes, in July 1994, calling to the outside world for help.

There were times when Carola reminded me that there were gaps in her story because she had either forgotten, or had never been privy to, the ins and outs of the secret negotiations which were taking place in mid-1994 between diplomatic channels assisting Taslima and her Bangladeshi lawyers. Like a good writer of non-fiction, she didn't invent what she couldn't recall. Three years had passed, she was no longer a PEN board member; Taslima had drifted out of her life. She'd heard nothing about her for a long time.

'You really need to speak to Gabi Gleichmann,' she urged, 'he is the only one who really knows. He was the president of PEN at the time,' she continued, 'but he was forbidden to tell us much because of the tight security arrangements. After we made the decision to give her the prize, everything became very hush hush.'

She frowned as she searched for the correct words. It is never easy sharing memories with a stranger in a foreign language, but that afternoon, sitting together in Carola's white-walled sitting room, on her white leather couch drinking steaming mugs of coffee, she shared with me the gift of her writer's memory and what she remembered of Taslima. The experience had obviously puzzled her but she expressed no ill will, only regret for what she didn't understand at the time.

'Yes, I remember thinking how beautiful she looked the night of the KT prize giving. She had only been in Sweden for a few weeks and nobody had seen her or talked to her—not even the press. She stood on the dais, flanked by the Foreign Minister, Margaretha af Ugglas, and the Minister for Culture and Immigration, Birgitt Friggebo, along with Gabi, who all made the usual official speeches.'

'You know,' she added, 'I can't tell you what she said exactly, but I remember thinking that it was a different kind of speech compared to Salman Rushdie's inspirational address the year before, when he came to accept the same prize from us.'

Later I read an extract from the speech Taslima gave that night, on August 18, nine days after her arrival. Her words were stilted, as if someone else had written them.

'I have a dream, a dream of a world without inequality and oppression, where women could be strong in their own right, and enjoy dignity and independence.'

The speech, delivered in English, didn't sound like Taslima's 'voice' at all, I thought.

'It was nothing that we did not expect to hear,' Carola said slowly and carefully like a woman thinking aloud. 'Maybe this is a strange impression for me to hold, but it seemed to me that the journalists were also expecting something different,' she said. 'We were all waiting to hear something more reflective, something, yes—something deeper, about her own situation and that of women in Bangladesh.'

Plainly speaking, they were expecting someone else: most likely someone in the mould of their enduring favourite, Salman Rushdie. Many members of the Swedish Defence of Rushdie Committee were also members of PEN. Well, it was too late to mark the parcel 'Return to Sender'. Following in the footsteps of Rushdie the author, philosopher and scholar was frightening. But that night Taslima touched the hearts of many in the audience, including Carola, who sensed that she was playing a role, but carrying it off well.

Her vulnerability reached out to her listeners. Tired as she was, she knew that she had disappointed a number of people. But the media, through its magic lens and with the help of the pomp and circumstance of the presentation, revealed none of this and turned it into a celebration, showing the world a triumphal victory for freedom of speech, as it was—on the surface.

Taslima could feel the expectations out there in the auditorium that night and other nights to come, but was helpless to meet them. Although she experienced problems expressing herself in English, she understood more than people realised. Speaking a foreign language was like perjuring her identity; she was not the real Taslima. Four years later the hurt was still there.

'They expected me to be an expert on everything,' she told me. 'They were looking for someone with a Masters in Literature and Islamic Studies. I felt terribly embarrassed when they asked me the solution to world problems like the Middle East Crisis, and how women and Islam fit into the modern world.' She could smile now, but her distress was real at the time.

'I think I disappointed them because my answers were not good.' She sounded like a child trying hard to please her parents, only to fail her exams and know she has disappointed them once more. In the back of her mind she wonders if she can ever please them.

She understood that she was a symbol, a heroic figure worldwide, wise beyond her years, but she couldn't make them understand that she was unable to discuss the topics they wanted her to discuss: in other words, she could not read the script they wanted her to read.

Taslima was out of her depth with the Western media. The Indian media had been adoring in the early days of her ascent and with the help of her friends from the Ananda Bazar [sic], the Calcutta-based publishing empire; they were pliant and eager to embellish her stories. Overseas, the European media was less open to manipulation, and to everyone's impatient eyes she was beginning to sound like a one-story woman.

'All I wanted was to tell them about my problems,' she tried to explain. 'I wanted to tell them what I saw in my country, and I wanted to tell them about my fight against religious fundamentalism.'

All very well, but after a period of time, journalists found this monotonous except for those papers dedicated to campaign journalism. Other papers began to move on in search of fresher game.

Carola and Taslima, from two different perspectives were telling the same story: how practically everyone the young woman met greeted her with unrealistic and, in the end, unfair expectations, how she felt suffocated by these expectations. There were times when she withdrew into silence.

What then unfolded was a tale of the best of intentions gone awry, shot down by a clash of expectations. The Swedes seemed to realise that Taslima badly needed rest—'peace and quiet' were the two words they often used in describing her needs, but Taslima needed more.

Completely alone, she needed emotional support, but found herself surrounded by strangers, all wanting to reach out and 'touch' Taslima as if their lives would be transformed by being close to her. Taslima was caught up in her own nightmares, and believed she would be murdered by a death squad following her to Sweden. Whether her family fed these fears in their communications is not known, but certainly they did nothing to allay them.

'When I was hiding in Dhaka,' she told me, 'my father sent me a letter and it was the most wonderful letter that a daughter could get from her father. He said, "You have written the truth and if you die, don't worry because you are giving up your life for the truth. Remember, don't compromise, and never surrender."'

She had not expected to live in hiding in the West, she told me, always under lock and key. Taslima received long-distance love from her family and sound advice from her lawyers, but there was no one by her side to quieten her hysteria, and once more she fell prisoner to her imagination.

Looking back now, Carola recognised signs she'd overlooked at the time. 'Life was so difficult for Taslima because the media didn't treat her like an artist or a poet, or a writer. They treated her like a celebrity, almost like some famous political figure or a great freedom fighter. They talked about her novel of course, but you could feel that it wasn't important for them.

'We were also to blame, because we treated her in a very ethnocentric way, without realising it; like a queen from the orient, and because of her reputation we also made the mistake of treating her with too much respect; we were in awe of her and this was not good for her—it was the wrong kind of respect, because I don't think she knew how to . . .' her words trailed off. 'It was tempting for her, I mean, it is nice to be treated like this,' she went on, 'but it is probably awful too,' she stopped suddenly. I thought, at the time, we were having language problems. Later, by talking to other Swedes, I filled in the gaps.

'You really must speak to M,' she said earnestly, 'she is the only one who got close to her.'

The next day I contacted M, Taslima's first real Swedish friend. She refused to see me. No, she wouldn't fuel the rumours about Taslima, she said; besides Taslima was vulnerable and needed protecting. Her response took me by surprise. I made no attempt to change her mind: it may have been because I admired her stance, or because I recognised intransigence when I heard it, or both. I put the phone down, a sadder, but wiser, woman.

Inadvertently, I was being told that I'd missed something right under my nose and so obvious that M assumed I must know all about it. Confused, and excited at the same time, I sensed that I was about to stumble onto a new piece of the Taslima puzzle. M was the first person (I hadn't met) who hinted at a major controversy. Nothing had caught my eye in the papers; Carola had closed ranks, although it was becoming clearer that her half-finished sentences had nothing to do with communication problems. Taslima, herself had so far remained *stumm*. Paradoxically, by trying to protect her friend, M had made a slip. I still had no idea what I was looking for but there was definitely 'something' out there, a large black hole, and while it might not contain a body it certainly needed filling in.

The next day I found a discreet Swedish PEN member, a woman who at the time had watched everything from the sidelines, who revealed, with only a little gentle pushing, that there were indeed a few things some people wanted hidden; for the first time the word 'scandal' was used—'the literary scandal, one might call it, of October 1994', which illustrated the old adage that the best of intentions can go astray.

⊕

Eugene Schoulgin is a PEN activist of long standing and a critically acclaimed novelist widely read in Nordic countries. He lives in Sweden, but is really a Norwegian by birth and predisposition. He describes himself as 'a Norwegian writer with strong ties to Russian and Italian literature'. An erudite, witty man with a wicked sense of humour, he watched what took place with a mixture of horror and a dollop of malicious delight, which the writer in him was powerless to stop.

We sat talking in the large kitchen of his spacious high-ceilinged apartment, where he prepared a simple but elegant lunch: a plain omelette cooked to perfection, ground black pepper, white bread, dry white wine and excellent coffee.

But before we began to talk of Taslima, he told me a fascinating tale which rivalled 'the Taslima affair' for intrigue and deception. And as this took place deep in the underground caverns of the Palace of Dragon Slayers, and tells us so much about the strange ritual and beliefs of these folk, I think it only right and proper that this be recorded in any fairy tale accounts of 'Taslima and the Dragon Slayers', although I must insert a disclaimer that the narrator's voice and the language used to record this tale is not Eugene's, but mine, and that he is not to blame for any 'allegorical flourishes'.

Eugene told me, what I'd long suspected, that even the Dragon Slayers fought amongst themselves, especially in the 1990s as the Cold War was coming to an end.

For years, a battle had been raging inside International PEN, which at the time was dominated by a fine old guard of Eurocentric warriors.

Over many decades, warriors in the West had used all their energy and fierce determination to defeat the two-headed Communist Dragon in what became known in legends as 'The Cold War'. They had completed their mission and the Red Dragon was no more.

But a new dragon had been discovered, a Dragon from the East, with a loud roar and a belief in itself that was terrible to behold. This dragon, feared far and wide, from the rugged mountains of Afghanistan, across the plains of the Punjab to the steamy jungles of Bengal, to the high Atlas Mountains in Northern Africa, and the oil-rich lands of the Middle East, had an insatiable, but discerning appetite, for not just any old sacrifice would do, he preferred disobedient women.

This new Dragon was called Islamic Fundamentalism, although there were times when the Dragon Slayers forgot this and thought that all Muslims were dragons and

dangerous, even more dangerous than the cigar-smoking Dragon, the last of his breed,
on the small island off the coast of Florida.

Now around this time, as well as taking on this new species of dragon, the slayers
also began fighting amongst themselves. A reform faction emerged from amongst the
Western Dragon Slayers, a younger breed who began to gather numbers from around
the world, for what would prove to be the last great battle in the annals of PEN
history, although it could never be written in the Golden Chronicle, the enormous
tome which non–Dragon Slayers, sometimes known as Dragon Slayer apprentices
Level Three, were allowed to read.

They rallied from far and wide to end the rule, the despotic rule, they believed, of
the Greatest Dragon Slayer of them all, a Grand Old Warrior of towering intellect
with charismatic powers who sat on the throne and refused to budge. So powerful
was his magic that it took many, many years to bring about his defeat and those who
rallied to his cause from loyalty, or habit, or because he always laid out a sumptuous,
twenty-course banquet for his friends, wailed loudly so that even the Dragons, snorting
and roaring as dragons tend to do when they are not devouring maidens, could hear
them in their secret mountain retreats.

But the rebels had won the day and a new Dragon Slayers' Council had been
elected to bring about change and compose a New Testament of Dragon Slayer Rules
and Regulations which all must sign with their blood in a mighty show of unity for
the new millennium. Amen

✿

'We used to blame everything on the Communists during the Cold War,'
said Eugene, 'they were the threat, the great evil. At the time most intelligent
people knew that it was propaganda and I think the same can be said today:
although Islam seems to be the new global enemy, people are only afraid of
the fundamentalist kind.'

The time had come to talk about Taslima. 'Ah! there hangs a tale,' he
said, pulling a face, 'a difficult case for Swedish PEN,' he added. 'We looked
at her through the eyes of the Western world, although we didn't realise we
were doing this at the time.'

I asked him what was by now an obligatory question. Were they expecting
a female Rushdie?

'Yes, a female Rushdie,' he repeated, 'and Gabi fell into the trap—
it proved his undoing. In Sweden, everyone had her well-being at heart
and she was wined and dined and generally feted. But they were soon
disappointed because she is not an intellectual—that she is not,' he said
emphatically.

I was beginning to understand that as well as being an expert on international relations, Taslima was also expected to know all about Western

literature. These expectations were based on an alarming Eurocentric vision
of the world. Perhaps it never crossed her new friends' minds that Taslima
was devoted to the literature of her own language, with a rich tradition spoken by more than two hundred million people, in comparison to the eight
million Swedish speakers. She spoke Bengali, wrote in Bengali, dreamt in
Bengali—Why should she be familiar with Jane Austen, Dickens, Günter
Grass or Toni Morrison? Were they familiar with the works of Tagore, the
Bengali Nobel Prize winner of 1933?

Eugene tried to be fair. So while he didn't expect Taslima to have a broad
arts background—he knew she'd been a medical student—there were still
universal standards that writers were expected to uphold. 'The trouble is,'
he said, 'that she has no idea of literature from a writer's perspective.'
He pronounced 'literature' as if it should be in italics. Eugene was a tall,
handsome man with a feel for drama, which gave him a definite presence
that would have served him well if he'd pursued an acting career. Probably
he'd realised in time that an actor is reading someone else's lines. . . . that it
is the words that are important, for the words never die.

Ironically, Taslima had sought sanctuary in a country with a very closed
definition of literature and found herself face-to-face with yet another
literary establishment which was just as puzzled by her as the one she'd left
behind in Bangladesh.

Eugene turned out to be a brilliant raconteur, with a story for every
Taslima occasion. 'Once when I was travelling with her in Norway, she
announced to me, "You know I have published more than twenty-four
books!" I mean what a nonsensical thing to say to me,' he said, sounding
cross. 'To be so precise is ridiculous—you might say, more than twenty—
okay, but . . . ,' he spluttered with an exasperation that he could still taste
four years later.

'And then, of course, she asked me, "How many have you published?"
and I replied "I have published six and I have been a writer since 1970,"
and she looked at me and I could see that I had lost all respect in her eyes
because she thought it was the number of titles you'd published that was
significant!'

Trying to give him some consolation, I told Eugene, that in Bangladesh,
writing books was often a hasty affair, 'In one year,' friends told me, 'writers
in Bangladesh produce anything between three to six books. But they are
very slim books—sometimes twenty pages; sometimes maybe a hundred.'

The Eugene–Taslima contretemps had taken place in the first few months
of her stay. Taslima now knew better. She'd been exposed to European publishers and understood that editorial standards were very different to those in
Bangladesh, where writers were constantly under pressure to produce more

and more. In Bangladesh, she intimated, some publishers don't even bother to read the book. 'In Europe the writer has time and there is editorial help,' she had told me. Not wanting to stand in the way of a good story, I decided not to share the news of her transformation with Eugene.

'I found it such a strange opinion,' he continued, 'for an author to hold about literature. You are an important writer only if you have written something important! It's not a question of the number of titles you have produced.' I was left to discover for myself that Eugene had spent thirteen years completing his trilogy, known as *The Frederico Trilogy*, a collection described by Nordic critics as 'a literary masterpiece'.

Taslima felt threatened by everything and everyone around her, Eugene maintained as he went on to tell me about an incident that still puzzled him. Eugene's brother is a doctor and had once offered to show Taslima and Eugene around the State Hospital where he worked, but she became very nervous, Eugene said. 'She—didn't—want—to—go,' said Eugene and he started to wonder about the standard of her medical education; whether she felt threatened by new technology she might never have had access to before, or whether she felt her Bangladeshi qualifications inferior by comparison.

His story had a familiar ring and reminded me of the time Taslima had been invited to visit a newly opened rape crisis centre for women at a university hospital in Sweden. Because of her reputation as a feminist, everyone thought this would be interesting for Taslima and the staff could learn a lot from her, they were sure. Nothing more than a quiet, low-key visit was proposed, but again that withdrawal, that quiet obstinate refusal. It matched Eugene's story exactly.

Everyone seemed to have their own Taslima tale and many of these stories had a common thread running through them. They showed Taslima's unwillingness—even fear—of exposing to outsiders, any 'flaws' in her background which might be detected by experts. Encounters which might affect her reputation as a writer, or as an international feminist, or a medical doctor, she would avoid. And those who'd built the Taslima mythology collaborated. Even foreign television crews on assignment, sensing that the Swedish honeymoon was over, avoided asking the hard questions; and continued transmitting the same messages with the old images of ranting mullahs and veiled women which they regularly fed their audiences.

Taslima supporters all believed in the same cause: promoting freedom of expression and opposing Islamist extremism. Anything which dented the Taslima mythology, which by now was well circulated, had to be kept hidden from the outside world. This seems the most plausible interpretation behind these numerous stories. It also explains why Taslima never corrected her host's impressions that she came from an upper, or at least upper-middle, class background. When she talked of servants and how she couldn't cook, they assumed she came from a sophisticated, elite family background like the many Western-educated professionals from the Indian subcontinent they'd encountered, the only ones I half suspected they felt comfortable around, because they were more like themselves. This was their only point of reference.

Underneath her glamorous public persona, there is a simplicity to Taslima. She is a product of her society, a woman from the lower middle class, and as people say in the Indian subcontinent, 'a daughter of the soil', meaning indigenous or non-Westernised. Taslima is typically Bengali in some ways, outrageously different in others. Foreigners who are more familiar with Indian or Pakistani women, educated in the West, with anglicised manners and upper-class backgrounds, find Taslima an enigma—it is the medical degree which fools them. They forget she is a local girl from a provincial background. This is her strength and this is why she writes as she does.

If you thought long and hard about these Swedish anecdotes, there were alternative explanations for her reluctance, but they presupposed a certain residue of goodwill and by now many Swedes had exhausted their supply. The other rationale for her 'strange behaviour' surfaced in my mind much later. Everyone expected an expert on international relations, philosophy, and comparative religions. Was she also expected to pit her medical knowledge against professors from the West? Did they think she could carry on a cross-cultural dialogue on rape trauma and rape counselling? The strain of undertaking visits and carrying on a specialist dialogue in a language you were just exploring would have worn her down. And we know that at the time Taslima was still unhappy and depressed. Seldom did she have access to interpreters, and when she did, they were usually well-meaning amateurs.

As I sifted through the evidence, I found yet another possible explanation for Taslima's reluctance. Taslima's medical career can best be described as intermittent after her first three years as a family planning doctor between 1986 and 1989. According to her second husband, Naim, Nasreen, as he always called her, and government service were not a good mix.

'As a government employee she was the most casual person I've ever met,' Naim had told me a year earlier in Dhaka. 'She didn't visit her office regularly. There were times when she would go to her country posting, sign on and then leave. I once saw her personal file in the Department of Family Planning, I used to act as her secretary, sometimes, and once her pay was stopped for eleven months, there were many complaints about her non-attendance and careless attitude.'

Even in Bangladesh, Taslima thought of herself as a professional writer. Naim believed that she stayed in the job because she enjoyed her doctor title, although, as he quickly pointed out, local journalists who disliked her refused to use her title whenever they wrote about her: by dropping her title, they lowered her standing in status-conscious Bangladesh.

It seemed plausible enough that once she became prominent as a writer Taslima started to slowly delete the medical part of her identity and finally resigned in 1993. Having closed this chapter of her life, she may no longer have thought of herself as a doctor. A logical explanation, I thought, certainly less judgmental, but lacking dramatic appeal.

So the good-hearted Swedes found themselves with this perplexing woman on their hands. She looked gorgeous, but said very little and when she did speak she often sounded arrogant. As Eugene told the story, they wined and dined her and were eager to be hospitable and sympathetic— whatever was called for. But some of them became fed up with her be-haviour. 'We still believe in the cause,' they would say, 'but don't bring her around to our house again, please.' She was developing a reputation for be-ing rude and appearing indifferent. There was the time she failed to arrive at a formal dinner organised in her honour, with twenty Swedish women writers waiting with a floral tribute, waiting and waiting—no message and no Taslima. Weeks later when the organiser ran into her and asked what had happened, the answer she received was along the lines of "Oh, I didn't feel like going. . . ." 'Never ever a hint of an apology for standing everyone up,' the organiser told me, still nonplussed by it all four years later. Many of her acquaintances would tell me over the next twelve months, sometimes with amusement, more often with bewilderment, that 'she doesn't know how to behave.'

Her deep depression at the time is only a partial explanation for her behaviour, for in Bangladesh also people remarked on her 'unique style'. It seemed that Taslima doesn't believe in, or always abide by, social niceties which influence most of us regardless of our culture. She seems as natural as a young child in this respect, with all the self-centredness of a child: if she doesn't like you she doesn't dissemble, if she's bored it shows . . . at sometime or other she turned inward displaying 'a self-involvement which was almost autistic', as a London PEN member once exclaimed in frustration to me. She doesn't appear to acknowledge social norms unless she's playing a role, or unless she wants something: the role of the hospitable Bangladeshi hostess when I visited her home for instance, or the charming writer bewildered by her celebrity, which she often played to her interviewers. Like a child, she tries to get her own way, either through tantrums or by withdrawing into a deep, punishing silence.

Taslima measured out her charm only on certain occasions, and if she was bored, she was very, very bored. Besides, the Swedes could never forgive her unpunctuality. The woman was always late! Taslima was being true to Bangladeshi custom, where socialising is an unhurried art form, rarely a punctual event. This doesn't endear you to the Western media, as she found out over time.

Eugene remembered one occasion when he had taken her to visit his elderly mother, who had prepared luncheon for her son's guest. 'She,' meaning Taslima, 'made life very difficult,' he sighed.

Sitting down at the table, Taslima announced regally that the bread she was being offered was not fresh. 'True,' admitted Eugene, 'it was a day old; my ninety-year-old mother had not been to the baker's that morning.'

' "I never eat stale bread," said Taslima and she tossed it aside.' In Eugene's memory she threw it down. He was shocked because he had always thought that Muslims were so respectful towards elderly people. How did his mother react? At the time she said nothing; 'We covered our embarrassment as best we could,' he said. Later she told her son that there must be something wrong with the woman.

People's patience was running out and no one seemed to understand what was wrong. The chances for a happy stay in Sweden were disappearing. Taslima was in a state of mourning for her past life and as the stress and the uncertainty continued, she revealed more of herself.

According to Eugene, the Swedes had never initially wanted Taslima. 'Gabi Gleichmann wanted her to come and he moved in very fast; he was the first on the scene before a lot of other countries.' Eugene made Gabi sound like an ambulance-chasing lawyer, or a tow truck that hovers around dangerous intersections waiting for accidents to happen. Meeting Gabi Gleichmann was becoming a serious priority, but my time was running out.

'How this all happened is still a mystery to me,' said Eugene, 'because you see Gabi did a lot of things we didn't learn about. But then perhaps I am wrong and maybe it was her idea to come to Sweden.' Although he seemed baffled, I could tell which version he preferred.

'She certainly came at the right political moment,' he said. 'She got the majestic treatment that Rushdie never received because, at the time, Government leaders were scared of the Iranians,' he leant forward in his chair eager and happy to impart this information to me. 'You see, Taslima was not as "dangerous" as Rushdie,' he said. 'The politicians and the venerable statesmen of Europe could meet her, pour honours on her head—the French soon got over their initial nervousness,' he said in an aside. 'She was wined and dined by German Chancellor Kohl, all the major French politicians and many others, and you know,' he wriggled in his chair like a school boy, 'in a funny way it seemed to make up for Rushdie—it made up for all the things they couldn't, or wouldn't, do for him when he was in desperate need of diplomatic help.'

The Swedish Defence of Rushdie Committee still existed and worked together with Defence of Rushdie committees in nine other capital cities. Trying to lobby the Government to be more forceful in its diplomacy on Rushdie's behalf was hard work, with little to show for it at the end of the day.

'Yes,' Eugene said, 'they could spout their anti-Islamist phrases loudly this time. They could look brave without taking risks.' He finished off his speech, filled our coffee cups to the brim and returned to the theme of Taslima.

'Of course we wanted her to have the KT prize, there was no debate over that . . . ,' he explained. 'It was exactly right for her. Every year this prize is given to a writer who is in danger in her own country: can't work there, who needs a place to hide away and work in peace for a year, it suited her case perfectly.' But that all seemed long ago, said Eugene. He did not see or hear much about Taslima. Nowadays she was very quiet inside Sweden and there'd been nothing about her in the newspapers for years.

'Nobody takes much notice of her any more,' he said. There was no malice; it was a statement of fact. 'She has her own friends of course and lives quietly. They say she talks of leaving Sweden for the USA, but I think she will be here for a while.'

Eugene and Taslima saw more of each other outside Sweden these days. 'Wherever I go abroad to conferences, we bump into each other at different literary sessions,' Eugene said.

'I'm not sure what she says when she goes around the world—well,' he contradicted himself, 'that's not really true—she says the same thing over and over again. She really has only one performance. That may be rude to say, but it's a fact!'

Because of this, he said, she was constantly on the move from one conference to the next. Taslima, of course, said Eugene, was always an invited guest, a necessary symbol, at events of this kind. Other women would give the lecture and then use Taslima as a figurehead—her speeches usually lasted about five or ten minutes and then the audience would respond with loud applause. It sounded formulaic and uninspiring, but then he'd heard it all before.

Lunch was over, it was time for me to go out into the cold streets, so I kept him talking a little longer than I should have. He was a kind man and didn't seem to think too badly of me and I knew he was 'between books'.

That very morning he'd received news that *Salto Mortale*, the last volume in his famous trilogy, would soon be out in the bookstores.

With the passage of time, Eugene's attitude has mellowed. 'I feel sorry for Taslima now,' he confessed. 'If anybody is a victim, she is: a victim of everyone's expectations, of all the political manoeuvres of the West, and also a victim of her own pride.'

She needed to return home, he said, and take up a normal life again. Eugene could hardly be expected to know that this was unlikely to happen. Taslima supporters were thin on the ground. 'They all support me secretly,' she had told me the day before. I knew from my own visits, that many progressives inside her own country preferred a Taslima-free Bangladesh.

'Nowadays,' he continued, 'I think she wants more than anything else to be left in peace and to be let off the hook.' Although they rarely saw one another, Eugene was still in touch with people who counted Taslima as a friend. 'They say she is really fed up and wants to get off this damned carousel and lead a normal life.'

Eugene believed that she should leave Sweden; that it was very bad for her development as a writer to stay here and how the isolation produced the same kind of deadening inner life for most non-Swedish writers.

'We have a lot of exiled writers here,' he said, 'some are published, but most are not.'

Everyone I met added narrative pieces to the story of Taslima. In Stockholm they were literary people who knew one another, shared similar passions and fell in an out of fights with a great sense of style. They loved carrying on feuds when the mood or a misunderstanding occurred amongst them. Many of them lived out their lives like the characters they created in their writing—always a touch of the autobiographical in between the covers of the book. In Denmark, Germany and France, I found similar circles of writers: authors, poets, translators, journalists: all disciples of the power of the written word. And they all shared something else in common, never failing to ask me before I departed, 'Who else are you talking to? Who else will you be visiting while you're here in Stockholm, or London, or Berlin, Paris, New York?'

Eugene was as curious as the next person. 'I'm trying to make contact with Gabi Gleichmann,' I answered. From his expression I could tell that he didn't approve.

'You say you want to talk to Gabi, and of course you are free to do so. How can I stop you?' he laughed at himself again, but then grew serious. 'I don't think he will give you anything new,' he said 'and the problem is that he is filled with hatred towards her—it was such a big scandal you know.'

Pride wouldn't let me disclose my ignorance, but curiosity demanded to be told: an interesting tug of war with curiosity winning in the end. And so I listened quietly to Eugene's version of the Taslima and Gabi saga, a truncated version because time had run out.

'It really came to a head at the Frankfurt Book Fair in October 1994,' he told me, as I inched my chair forward, 'and here I must defend Taslima, I really must,' he said as he drew me into another Byzantine narrative. It was an intriguing, fragmented story about two people whose lives were linked together for a short, intense period, almost like soldiers of fortune. Their personalities were bound to clash; it was only a matter of time. Eugene gave me only a short introduction to what had happened, admitting that he and Gabi had had their own difficulties working together.

By now I was convinced that I could not leave Sweden without talking to Gabi Gleichmann. Of course he might turn to stone and prove as immovable as *M*. In less than a week I would be leaving Stockholm, barely enough time to persuade him, if he proved reluctant.

That same night I rang his home. Suddenly it mattered very much that I talk to this man. Gabi's voice was husky and attractive, his English fluent, with a slight American accent. The voice on the other end of the phone didn't belong to a man with thick glasses and a receding hairline, yet this was the likeness I'd seen in a poor-quality black-and-white newspaper photo in which he'd worn a suit and looked like a good burgher pleased with the occasion.

He was exceedingly pleasant to me on the telephone and agreed to talk about the behind-the-scene machinations at a diplomatic level, which were an essential part of the story. He would not talk about any personal matters whatsoever, he told me politely but firmly.

'We have a saying here,' he said. 'If you can't say anything good about someone then say nothing.' It was nice to know the Swedes were in tune with the English-speaking world with regard to homilies. He was being direct and I liked that too; not having to go round in polite little circles saved time.

We talked for nearly an hour that night over the phone. At the end of our conversation, Gabi mentioned that he'd be happy to see me if I ever returned to Sweden, and by now I had the germ of an idea that returning to Stockholm next summer might be possible. Next year International PEN was holding its Annual Congress in Helsinki, Finland, and I had plans of infiltrating the Dragon Slayers' meeting at the end of the northern summer next year. Sweden and Finland were neighbours ... I would definitely return in 1998 and talk to Gabi face-to-face.

Eugene's last words came back to me. 'She's been mistreated,' he'd said; 'she's been used by people.'

At the time I wasn't sure if he'd meant anyone in particular. Gabi had been resolute in insisting that he would not discuss anything outside of the political and diplomatic context surrounding the story of Taslima's 'rescue'.

'Nothing personal,' he'd warned me.

Ten months later, he would change his mind.

Chapter 3

A Tug of Wills

I'll no more pour my nectar into an undeserving vessel.
If you beckon to me once again you'll get no response.
I'll be your veritable God, a motionless rock.
                    Taslima Nasreen, translated by Prof. Kabir Chowdhury

Meeting Gabi lay ahead of me in the warm summer months to come, eight months away, with the fragile promise of a breakthrough if everything went well. Meanwhile I was preoccupied with Taslima: frustrated by the obstacles she placed in my way, for she delighted in keeping secrets, just as I was driven to perversely breach them.

One day followed the next as I faithfully made my way to Taslima's like a suitor doggedly following in the tracks of the beloved: in and out of the subway station, Central Station, bus station and then a short walk loaded down with briefcase and tape recorder; running through the themes in my head that I wanted to cover that day, yet knowing it was impossible to follow the skeleton of a semi-structured interview. Each session followed the same routine: I would be handed a mountain of press clippings, there were videos for me to look at starring Taslima in different locations: Taslima looking out to sea, or walking alone beside the banks of a lake in Munich, or crossing a bridge in Prague—a romantic, melancholy figure. We would stop for lunch and each day I was treated to her mother's fine cooking. The afternoons were spent in her office, face-to-face: Taslima talking, me listening, with only now and then the sound of a tug of wills, whistling through the air like an arrow.

I watched Taslima and her mother together, noting how Taslima had reversed the roles of mother and daughter, as adult daughters often do. From the downstairs lounge-room where I sat, I could hear her above me cooing little Bengali songs, to her mother, which to my untutored ears, sounded like lullabies. I was seeing a Taslima absorbed in someone other than herself. Concerned about her mother's health, she fussed around her like a mother hen: watching what she ate at lunch, carefully counting her pieces of chicken; checking to see if she was dressed warmly before leaving the house, adding an extra scarf; making sure she'd taken her medicine and monitoring her diabetes. When she thought nobody was watching she showed her love in small tender ways, which took me by surprise.

In media interviews she always painted a negative, one-dimensional picture of her mother, scorning the only consolation her mother found in an otherwise miserable married life. Taslima's comments against religion were harsh. She was full of praise for her father's scientific mind, but used her mother to illustrate the oppressive lives of women as if she were talking about a stranger, exploiting her as subject matter, as writers are wont to do, in most of her tabloid interviews with Indian journalists. In public she seemed incapable of understanding the reasons why her mother took refuge in a devotional style of Islam. Taslima displayed no sympathy whatsoever—Islam was the disease and she was the doctor.

When talking to journalists she would select which details of her personal life she gave away, picking examples which reinforced stereotypes, made for good sound bites and helped mould her image into the woman she wanted to become. Taslima never tired of telling her foreign audiences how fearless she was, using examples that might on reflection have been dubbed reckless had her public not been carried away by the 'perils of Taslima' and the need to see her as a victim, a figure reflecting their own vulnerability. Away from the cameras, however, she was quite capable of contradicting herself. The dissonance was hard to reconcile, so at the end of the day, you weren't sure what to believe: first you would have to consider the context.

For most of her life Taslima lived under the same roof with a superstitious, religious person who prayed five times daily and visited her own local *pir* for spiritual guidance. As a little girl Taslima had been made to recite the Qur'an in Arabic, which she could not understand. After finding a Bengali translation she started asking questions her mother could not answer. 'Just recite the verses,' she was admonished. The author says that she turned atheist when she was twelve, and in many interviews talks of her disillusionment after reading in the Qur'an that the sun moves around the earth. After reading her science book she learnt the truth. 'Allah is a liar,' she told her shocked mother.

Mother and daughter lived out an uneasy truce, the kind of family relationship seething with contradictions and unresolved tensions, feelings that we usually accept as the price for intimacy and a sense of belonging.

Taslima loved her mother but, as a young girl, dreaded following in her footsteps. She loathed the kind of domesticity she saw played out before her eyes: the subservience, the sacrifice, the extinction of any creative impulses. The women in the large extended family on her mother's side, that she was a part of during her formative years, reinforced the kind of life she could expect. Love and shame pulled at her.

"A lucky man's wife dies, an unlucky man's cattle die", she quoted in a 1993 newspaper column, commenting on an old Bengali proverb. 'If your wife dies you can always get another and she may bring money with her, while for new cattle you have to pay hard cash.'

Taslima's admirers in the West often talk about how she escaped from Bangladesh, from the danger of escalating violence. And certainly, by leaving, she was able to avoid this prospect, although it meant becoming an outcast. Most women in her society suffer their agonies silently while trying to negotiate a bearable existence.

Taslima made her escape years before by doing the unthinkable. As a young woman she dared to believe she could change her life; dreaming of a world where she had a choice and need not meekly live out her life according to the silent laws laid down by men for women to follow since time immemorial. She did more than dream; she acted on this belief out in public, taking charge of her own life in a way that very few women in her society had done before. She avoided her mother's fate and escaped from the suffocating provincial life of Mymensingh. Some of her former friends say that, by leaving Bangladesh, in the end, she made one 'escape' too many, and that now it is time for her to stop running and to reclaim her life.

❦

There were times when Taslima seemed to be toying with me like a cat plays with a mouse. Now and then we disagreed—even clashed. More often than not it was a communication problem, a colloquial expression or an English word new to her that caused a temporary breakdown, but I guessed I might also be there for her amusement, or at least to satisfy her curiosity.

Once or twice she looked at me dumbfounded. 'How do you know that? Who told you that?' she would demand when I revealed a particular story because I needed to have it verified. Well, it seemed a small price to pay for access to the writer, and by revealing some of the information I'd gathered, I ensured that she told me more than if I'd stayed at her feet in an attitude of obeisance. She quickly realised that I knew more than the usual interviewers she met. I'll swear that once or twice she may even have wrong-footed me deliberately just to see my discomfort, or was I being tested? Taslima isn't much interested in resolving misunderstandings if it means listening to another point of view—clarifying conflict is not her strong point.

Early in the piece it became clear that my usual technique of listening would have to be abandoned if I wanted to try to locate her real self, to discover what lay behind the face Taslima presented to the world. Everyone has a story and most people will tell the stranger passing through their lives what they conceal from friends and family. Yet Taslima favours dissimulation rather than openness. One had to joust with her from time to time or else be served the same old fare.

Taslima was ever ready with a sharp answer to show how self-sufficient she was: pretending she'd made her own way as a writer was part of the myth she'd adopted and a prop for her self-esteem, but I soon discovered that this was not the truth.

Taslima passes lightly over the men who have figured in her life like a pianist running her fingers over the keyboard. With each passing year they slide further into the background. Occasionally they find themselves picked up, dusted off, mentioned in a speech on women and violence, or as another example of male tyranny, but these interludes become less frequent as the years pass. She has schooled herself not to remember.

Not everyone has forgotten. Dhaka's journalist corps remembers classmates and friends who helped her along the way: men who became writers or newspaper editors, or small-time publishers; successful men of style who were all better known than she was at the time. They sympathise with their old friends, electing to believe these men suffered professionally and personally because of their association with Nasreen, as she was then known.

The myths surrounding Taslima are seductive as all myths are; it is hard to resist their pull. During my visits to Dhaka between 1996 and 1999, I came across scores of men who remembered the rise and fall of Taslima Nasreen. After interviewing Taslima in Sweden, I used their observations to balance Taslima's interpretation of her life. I found them a healthy corrective— everyone had something to say.

Talking to Taslima's contemporaries helped me answer a question which has never fitted neatly into the annals of the Taslima Nasreen mythology; it is always missing from stories we read in magazines or newspapers. But it's a question well worth the asking, because it opens the doors to a number of chambers which Nasreen prefers to keep under lock and key.

The years between 1989 and 1992 were crucial years as she matured as a writer. How then did Nasreen become so well known in Bangladesh and then India, in a matter of four years? Her rise becomes more intriguing because the literary world of Bangladesh is dominated by men: writers, publishers, newspaper editors, and academics. Women are often tripped as they try to make their way because they are exposed to rumours. Decent women in conservative Bangladesh do not easily occupy public space as individuals unless they are someone of enormous moral stature, like the country's great poet and feminist leader, Begum Sufia Kamal (who died in 1999). If they are to advance as writers, they should be married and their patrons beyond reproach—and even then women can be dragged down. Men made no bones about discussing Nasreen's private life, but women confined their criticism to her writing, showing empathy when her personal life came under the knife. Still Nasreen delights in presenting herself as the only female writer of any merit or reputation in her homeland, a conceit she can only pull off if her listeners are ignorant of Bangladesh literature and social history.

India, Bangladesh and Pakistan ride on the back of the patron–client relationship. Every minute of the day, a patron is interceding with a third party, using their influence on someone else's behalf. At some stage of their life, everyone needs help to find a job; win a promotion; lend them money; place their son on a scholarship list; plead with the editor of a paper to publish a poem; ask a famous doctor or lawyer to see you. Your patron may be a relative, or a family friend, your employer, a classmate, the friend of a friend, or someone you've done a favour for in the past. It is a duty, not a burden.

Men have their tea house culture, where other men gather to hang on their words and sing their praises—the patron–client system clicks into place in this traditional form of entertainment, known as *adda*. Fans adore listening to their guru as he reads passages from his books and ponders some of the social and philosophical dilemmas of the day. A woman writer in Bangladesh stands outside these circles because the silent law dictates that decent women do not mix socially with males from outside their family group—presumably they have to be protected from 'indecent' men. For a woman writer it's hard to advance unless you can, in the style of Taslima, infiltrate this masculine world. Nevertheless women make themselves into writers. There is a fairly long list: Begum Sufia Kamal, Selina Hossain, Jahanara Imam, Razia Khan, Nasir Jehan and many others.

A poet is adept at manipulating language and Nasreen became accomplished at manipulating people as well. Her assertion that she rose on her own merits is the claim of a boastful child; hiding behind them is a self-absorbed and lonely individual.

On reflection, it's really not surprising that the young doctor became a writer; she'd been writing romantic poetry for years; was a thoughtful person with a powerful imagination, a natural gift for communicating in simple lyrical language and an unorthodox way of looking at the world. And hidden inside was a deep-seated anger which she could release only through writing. Nasreen's feel for language and her ambition and drive made her stand out, but she had no experience of the world outside the provincial town of Mymensingh until she met a popular young poet, with a cult following, five years her senior by the name of Rudra, who opened up a new world of ideas and introduced her to writing circles in Dhaka so that gradually, opportunities rarely available to other writers—male or female—were hers for the asking.

The two young poets met when she was a seventeen-year-old medical student, married in 1981 when she was nineteen, and divorced seven years later. Through all the ups and downs of their relationship, they remained friends until his death in 1991.

His full name was Rudra Mohammed Shahedullah, but everyone knew him as Rudra, the poet, an angry young man who wrote strongly voiced protest poems on social issues in sharp contrast to Taslima's adolescent love poetry. Their contemporaries swore that at first Rudra heavily edited her poems and helped get them published. Taslima denies this. They first met after she wrote to him in Dhaka inviting him to contribute to a small magazine she was starting up at the time, not unusual in Bangladesh, where the 'magazine movement' led to the establishment of many small magazines, some no more than a few pages stapled together, others more sophisticated.

'With Rudra, I danced on the edge of air, on open fields, walked through the light-tight woods; crossed one by one the milestones of time scripted in the letters of my age—eighteen, nineteen, twenty and twenty-one,' she recalled.

Rudra became obsessed with the beautiful young medical student of seventeen who looked as delicate as a rose but who thought and behaved differently to other girls he knew. He fell in love, and with Rudra by her side, within a short time, Taslima started to achieve a profile.

From about 1978, Rudra would make the five-hour round trip twice a week just to see her. They would meet secretly at his friend Bibagi's house, whose mother, worried by Taslima's reputation, tried her best but failed to put a stop to their meetings.

Rudra came from a well-off family of higher social status than Taslima's clan; they were from Khulna. He was an exuberant young man full of ideals, and young people wanted to be in his company whenever they could.

'Rudra had a soul that was infinitely larger than that of most,' wrote Taslima many years later in his obituary. She described herself as an innocent girl who was stunned by his raw, intense vision.

Aside from a few senior poets jealous of his popularity, he seemed not to have an enemy in the world—except himself. He was unstable and powerfully self-destructive. Like many young poets of the time, he believed that you must suffer for your art and suffer is what he did.

Bohemianism was rife among the younger poets at the time: influences like the Baul culture of bards, or travelling singers, was 'in their blood', as certain young poets were fond of saying. Owning a house meant you were not a bohemian; you had to be without possessions, drink, smoke hashish and wander around in a *lungi*, a sarong, with a hangover. In the late sixties, the Beat generation poets also hit Bangladesh and for a while Allen Ginsberg lived in West Bengal, India. While the Beat influence didn't improve the quality of local poetry, being a poet gave young men a license to be unconventional. 'Oh! He's a poet' their patrons would say as they, found 'their poet' a job, lent him money and excused his behaviour.

Bangladesh is a land of poetry and poverty; there are millions of poets in Bangladesh. The oral tradition is strong: peasants sing favourite songs and play drums at harvest time, fishermen sing while they pull in their nets and then there are the months and months of rain—plenty of time for telling stories and making up verses.

Wealth, position, a career, all of these things meant nothing to Rudra. What mattered was his writing; the cultural politics of the day, which all of the young artists were involved in; and a Utopian vision of the world, based on a type of raw Marxism popular at the time with many young students at university. He was addicted to all of these heady things.

He was also addicted to *ganja*, cheap country liquor and prostitutes. At the time, most, if not all, of this was concealed from Taslima. In every district there are many outlets, most of them illegal, for selling liquor made from fermented rice. Magazine and newspaper articles regularly report this addiction and how it inflicts misery on countless families tied to their alcoholic husbands and fathers, men who are manual labourers or unemployed, who over the years lose their energy and health and often die prematurely.

Rudra had none of Taslima's self-discipline and never applied himself to his university studies in Bangla literature. A former professor of his I spoke to at Dhaka University remembers him as an engaging, but hopelessly lazy, student who never turned up for tutorials and whom he failed in the end— he was one of the few not taken in by the young man's charm and good looks.

Taslima fell badly in love with the handsome young poet, with the dark beard and wicked engaging smile. A forbidden, romantic love affair between two poets captured the imaginations of their circle of friends. Close friends, like expatriate Ali Riaz, teased Rudra unmercifully, as he set off each week on his love pilgrimage to Mymensingh. 'So you're in love with a girl who writes letters to the papers!' Ali laughed.

'No,' answered Rudra. 'I've told her she has to stop this letter writing business! It's making her ridiculous and nobody will take her seriously as a writer.'

Taslima badly wanted her poems published in the national dailies and Rudra and Bibagi had useful contacts. Many of Rudra's friends were a clannish lot and very unkind towards Taslima. They became jealous that their hero spent so much time with her and spread stories that he wrote her poems. People, who know how much Taslima hated even to have her work edited, refuse to believe these stories.

Taslima's father knew nothing about her secret meetings with Rudra, which went on for years behind his back and were usually conducted at the Mymensingh Press Club and friends' houses. At the time of meeting Taslima's father and brother, I also visited the Mymensingh Press Club, where Rudra's friend Bibagi helped the young lovers hold their trysts. The club is a modest structure: a narrow single-storeyed building in the centre of the small, dusty town with the din of clanging rickshaw bells and car horns bouncing through the windows so loudly that, at certain times of the day, conversations turn into shouting matches. The journalists' haunt was hardly the place you would choose for an assignation. Reporters meet to socialise, eat and share information. I was the only woman present on the three occasions I visited there under the aegis of my journalist friends.

In 1981, while Taslima was still a medical student, the pair were secretly married at a registry office in Dhaka; they were thought to be very avant garde because they sent out their own invitations to their celebratory dinner in Dhaka (far away from Mymensingh and her parents). Not only was their marriage not arranged, there was no involvement by parents on either side—something unheard of in Bangladesh. They continued meeting as before. Taslima says that the marriage was consummated two years later in 1983. Her father refused to ever allow Rudra into the house and he was never accepted as a son-in-law. Of course many Rudra fans believed that Taslima trapped Rudra, but this was untrue.

On the night their marriage was consummated, Taslima, who could not have been older than nineteen, discovered her husband had syphilis. As a doctor, she knew a syphilitic ulcer when she saw one. This was the first time she treated him. Rudra broke down, promising that he would change his ways now that they were married; he would find regular medical help, he promised. He swore to give up visiting brothels, but seemed unable to do so for very long. When later she wrote about this, for everyone to read, Bangladesh society was scandalised—not at Rudra, but at Taslima for making public a vice that should have been concealed forever. Later a circle of his friends would punish her by smearing her reputation, claiming that Taslima had driven Rudra to prostitutes.

In 1985, when Taslima was a young woman of about twenty-three, they began living together regularly, but from the time she joined Rudra in Dhaka, their relationship started to fall apart. Before their marriage she must have known that he drank, but it was not until she lived with him as his wife that she began to understand the full implication of his three addictions: *ganja*, alcohol and prostitutes.

At the end of every day he would return to her drunk, something difficult to hide in a Muslim society like Bangladesh. He was popular but nobody would employ him and all his business projects failed; like many young men of his class, his family supported him. Taslima tried to isolate herself from his circle of drinking friends, other young poets and intellectuals of the time. She began to seek the company of senior writers like Shamsul Huq and Imdadul Huq Milan. She did her best to persuade Rudra to move away from his friends; as a doctor she was also concerned about his health. This increased the enmity of many of Rudra's friends; secretly, many of them were horrified by the extent of his drug addiction.

Rudra and Taslima quarrelled incessantly and separated and tried again many times. There were weeks when they were apart when Taslima had to work at remote district hospitals as a junior family planning doctor. By 1987 they were still together but the marriage was almost over. Her poetry and her prose writings later expressed her sexual frustration. 'Every night I sleep next to a eunuch,' she wrote in one of her verses.

Wazrul Huq, senior editor of an English-language paper in Dhaka, witnessed how distraught she became over the breakdown of her marriage. She found it terribly hard to end their relationship, he said. 'He infected her more than once,' Huq says. 'It was a cruel marriage, but she agonised over her decision although it was obvious that she must get out of this destructive relationship.' Huq believes that this coloured her later writing about men; even so-called progressive men were monsters to their wives.

In an interview with the Indian magazine *Savvy* in 1993, Taslima did not hold back: she thought Rudra was 'broad-minded', she said. 'But I was wrong. He did not like my freedom. He wanted to see me as any other slave woman—to cook for him, to wash his shirt, to massage his body. . . . He wanted my body, my mind and my life fully for himself. He used to drink and beat me most nights. If I denied him sex he went to prostitutes.'

After their divorce Rudra fell into a deep depression and drank more and ate little, keeping up his brothel visits, more from habit than passion or sexual desire. He became a physical wreck, fell ill and lost his remarkable zest for life, a man watching life, but no longer participating. But Rudra and Taslima kept up a close friendship until his death in 1991.

One of the few times Taslima has expressed her deep love and gratitude publicly to anyone came in the eulogy she composed for her former husband. In his parent's eyes, she was a divorced woman, who had no place in their son's life, and she waited hours outside his house before she was allowed to see his body.

I have read an English translation of the obituary she wrote for Rudra; it is Nasreen at her best: powerful, moving and direct. She tells how Rudra influenced her life and how they finally realised they could never live together without destroying each other. She writes with some bitterness of his 'friends' who could never find him work and how he hid his sickness to present a bright smile to the world: how he never let his contemporaries know how hurt he was that no one would publish his poetry.

'Has he died,' she asks, 'to give publishers an occasion for bringing out his complete works?' She was attacked by her old enemies for writing the obituary.

❋

After Rudra there were other men, including prominent writers like Shamsul Huq and Imadul Huq Milan, and a young publisher called Kokha; her rise seemed well charted. Established writers introduced her to their own publishers, for at first she was forced to self-publish, like many other writers in Bangladesh. Others helped her distribute her first books of poetry and persuaded their colleagues to write reviews. Her first breakthrough into writing prose came in 1989 as a newspaper columnist for the paper owned by Naim, who became her second husband and introduced her to other newspaper and magazine editors. Her biggest breakthrough came when, through him, she met powerful publishing figures in nearby Calcutta.

Without the Indian connection, Nasreen's career would never have developed beyond the borders of her own country. Certainly if she had not been published in the national dailies of both countries, if she had not enjoyed such a high profile, she would never have come to the attention of the religious bigots of her own country and the international lobby groups dedicated to freedom of expression.

Someone else might find a kind word, or at least recognise in passing, the men and women who assisted her—Nasreen does not. Those of the older generation, who have defended her in the past, understand how hard it is for her to acknowledge anyone's assistance publicly. She waxes and wanes from one day to the next, telephoning an old supporter to thank him for everything he's done and the next day declaring in an interview that her fellow writers are all cowards, and Taslima stands alone against the world.

Professor Kabir Chowdhury, who holds the country's highest academic honour, the title of National Professor, is both a scholar and translator of many of her poems. He is a brave, gentle man with impeccable pro-Liberation credentials and has always defended her right to dissent even though there are times when he shakes his head in frustration at Taslima's wilfulness and indiscretion, like a father with a wayward child.

'She was scarred by her adolescence,' he told me on the day I first visited him in 1997 at his modest home in Gulshan, a quiet residential suburb of Dhaka where most of the foreign embassies are located. 'And when you consider the harsh treatment she's been meted out by the people she has loved, and her own society, you begin to understand why she can't seem to bring herself to acknowledge any help she's ever received. She hasn't learnt a great deal about empathy,' he said.

His last sentence surprised me until I remembered that Bangladesh looked at Taslima with different eyes—even someone as sympathetic as Professor Chowdhury was not blind to her weaknesses.

Nareen's first two husbands were very different in temperament and background. Rudra was spontaneous and undisciplined as a bohemian poet should be, with little interest or talent in making money. Naim, her second husband, was, above everything else, correct, if a little on the staid side—a young man who wanted to advance professionally and who liked the comforts of life. Yet each man, in his own way, marked an important stage in her development as a writer and how she saw the world.

Her second husband was a well-connected man who proved as obsessed with her as Rudra. Naimul Islam Khan was a smart young man with a view to the main chance. Although not a writer, he had a discerning eye for good writing and was a rising young newspaper editor by the time he and Nasreen became intimates. Naim, as he was called, knew how to organise and administer cultural festivals; he was someone who liked to control people as well as events and was not always good at disguising this tendency, as I soon discovered when I met him in late 1996.

Naim came from a 'good family' in spite of one major drawback: a politician father in the National Assembly who'd been pro-Pakistan in the 1971 War of Liberation. The family background was upper middle class, not wealthy, but a stylish family with only this one blemish to its name, which over the years didn't seem to hinder young Naim's advancement. Naim's family background and sense of style attracted Taslima.

At first Naim was cautious about meeting me but, in the end, sent word through an intermediary that we should meet. He was no longer an editor, and in his own eyes had come down in the world. Now in charge of a small foreign-sponsored non-government organisation (NGO), Naim worked on media projects. He employed a personal assistant, wrote papers and made overseas trips to conferences, and he ran his small office as if he was still the editor of an important newspaper.

Nasreen and Naim's paths first crossed in 1987, when he was approached one day by a friend who begged him to include Nasreen in the program of the 1987 National Recitation Festival which Naim was organising that year. He assured Naim that the young poet from Mymensingh would prove a hit with the audience.

Young people at the time were active in the strong pro-democracy movement against the authoritarian regime of President Ershad. Naim was one of many young men involved in *Shammilito Shangskritik Jote*, which brought together several cultural organisations under one umbrella, involving poets, playwrights, authors, dancers, singers, musicians, painters. It was a huge bloc of artists who believed in Bangladesh nationalism and opposed Islamist politics.

Poetry was a form of dissent and poets became leaders, playing a major part in marches and protest meetings. This is something unique to Bangladesh; it has not happened in West Bengal, India, where language has never been threatened. The political role played by Bangladeshi poets goes back to the Language Movement of 1952, when Urdu was imposed as the official language on the Bengali (Bangla)-speaking people in the days when Pakistan consisted of two wings, nineteen years before Bangladeshi independence.

Poetry festivals are enormously popular in Bangladesh, attracting the numbers that rock concerts do in the West. Festivals start at four in the afternoon and end at ten thirty at night. Their neighbours in Calcutta, where verse is popular also and whose language is also Bengali, think Bangladeshis are crazy about poetry; everyone yearns to be a poet: lawyers, doctors, soldiers, social workers, bureaucrats. Even former President Ershad was a poet, and it was rumoured that if your paper wanted to avoid being censored and to continue buying the government-controlled newsprint and receive government advertising, then it was a good idea to publish his poems.

Naim agreed to help but, to his surprise, his own program committee turned him down. Finally, after a little table thumping, on his part, they reached a compromise: Nasreen would be invited as a reciter, but not as a poet, which meant that she could not read out her own verses but would recite someone else's poetry. In the committee's eyes she didn't belong to the top twenty poets—yes, she was good, they agreed, but she still had a long way to go.

Reciting poetry in Bangladesh is an art form and audiences react enthusiastically to their favourite reciters; their dramatic renditions often prove more popular than poets reading their own verses. Reciters perform solo or in a choir. On this occasion, twenty-five-year-old Nasreen did both.

Naim only saw her from a distance but remembers that Nasreen stood out at the festival: she had a way of wearing her sari, 'like a Bimani air hostess,' men would say, not like the air hostesses of today whose saris are more conservatively draped, but the more glamorous drape of the eighties, which sometimes bared the navel and revealed clinging choli blouses (hint of cleavage if you were lucky); her hair she wore medium length, when other women's hair was long.

Naim knew many important poets in Calcutta, West Bengal, India, whose works were read in Bangladesh. During 1987–1988, he took the thirty-minute flight from Dhaka to Calcutta, as often as four or five times in a two-month period on the excuse that he was organising the poetry festival. He wooed important West Bengali poets, all expenses paid, to Dhaka for poetry festivals and the like.

When they finally met in late 1988, Naim and Nasreen's lives had both changed. Her marriage to Rudra was over and Naim was the founder and editor of *Khaborer Kagoj*, a liberal weekly paper. Nasreen had returned to Mymensingh, where she worked as a Family Planning Officer but, according to Naim, she needed a platform in Dhaka. Life was difficult for her as a divorced woman, so she returned to Mymensingh, where she could live in her father's house. Even today any young, single or divorced woman living by herself is regarded as suspect; it is impossible for a young woman to negotiate the kind of personal space which other women, in non-traditional societies, take for granted.

Every night Taslima's second husband rehearsed the themes that he thought we should discuss the following day in his office. Our conversations were long and convoluted, but Naim, a handsome man with a pale brown face—which never seemed to perspire—and a light pencil moustache, was always in control. He sat behind his desk, pen and papers neatly arrayed before him while I juggled my equipment and notes on my knees or on the edge of his desk. Now and then he would lean across and with his long elegantly tapered forefinger, switch off my tape recorder as it suited him. He explained to me on our fourth meeting that he wanted to understand the role he had played in Taslima's life; sometimes he seemed to be making sense of it as we went along and I began to feel like a therapist. Naim had a reason for every secret he gave away and there were two subjects where he was as slippery as an eel: I had no idea where he stood politically and I was very confused about the legality of his marriage to Nasreen.

By early 1989 Naim and Nasreen were close friends, although he was deeply wounded when she made her first trip to India some time early that year in the company of a male writer. He followed her to the airport to learn her travel companion's identity, but had the sense to keep this to himself. The young newspaper editor was besotted by Nasreen. People in his circle were starting to talk about Naim and Nasreen as a glamorous new couple and Naim didn't mind being the envy of other men, although the strain of travelling by train to Mymensingh every week was mounting.

Later Nasreen boasted in her columns that she travelled to India by herself and turned this into quite a psycho-drama, daring her readers to tell her why she shouldn't travel alone just like a man! It made for a far more interesting story, even if it wasn't true. The idea of an adventurous young woman travelling alone, on the thirty-minute flight to Calcutta, fitted in with the unorthodox image she was cultivating.

Through his connections, Naim helped Taslima obtain a medical posting back to Dhaka in 1989 and continued to promote her writing career. A new writer could not advance a career from a district town like Mymensingh. And even in Dhaka, you were regarded as a top writer only if you were taken up by West Bengali publishers in Calcutta—Naim helped make this happen for Nasreen.

Not long after she moved back to Dhaka, Nasreen began writing a weekly column for Naim's paper, called 'Inside and Outside'. A prominent writer called Shamsul Huq, who was a guru-like figure in Nasreen's life between 1987and 1989 after her first divorce suggested it to Naim. At the time Nasreen was a rising poet who'd self-published a few slim volumes of poetry but was not known for writing prose. Usually only well-known public or literary figures, writers and academics have their own columns, and the news that Nasreen, the medical doctor, poet and divorcee, would move to another echelon of writing infuriated many in Dhaka's cultural circles. 'Why should this upstart have her own column? She was a nobody,' they complained.

When she first began writing newspaper columns, Naim warned Taslima on numerous occasions not to write about Islam and she promised faithfully that she would be careful, but self-censorship was anathema to her and she never kept her promises for long. It struck me that Taslima's newspaper columns upset readers, far more than her poems or novellas: people didn't castigate her for her verses, perhaps poetry readers accept rage, passion and bitterness more readily than newspaper readers trying to eat their breakfast. Or was it because a broader cross section of the community read the papers and were exposed to her views? Religious fanatics were always looking for a bandwagon: they could write letters to the editor, start up a debate, have their names in the paper and then sit back knowing that they were heroes in their followers' eyes.

Nasreen's articles protested against society, religion and men, while other writers mainly concentrated on the theme of national independence and nationalism. Bangladesh is a country that continually looks back to its armed struggles to bolster national pride. Its psyche is dependent on an ongoing observance of ritualised national days of remembrance: pain, suffering and sacrifice are honoured. Themes which have dominated the arts for nearly fifty years have been those of heroism, martyrdom, of courage and patriotism.

On the calendar, two days stand out in particular. National Language Day on 21 February and the War of Liberation celebrated on 26 March. These remind Bangladeshis of the two things they can be proud of: language and independence. Numerous other celebrations are linked to these two events. Nasreen loves her country but displayed none of the automatic deference she saw around her, daring to ask, 'What did the War of Liberation do for women?'

Now that she was writing a weekly column, her profile increased and she had the perfect vehicle for disclosing her views about the unequal relationships between men and women and simultaneously drawing attention to herself. She still continued as a doctor, although by now she was working in the gynaecology department of the Nancy Mitford Hospital as an anaesthetist. According to Naim she had no post-graduate qualifications for this. She read a textbook and that was the end of the matter! I found it difficult to believe that it was quite as simple as he made it sound, although he was quite insistent.

Her brother Noman noticed that after she began writing her columns, women from different towns 'rushed to her', and she collected their individual histories and used them as if these were part of her own experience. This may have been the beginning of 'Taslima, the fabulist', who always 'owned' the terrible things she described in her articles—perfectly legitimate in fiction, but something new in column writing and journalism in Bangladesh.

Years later, she would tell her enthralled European audiences that, as a doctor, she had personally delivered several thousand babies. Juxtapose this bizarre tally against an earlier speech where she claimed to have performed a thousand tubal ligations, and you were left wondering. Given the intermittent nature of her medical career, which lasted from 1986 to 1993, and the fact that for the last three years she seems to have worked as an anaesthetist, Nasreen must have been labouring night and day to reach the magic quota of thousands of deliveries and a thousand tubal ligations to boot—another example of her writer's flair carrying her away.

Naim turned a deaf ear to his friends' warnings and proposed to Nasreen formally in a badly lit, discreet little coffee shop in the heart of downtown Dhaka on crowded Elephant Road, in its heyday a rendezvous for young lovers. She promised to consider his proposal. Naim, head over heels in love with the wrong woman, went to Newmarket to buy a gold coin for his beloved, an old family tradition.

Naim is not given to flashes of humour or playful interludes; as sombre as a man facing surgery, he revealed how he'd made a clean breast of all his shortcomings as a prospective husband. 'There are certain negative things about me you should know,' he told Taslima. 'I once failed an exam and academically I am your junior; I have false teeth because of an accident, and my father was a collaborator in 1971.' For a day or two he heard nothing from her. Later he discovered that she talked to many of their friends about his position in society.

They visited Calcutta together before they were married; Naim became fixated, as if this would discharge the earlier slight to his manhood. During this trip, sometime in late 1989, Nasreen's Indian connections were established and she came into contact with certain senior figures in the famous publishing house of Ananda Bazar (sic), which around this time began to market her first book of poems.

Popular Calcutta writer Sunil Gangopadhyaya remembers her as an unknown writer in Calcutta at a time when she wrote only love poems; he reminded her of their first meeting in Dhaka. Surrounded by fans, all clamouring for his autograph, a young woman had approached him. 'Everyone wants your autograph,' she said, 'would you like mine?'

Naim knew his parents would oppose their first son marrying a divorced woman, so he avoided telling them he was now married. Unfortunately his subterfuge led to him being impotent on their wedding night and it was only after a psychologist asked him bluntly a few days later 'Do your parents know you are married?' that the reason for his problem became apparent. In Bangladeshi society, where arranged marriages are customary, a dutiful son would never keep his marriage a secret and this preyed on his mind. Once he announced his marriage to his disappointed parents, his sexual problems were over.

Trying to unravel the mystery of whether Naim and Nasreen were legally married or not is painfully difficult. At first Naim said that a civil ceremony took place in 1990, as his atheist wife would never have agreed to a religious ceremony. A week later he told me that, through some technical error, they may never have been married at all and mumbled something about a legal agreement to live together. Later in her career, Nasreen would insist that she had only been married twice, although she has never disclosed which, if any, of her three marriages wasn't legal.

Some of their friends were suspicious because, although the couple would say they were married, the couple held no celebration, nor was there a certificate for anyone to see. In Bangladesh, marriage is always a public affair but whether their marriage was registered or not, they lived as husband and wife, and Naim is always described as Nasreen's second husband.

In an unusual turnabout, Nasreen divorced Naim in the Islamic style, pronouncing the three *talaqs*, whereby the husband—and it is usually the husband—or wife repudiates their partner. I thought a religious-style divorce a surprising decision for an atheist who had refused a religious marriage ceremony, but it was certainly the fastest way of ending their union. Many of his friends shake their heads, even today, and say that Naim fell into the hands of an overly ambitious woman, metamorphosing 'Nasreen's men' into listless wooden figures who danced to Madam's tune.

Naim rejects this out of hand. 'She didn't manipulate me. I played a role and I am not blameless; nobody forced me,' he says.

Naim lost his first paper because of financial problems not long after they broke up in 1991 and his reputation suffered, although he joined another paper shortly after and re-married, as he admits, on the rebound; but he was still in love with Nasreen and his second marriage failed.

However, before coming to Sweden, word reached me that Naim had fallen on happier times; he is now married for a third time and reportedly very happy with his new wife, twenty years younger than himself. *In 2006 Naim is once more the editor of a popular newspaper.*

❀

Taslima liked collecting new English words, testing them and letting them roll softly off her tongue. One expression, however, she rejected out of hand. The word 'mentor' was strange to her ears and she examined it with the suspicion of someone waiting to be ambushed. In spite of her denials, Taslima had been helped by a number of men in the world of writing and publishing—whether they were friends, husbands, lovers, or colleagues was irrelevant to me.

Leaning back in my chair, sipping my third cup of tea for the morning, I felt our conversation was going along smoothly until, thoughtlessly, I suggested that it was good for her reputation (meaning her reputation as a writer) to have Shamsul Huq as her mentor and to be introduced into literary circles under his patronage. And it was here that an act of miscommunication, or pure contrariness, took place that coloured the rest of our discussion and assigned the word 'mentor' to the rubbish heap.

After her first marriage ended in 1989 and before her close friendship with Naim developed, Nasreen received help and advice from the well-known senior poet Shamsul Huq. He was a highly respected man of the world who made the young men of the day jealous, although they passed it off as a joke. 'We respected him,' said Naim, 'but we used to laugh and call him our rival. "He's stealing our girlfriends! How can we compete with the great man?"'

Huq would talk to Taslima on the phone for hours, and whenever she visited Dhaka he would invite her to lunch at restaurants. He acted as a guru figure in her life, even introducing her to his own publisher. The famous writer and intellectual was in his early fifties and Nasreen in her mid-twenties at the time.

'Huq *bhai*' she called him, which indicated that they were personal friends. Huq would talk to her of world events and international feminism and was associated with her for quite a significant time—it was Huq who suggested that she should start writing a column. When I met him in Dhaka in 1997, he declined to discuss Taslima with me because, as he said with a charming smile, he made it a rule never to discuss other writers. I accepted Huq's refusal at face value until I met Naim and understood that I'd stepped on some sensitive toes.

From all accounts it was a delicate relationship and after Nasreen became a popular writer, and even began to outsell the master at book festivals, their friendship cooled. By 1989, when she and Naim were together, her association with the older poet had wound down. She poked fun at him in her column by alluding to older writers who enjoyed taking young women out to lunch in dark restaurants.

'No,' Taslima argued, 'I didn't take up with Huq *bhai* to improve my reputation. He was good to me and I liked and admired him; he took me as a little sister, as a rising poet. . . . I knew him and my family knew him before I came to Dhaka; he would sometimes visit us in Mymensingh. He was a friend and not a mentor,' she finished off neatly but emphatically.

In 2003 Shamsul Huq takes out a libel suit against Taslima because of the revelations in her latest memoir about his love life and extra-marital affairs.

I tried to retrieve my position by explaining that the concept of a mentor was positive in my society and did not hold any sexual connotations. But she would have none of it and saw it as an admission of weakness.

'I don't think I needed anyone to help me,' she said. As if to prove her popularity, she went on to tell me how her poetry books went into several reprints and I thought to myself that the 'I' creates itself and its relation to the world.

I gave in and moved on to her second husband, Naim Islam, years later still trying to make sense of the Taslima interlude in his life.

'A good man,' she said, 'but he was not for me and I was not for him.'

I preferred Taslima's terse summing up to her ex-husband's nostalgic re-enactment, for I could tell that right from the beginning, one of the parties was emotionally involved and the other was not. Many of their arguments were about money, Naim revealed. She would scream, he would push her away, she would scratch and he would hit her. There was a lot of shouting, and like many marriages in the Subcontinent their problems were never 'talked out'. Naim could not afford the life she wanted: moving around at night, eating out in restaurants, staying at five star hotels, flying to Calcutta, buying expensive presents for friends—they were living beyond his means and his paper was in financial difficulties.

'She is the kind of woman who makes men shout,' he told me in the universal lament of misunderstood males around the planet.

Nasreen, on the other hand, disliked Naim's sense of correctness. His habit of waving his elegant fingers in people's faces, as he corrects them, can be infuriating—I knew from experience. As a young woman, Nasreen might bend herself to her father's will but not to her husband's. Like many young wives, she was also unhappy that at first they lived with his parents and she behaved distantly to her in-laws, refusing to *salaam* them, an old custom where a younger person, or someone of lesser status, bends to touch the feet of an older person as a gesture of respect when they meet for the first time. Naim didn't bother to hide that he felt his patrician taste was vastly superior to hers. They quarrelled over hundreds of small things.

Accordingly I wasn't surprised when she rejected any suggestion that Naim had helped her professionally. 'He was not a mentor,' she said, looking me straight in the eye, daring me to disagree.

Poor Naim. Suspended between the past and the present he summarised their four-year affair and brief marriage. 'Nasreen, you know, always expected me to be a huge tree and under my enormous shade she thought that she could move around freely. But,' he added, with a small pinched smile on his face, 'she discovered that in the end, I was just a small plant without any shade. If she mentions me at all it will be in a dismissive way. I am an unimportant part of her life which is now over.'

'Nasreen is the Bangladeshi girl who became a legend and was turned into "Taslima" by the foreign media, and is "Nasreen" no more. But once upon a time she was Nasreen *bubu* (older sister). Then we all started to believe the legend. Sometimes it is hard to remember that the woman I loved was called Nasreen.'

I decided not to share his ode to the death of their marriage with Taslima and, in the end, I surrendered on the whole business of 'mentors'—it seemed the wisest course. Taslima had already curled her lip and told me that the hours I'd spent in Dhaka talking to Naim were a waste of my time. Once she had finished with people, she disposed of them with no sentimentality.

Taslima's poems and columns make no secret of her antipathy towards men and her low opinion of marriage as an institution. Yet men flocked around; life was dull without them, and she much preferred the company of men to that of women: the company of the slave master to that of the slave. Her rage was directed at men in general, for in her private life most of her best friends were male. She enjoyed controlling men and manipulated them to serve her own material, physical and intellectual needs. There were two aspects to Taslima at work: the first scorned men, the second used them.

I put it to her without any shilly-shallying that for a woman who publicly disapproved of marriage, husbands and men, she'd certainly had her share of all three.

She found this very funny. Naim, she explained chased after her for a long time and her parents were angry at the mounting gossip his visits caused. 'Either you have a husband or you have male relatives—there is no other relationship possible, with a man, for any decent woman.' The pressure from Naim and her parents mounted until she could stand no more and she gave in.

'I was angry,' she argued. She was not really giving in to her family's badgering but was showing a kind of anger by marrying Naim: a "to hell with them!" attitude? I wondered. Taslima tries hard to disguise any compromises she's forced to make. Her way of rationalising any behavior that contradicts her writing is by now entrenched.

For a long time men had been a problem in her life. I put this view to her. She was caught on the horns of a dilemma I suggested. She liked men, they were more interesting than the women she met, as she had told me, you could talk about literature with men: their world was limitless and the reflection she saw of herself in their eyes was gratifying. But her parents were right when they warned her that in Bangladesh it's impossible to have men as friends, not only because of gossip but because men wanted more than friendship from Taslima. In my head was a list of men who at one time or the other had pursued her or behaved like love-sick calves. She challenged me to say who they were. I obliged reeling off five or six names and then told her there was no point in continuing—it was a long list.

She sounded amused. 'So are you going to write a love life of Taslima?' A note of scorn sounded a warning and I watched her small fingers tap out a tattoo on the arm of her chair. I tried explaining that it wasn't a prurient interest in her sex life that was motivating me, I was trying to understand her, especially the contradictions between what she wrote and how she lived out her life.

I continued trying, long after I should have stopped. Surely it was a problem in any society I argued, for a woman of independent mind and means to function if her society wouldn't hold with men and women being friends. 'Hm,' she said; I hastened on. Now, I told her, if you can't have men as friends, if people misunderstand—and even progressive men are not progressive in their views about women—then men become a problem in that sense.

Her mother silently entered the room carrying a round metal tray with tea and some *paan*. I proved inept at chewing, which amused Taslima. 'You don't know how to do it eh?' she said, and gave me some hints. Taslima had once described herself in a poem as the girl who takes the lime out of the *paan*, a rebellious image, friends explained to me, adding that lime also stings the mouth and has an addictive quality. I liked Taslima's explanation better. 'It is dangerous to remove the lime from the betel leaf.'

'Yes, it is true,' she finally agreed. 'The only man I ever loved was Rudra. The other relationships were with friends, sometimes marriage came later, but that was only because of the circumstances.' She was unable to convince the men in her life that their relationship could continue without marriage, or that 'piece of paper' as she called it. Taslima saw herself as a victim of social custom. The word 'victim' came from her own mouth and I thought it a strange choice; it is a word that I would not use to describe Taslima Nasreen.

❈

In Dhaka circles they seem to enjoy blaming Nasreen for ruining her husbands' careers. But Rudra, the poet, was bent on self-destruction and Naim, the editor, ruined his own career with only a little help from Nasreen. And her third husband, Minar Mahmood? Perhaps next year, when I visited New

York, I would find out for Naim had mentioned that his former colleague and friend, the one-time editor, now drove a Yellow Cab in Manhattan.

Nasreen's relations with men were disastrous. The men she lived with were mainly abusive, self-destructive men like her father in some ways, although the evidence shows that Naim was different. One side of her yearned for romantic love, yet the other part of her knew this was hopeless and that she would never be happy in any marriage. However much Nasreen might rebel, she was not foolish enough to live together with a man without benefit of a marriage certificate, and neither were her men—they all wanted to own her to some degree. Informal liaisons, quite normal in Western societies, are beyond the pale in Bangladesh unless there is at least some pretence of a formal marriage.

The wound which never healed goes back to her early childhood and to the unloving, rigid behaviour she witnessed as a child within her family's four walls; this was later compounded by her first marriage to the violent, yet tragic, Rudra. She felt betrayed by her father and Rudra: betrayed by their vices, by their contradictory natures, the way they pretended one code, but lived out another.

Her first disastrous marriage marked her transition from romantic poet to protest writer. In an interview with the Indian magazine *Savvy*, in late 1993, she told her readers: 'I divorced Rudra not because he had syphilis, not for beating me, but because he didn't support a woman's freedom.'

To the feminists of Bangladesh it seemed a strange comment, a flowery poetic gesture without much substance. The reference to Rudra's infection they considered to be in poor taste, and shameful to his family—gossip mounted.

Taslima knew all there was to know about gossip. 'You meet someone and the next day everyone says he is your lover!' she said, drawing on her cigarette fiercely. She found herself attacked so often that in the end she stopped caring and became indifferent. Meeting and mixing with men, breaking the social taboos, were all part of her protest, she said.

I'm not sure if Taslima ever really understood why I asked the questions I did that day and at first it worried me. I felt that I'd failed, that my literary hunt might have crossed over the line into tabloid research. Face-to-face with Taslima at last, I wanted to understand the contradictions. In the end I forced myself to stop worrying because I sensed that I might be falling into a trap, that Taslima wouldn't be at all troubled if I continued to fret.

Writing, for Taslima, was the only way she had of expressing her rage and I wanted to know its source, but she veered away from any discussion of this and I was in danger of putting words into her mouth. I was probably too eager and may have set off a warning in her head. Or perhaps she belonged to those writers who believe that by analysing their writing they will lose their 'gift'. By now I was confused. What kind of a book did she think I was writing? A literary critique that discussed her poetry and other writing and not much else it seemed. But this made no sense: I couldn't believe for one minute that Taslima had forgotten the names of all the people I'd met, including her lawyers, critics and supporters—even her own family. Why play this little charade?

❀

Her friends and enemies in Dhaka would be surprised to hear the word 'humility' and Taslima used in the same breath. She has a better understanding now of Western literary standards than when she affronted Eugene three years earlier in an unsophisticated show of literary arm wrestling. She now makes it a point to emphasise that she had never studied literature, 'so maybe my books are not such high quality literature.' She takes more care about what she says concerning Rushdie than she did in Bangladesh. There has been time to appreciate how widely respected he is and to better understand the pressures of exile and its sense of permanent sadness.

'When people try to compare us, I tell them he is a great writer; I'm a simple writer who writes from the heart.'

In the first three years of her exile Taslima fretted about her literary output. I thought she was worrying unnecessarily: there were her new poems in exile, many of which were included in a new anthology edited by American poet and academic Carolyne Wright, *The Game in Reverse*; she wrote some columns for *Le Monde* and during my visit was struggling with her memoir about growing up in Bangladesh. In addition there were papers for the numerous conferences she attended each year and although they are what academics like to call 'traveling papers' they still required time and attention, a new paragraph, a reference or revision here and there. At first friends helped her with her speeches, which she wrote in Bangla and had translated. New poetry, newspaper columns and a book—all written between 1995 and 1998 within four years of quitting Bangladesh in terrible circumstances. A very respectable output I thought, given the amount of traveling she undertakes. (*Since 1999 Taslima has completed four memoirs, one novel and a new poetry anthology.*)

'Maybe because I'm not writing that much, people are forgetting me. Their reception is still warm, but I'm no longer in the news.'

The feeling behind her words was ambivalent: on the one hand she said she disliked giving interviews because of the frenzy she remembered from the past when she was front-page news everywhere; on the other hand she seemed to regret finding herself relegated to the sidelines, out of the spotlight. During the four days we met, she often repeated herself: people were forgetting all about her, she said, and this clearly disturbed her. To be forgotten is to be ignored.

News from home forced her to accept that she was fast becoming the forgotten woman to her hometown critics, but to live through that twice over, again in exile, was like a small death to her, I think. As I've said before, Taslima is a proud woman: once the darling of the international press and TV networks and now languishing in the wings. These are painful, private matters for her to discuss.

Treading lightly, I reminded Taslima that both the mullahs and the modernists accused her of being publicity crazy. 'People are jealous,' she answered. 'I was a little girl in little Bangladesh and I suddenly I made headlines all over the world. Thanks to the fundamentalists, everyone knew my name,' she smiled.

I smiled back, relieved that we were in agreement. I much preferred a smiling Taslima with her dimples showing. 'They gave you a million dollars worth of publicity.'

She jumped in, 'But I didn't get the million dollars!' We laughed.

Taslima likes to think of herself as a 'gypsy' moving from location to location. 'I come alive,' she said, 'for if I stay in one place too long, I remember I'm in exile and feel trapped.'

Moving around on the international celebrity circuit acts as a surrogate for the excitement of Bangladesh with its volatile politics; its literary fever and newspaper debates, its poetry festivals and yes, even its danger. Sweden is safe but Sweden is not the most exciting of societies, as Swedes are quick to point out. She badly needs those quick, now-and-then trips to Calcutta, India; to the Bengali-language environment she misses.

Taslima has been an angry woman for most of her life. Anger is very creative; the energy it unleashes propels you along and if someone is used to living with anger it is a hard companion to lose. Now that she finds herself locked inside Sweden, where does all that rage go? Did people at home ever talk of her returning? she asked. What could I say without hurting her feelings?

There was little sign of a 'Bring Taslima Home' movement when last I'd visited Dhaka earlier that year in 1998; there was no point in pretending otherwise. Taslima has never been good at building alliances: she has never seen the need to belong to a group outside of her family. Friends and supporters in Dhaka were small in number and any voice calling for her return was drowned out by other voices. Her potential allies have long memories: the women activists, the writers, and the anti-communalists have remained at home and continue their fight against obscurantist forces using the traditional methods that Taslima was once so fond of criticising. But she is not a silent observer and many dislike her ongoing criticism. The liberals continue to punish her with their silence. In their eyes she has run away to safety and the easy life, while they continue the fight.

'I thought some people would help,' she said quietly, 'but nothing has happened. Too many people are afraid of the fundamentalists, they don't openly give their support.' She made no reference to leading public figures like Shamsur Rahman, Kabir Chowdhury and Ahmed Sharif, who had always supported her.

We talked about her controversial book *Lajja*. Many of the progressive-minded people I'd met expressed a feeling of betrayal, insisting that it wasn't a true picture of Hindu–Muslim relations in Bangladesh at all.

'I don't know why they should feel betrayed,' she said, looking up at me as if she was hearing this indictment for the first time. 'I didn't betray anybody. I just wrote a book and I told the truth.'

Was she deliberately underplaying the impact her book had made on the secular community of Bangladesh? I knew of no journalist, academic, lawyer, activist, writer or businessman who did not have a strong reaction of one kind or the other to *Lajja*, and nine times out of ten, it was a negative response.

'Many progressives tell me that they support the religious minorities in your country.' I was interested in her answer and if she realised that there was a sadness on both sides: her own disappointment and the unhappiness that expresses itself in the slow anger of those who feel they have been misrepresented.

I strained to hear her words; her voice had dropped to almost a whisper. 'Yes,' she replied, 'I included that in the preface of my book and again in the story. They showed support, but I wanted to tell everyone that this is not enough; the acts of individuals are not enough. Hindus continue to leave the country in huge numbers; they do not feel safe. I never said that nobody protested against the attacks on Hindus. But their way doesn't work: organising processions and placards, signing petitions, they just don't work,' she told me earnestly. 'The minorities don't feel safe and they continue to leave.' Statistics support what she says.

I asked her about the great disappointments in her life. 'What has been the great disappointment in my life?' she repeated.

'Maybe that I couldn't stay in Bangladesh,' her voice was soft and sad, 'that my countrymen didn't keep me there because it all depended on them in the end, you know. It might have been possible for me to stay, if they had wanted me. . . .' When she talks of her 'countrymen', Taslima is not referring to religious fanatics.

There is a Bengali word which Taslima tells me has no translation in English, *obeeman*, an emotion or feeling between lovers or a strong attachment to something you love dearly—perhaps your country; sometimes there is a falling out, like a quarrel between lovers. A terrible feeling of disappointment fills your soul. Friends would try later to explain the meaning to me. 'It lies somewhere in between anger and disappointment,' they would say, 'but it is neither of these.' From their description it sounded like a terrible wave of sadness, an intense feeling of estrangement that you hope will pass. A person with a strong sense of being aggrieved has this feeling, but whoever, or whatever, has wounded you can easily be forgiven in the future by, saying the right word, or healing the breach in some other way. Taslima is right, there is no word in English.

❀

The last time I saw Taslima she was not pleased with me, and a feeling of deja vu swept over me. Were we going to re-enact our initial meeting all over again? We'd been sitting in her office laughing and talking with one another when it must have happened. Somehow or other Taslima and her computer came to grief and she lost fifty pages of the book she'd been laboring on each of the four days I was there—she had not made a back-up copy. Every writer in the world lives with the dread of this happening one day. She immediately rang Gunnar begging him to come home early and solve the problem. 'I don't know what has gone wrong. Please come home! I'll just die,' she whispered.

To add to her distress she had also mislaid a speech she was working on. I left behind an agonised writer. The next day she rang asking me if I had such and such a paper. It made no sense, but she sounded so sad and my concern mounted. She cancelled an outing we were supposed to go on and I felt that somehow I was being blamed. That was the last I ever heard of her.

She once told me, 'If I am angry, I don't shout, I don't explode, I just leee..ave. That is my way; I have done that all my life . . . I just leave.'

I was sorry that she had decided to withdraw from me, but slowly I came to understand that I had joined a select group of people who'd had similar experiences. By denying you the opportunity to resolve misunderstandings, you remain attached to Taslima, like it or not, while she simply withdraws herself and moves on, in a slow dance of passive aggression.

Originally I'd been drawn to the Taslima story by 'silences', by a feeling that there were things left unsaid. Nothing had changed for me.

Chapter 4

Fallen Prose of a Fallen Woman

Lajja is a document of our collective defeat.

Taslima Nasreen, 1993

I left Sweden and returned to Australia convinced that nothing was what it seemed any more. The Taslima mythology stood primed to defend itself, but in spite of the silences, the fabrication was loosening and starting to drift between Europe and the Indian subcontinent—myths are vulnerable, and so are mythmakers, was the message I took home with me.

Faced with her past, Taslima had become wary: drawing a line in the sand she had left her interrogator stranded on one side while she acted out her role. Her performances were a synthetic blend of naivete and bewilderment—the dramatic events in her life were beyond her understanding she was fond of telling me but, on one occasion, when quizzed about the great disappointment in her life, her response was immediate and heart-felt, of that I was sure.

'It might have been possible for me to stay, if "they" had wanted me,' she'd whispered.

To discover how Taslima 'the stranger' became transformed into Taslima 'the enemy', my story needed to move back to Bangladesh, to the time of her best-seller *Lajja*, a catalyst in the chain of events in 1993 and 1994. Why were progressive men and women distancing themselves as early as mid-1992 and why wasn't she adopted as one of their own? The Greybeards' animosity came as no surprise; it was even a badge of honour to activists who travelled in her circles, but to be rejected by the progressive elements in a solid show of silent hostility was a hard blow, even if she pretended otherwise.

89

I believe that it was a combination of events which finally 'did her in'—
some of them personal, some tainted by the domestic politics of the day
and some triggered by outside events. But the response to *Lajja* brought
everything to a head: her unpopularity, isolation and the orchestrated moves
against her, by the religious hardliners at first, and then finally by the
Government.

Taslima Nasreen was subjected to a stream of personal vilification that was
shameful. Her family had neither the status nor the connections to protect
her. By removing herself from her family's guardianship and trying to carve
out her own personal space, she flouted the unwritten laws of her society.
Her vulnerability increased when she married and divorced too often for
society's tastes. Moving from Dhaka to Calcutta I couldn't help but notice
the difference: Dhaka gossiped about her morals, while Calcutta cared more
about her writing.

Finally, at a political level, she outraged many people by her irrev-
erence towards Islamic texts, giving extremists the pretext they needed;
she upset the Government and the community when she accused them
of ignoring the position of the country's Hindu minority. In effect she
broke the Subcontinent's three taboos, in writing about gender, religion
and communalism—men, not women, wrote about the last two subjects.

When the West looked at Taslima they saw a victim, but in Bangladesh,
even human rights activists conceded that she was a woman complicit in
her own downfall. Her ambition, her self-involvement came at a price:
she gave no thought to the consequences of her writing, nor to the expectations her community had of its writers. She wanted absolute freedom
and glory, while they would respect her only if she stayed within certain
boundaries.

Nineteen ninety-six was the year I met David Davidar in New Delhi. At the
time, Davidar was the Publisher of Penguin India who had first published
the English edition of *Lajja* in 1994. I wanted to meet the man who in an
newspaper interview that year had said:

A sensitivity where religion is concerned is one of the realities you accept in India.
You are working on a knife's edge because if you write a book where someone
slags someone else off on the basis of religion, you can be fairly sure that tomorrow
twenty people will die. I am not an advocate for self censorship but writers do have
to take it upon themselves not to be stupid. Don't mess with religion, use sex and
violence instead.

Davidar examined Taslima's book before reaching a decision and in the end rejected arguments that it attacked religion. The book's descriptions of the violence and rape underlying communal attacks was hardly the kind of soft porn sex found in Indian fiction, manufactured for the mass market, which I judged Davidar was referring to in his flippant aside warning writers not to mess with religion. He published *Lajja* because he recognised its significance.

Shame was the English title of Nasreen's new book, a work of documentary fiction with the same title used by Salman Rushdie in an earlier novel. It is a harrowing story which tells of the plight of Hindus in Bangladesh through the life of one family who lose everything and a community which sees its property seized, its temples destroyed and wives and daughters raped. In the first Bengali edition, a rushed seventy-page version, there is not one instance of a Bangladeshi Muslim shown as anything but 'communal' in outlook. Muslims are portrayed as aggressively anti-Hindu. No one protects Hindu life or property; there are no simple acts of compassion; the Muslim community turns its back.

The attacks which Nasreen chronicled were not imagined, but in her account the context of the attacks is distorted. What happened in Bangladesh came in reaction to the destruction of the Babri Mosque in Ayodhya, North India, on 6 December 1992 by Hindu extremists, where over twelve hundred Muslims were killed in outbreaks of pogroms throughout India and thousands more lost heart when they realised that, in the eyes of their attackers, they had become 'the enemy', they had become non-Indian.

These acts of insanity made mockery of the soul searching that Muslim and Hindu families had put themselves through in 1947 when British India was divided into two, in the period called 'Partition', and the question of self-identity came into play. Were they Muslims or Indians? Hindus or Pakistanis? Could they be both? Where did they belong? Millions decided they were Indian Muslims, not Pakistanis, and stayed behind in India. Just as millions of Hindus made the reverse decision by greeting independence as Bengali-speaking East Pakistanis, rather than moving to India to become Indian nationals. These decisions often left extended families divided, just like India, and millions of terrified people from all walks of life were uprooted.

Not everyone made the same choice and a million or more families dashed to the new borders of India and Pakistan before the curfew of independence sounded. The country was in the grip of a communal frenzy. Untold numbers died or disappeared; thousands of women were abducted. Hindus,

Muslims and Sikhs slaughtered one another out of desperation, revenge or as part of the politics of hate which swept the country. Communal politics still lives on in the Indian subcontinent: when the religion of one community or individual—Hindu, Muslim, Christian or Sikh—is used against another for political or economic gain.

Taslima Nasreen's indictment shows how Hindus in Bangladesh have been driven into a situation where their identity and their loyalties are now decided for them by the majority Muslim community. She becomes the voice of the Hindu community as she reveals how they've been leaving for India, in steady numbers, for years. This silent exodus has always been played down by the authorities and ignored by others.

Nasreen's story is set thirteen days after the Babri Mosque incident in India, seen by many political experts as the most serious political crisis India had faced since independence. The timing of her book, only ten weeks after the destruction of the mosque, aroused suspicion. Bangladeshis saw its release as a sinister move to divert attention away from India's predicament, which at the time was attracting international condemnation—they did not see the book's release as a clever marketing ploy. The book's contents were debated in Dhaka at the time of its first publication in February 1993. But after the Hindu fundamentalists across the border began using the book as a counter voice to the Ayodhya anti-Muslim riots, there was no room for rational debate—everything degenerated into an ugly affair and Taslima was tainted by the sequence of events, and the hype surrounding her book's promotion in India by Ananda Bazar.

Within a few months millions of pirated copies were quickly sold in India in the streets, at railway stations and bus depots for a few rupees by the Bharatiya Janata Party (BJP) Hindu extremists who used *Lajja* as a propaganda tool to vindicate their actions and deflect international criticism. 'Read *Shame*,' they yelled, 'Read *Shame* and learn what Bangladeshi Muslims do to Hindus!' Their national leader carried a large picture of the author in a procession, calling her 'Mother Taslima.' The Bangladeshi Government's embarrassment increased.

At home in Bangladesh, the Greybeards began calling her a traitor, while the progressive elements started questioning how progressive she could really be to let herself be used like this by the Hindu Religious Right. They decided that Taslima wrote what she did out of self-aggrandisement and were angry at the book's lack of balance, but central to their feelings of injustice was a layer of resentment that she had dared broach a subject rarely discussed in public and never by a woman.

Activists prided themselves on their non-communalism. While they admitted that outbursts against Hindus took place in 1990 and 1992, because it was not on the scale of the Indian anti-Muslim riots, and because they excused it as a reaction to Hindu attacks, it was either glossed over or blamed on politicians wanting to put up a smoke screen. There were always good reasons why Bangladeshis described 'communalism' as an Indian disease. After Taslima's book was released, this pretence was torn away.

Communalism was a topic which many of the younger men I met shied away from discussing. They could well imagine what it felt like to be a Muslim in India, but because many of their own friends and colleagues were Hindu, Christian or Buddhist, they were blinded to the prejudice living inside others. Proud of their democratic constitution, they would not—or could not—confront the reality of systemic and personal discrimination; our conversations usually floundered. Communal disturbances were always blamed on the politicians and their *goondahs*, the criminal elements found across most political parties, I was told, and there was no denying the trouble that these gangs caused before the authorities stepped in. The only political party apparently keeping its cadres under tight control was the religious party Jamaati—Islamist to the core, but not given to organising violence against Bangladeshi Hindus.

Members of the Hindu, Buddhist and Christian Committee understood the meaning of exclusion. When I visited the home of their leader, retired Colonel Dutt, I saw life through their eyes. The man too scared to speak out when hooligans steal the mangoes from his trees is a victim of communalism, the soldier or civil servant overlooked for promotion year after year, or the farmer forced to sell his land at less than the market price because he worries about his family's welfare and will soon leave for Calcutta. The day is coming, he thinks, when they will be the only Hindus left in the village, and who will help them celebrate the rituals which give meaning to their lives?

Other stories reach my ears and so great is my need to drown out the insane voices of communal hatred that I seize on them: I only want to hear stories where Muslims protect their Hindu neighbours and I tell myself that all is not lost for there are many such tales. The same narratives are told in India, only this time Hindus are protecting Muslims – and they are all true. In Bangladesh a Hindu widow's face lights up as she tells me how Muslim neighbours formed a human circle all night around her house to protect her; an eyewitness tells me about other Muslims who razed the temple and houses of a Hindu village not far outside Dhaka, who stole tools and animals and then returned a week later, ashamed, seeking redemption, to rebuild the village they'd torn down—a project which took months and was led by a writer-activist and implacable enemy of Taslima, a man called Ahmed Sofa.

But fear crowds out compassion and I also hear first-hand accounts of Hindu women too scared to leave their houses in the old parts of Dhaka in 1992; some stop wearing the vermilion-coloured *bindi* on their foreheads, the dot which symbolises they are married Hindu women, in case they are attacked.

✸

Most Bangladeshi writers found no literary merit in *Lajja*. I was only able to read the English translation published later, but from listening to others it seemed that the original novella belonged to the tradition of the pamphleteer and that each revised edition and translation has destroyed its original charm and raw passion. The Indian publishers could not avoid the temptation of trying to improve on the original: six chapters became thirteen and it grew from seventy pages to over two hundred, which can't be explained away in terms of translating from Bengali into English. Some may ask the question whether extensive revisions like this are legitimate in literary terms, but it was a commercial necessity, as the hastily written novella would have difficulty attracting reading audiences outside the Indian subcontinent without some revisiting. Certain sections may also have been inserted to deflect criticism that the book was not a balanced analysis of Hindu–Muslim relations in Bangladesh. The first English edition was published by Penguin India, at the time fifty-one per cent owned by Taslima's publishers, Ananda Bazar. David Davidar, Head of Penguin India, used a team of people to work on the revision, including Nasreen, he told me. But by then Taslima was living overseas burdened with new problems, so that I was never sure how much of the new English edition was her authentic voice.

New York–based Indian writer Amitav Ghosh was a staunch defender of Nasreen and saw in *Lajja* what others were blind to. He defended it as a new form of writing that he calls 'polemiction', a hybrid form where polemics and fiction merge, and compared her to Egyptian feminist Nawaal al Sa'adawy. He thought *Lajja* a work of considerable insight, but was not blind to how the text distorts the events leading to the attacks in Bangladesh. Ghosh blamed the appalling reviews *Lajja* later received in America and Europe on the poor quality of the English translations; he had the good fortune of reading it in its original Bengali version.

The Bangladeshi men who look kindly on Taslima and admire her for writing *Lajja* belong to an older generation. 'As a man I would not have dared to write this,' British-based Mr Abdul Gafur Chowdhury told me. 'It is a shame on the entire Bengali Muslim community that they did not stand up like this girl!' Editor Wahid Huq argued that an exposé should have been written years ago. He was 'grateful to Taslima for writing this book'.

Two years after Nasreen's controversial book came out, and a year after her departure, a Bangladeshi journalist called Fazlul Bari wrote a book about a homosexual mullah who seduces a Hindu boy. In revenge the boy cuts off the mullah's penis. Bari's statistical information came from the same source used by Nasreen; his account, however, includes incidents of Muslims helping Hindus. The reaction to his book was revealing: a few murmurs from the Bearded Ones, articles in two pro-Islamist dailies, but the book was neither banned nor were there any death threats. Twenty thousand copies were sold.

Bari walked away with his reputation intact. What saved his book and why wasn't he sanctioned? First and foremost, said Bari, he 'escaped' because he was a man; secondly Taslima already had a name for being anti-Islam; and finally, the BJP in India used her book to stir up trouble, which, in turn, led the Bangladeshi Government to ban *Lajja* because it was embarrassed by the publicity.

❀

Why did Nasreen write *Shame*? According to those who knew her, she'd never taken an interest in Hindu–Muslim relations before; and she stood outside the popular anti-communal movement sweeping the country in 1992–1993, led by the progressive secular forces

A year before *Lajja* came out, the Hindu, Buddhist and Christian Committee of Bangladesh had released their own small publication documenting their plight—it was banned. Hoping that other writers would break the silence, they sent their materials to journalists inside and outside of the country. Taslima, who was writing columns in Dhaka at the time, either received this research dossier directly, or else it was passed on to her by some of her Hindu Bangladeshi friends. From this base Nasreen compiled her own novel using a similar title to the Committee's whose document was titled *Glasi,* which meant in English 'The Disgrace'.

Two of Taslima's close friends who influenced her at the time were a married couple, well-known intellectuals from Hindu backgrounds. Taslima and her friends strongly believed that if you followed any religion, you were inherently 'communal'—the seeds of hate were there and would grow, no matter what your religion, no matter how tolerant you thought yourself. Taslima wanted to please her friends who were only expecting a newspaper column, but she would do much better than that, she told them.

And as Naim would have it, Taslima needed the money and knew that *Lajja* would be a commercial success in India, as well as in her own country. No other writer—Hindu or Muslim—had ever before written a book in defence of their respective minority communities. Taslima told everyone that she was an atheist, but Indians preferred to see her as a Muslim girl who turned on her own society and exposed what she saw as terrible wrongs. This was something new; it would cause a sensation and by now Taslima's writing was her main source of income.

Dr Fazlul Alum describes his flat to me as 'servantless', which makes him an eccentric in Dhaka society. Life in the UK has trained him to look after himself and he is a man who likes his privacy, impossible in a house with servants. For the moment he has returned to Dhaka and holds a senior position in the Dhaka University Library.

Fazlul Alum discovered Nasreen through reading the local Bengali papers in London. He liked what he read and, in 1991, when he came home on a short visit, he made up his mind to meet her. Soon after he arrived, Alum wrote an article defending Nasreen from accusations of blasphemy which some minor religious figure was using to make a name for himself. Nasreen wrote him an emotional letter telling him that, 'the whole world is against me and a man I hardly know has defended me. Thank you, I am very grateful.'

The two became friends and he started to feel that she liked being seen with him. 'Genuinely, I'm a nobody; just a migrant, an expat who comes here, off and on, and writes a little of this and that,' he said, but this portly, dignified man was being overly modest, for Nasreen was not known for picking up nobodies. He translated some of her poems into English and she helped him in return.

Alum was scathing about Dhaka intellectuals, who in their heart of hearts, he said, never supported her. 'Never for one minute did they believe she should be saying those things; nor be so prominent.'

Some writers were jealous that by 1993 Taslima was able to live from her writing. The editor of a popular weekly told me, 'People don't want to believe this, because in Bangladesh, only Taslima and one other writer existed solely by their writing. This is a country where you don't have to pay a writer anything! You can tell them, "I have printed your poem, or your story, and you should be grateful to me", or you can pay them 100 or 200 taka [US$1.50].'

What drew me to Fazlul Alum's story, however, was not the envy of other writers but his open cynicism when he began talking about *Lajja*.

'*Lajja* was just a political novel,' he said, 'and it was politically geared to cause trouble. I know the background of it and I know the background of Taslima's passport being confiscated at the airport, which shot her into international fame. I have always believed that someone must have engineered that. It may have been her well-wishers or her enemies, who knows?'

I was sure that Alum did know, in spite of his 'vagueness'. His habit of hinting at conspiracies and then trailing off at the last minute left me hanging, wanting to know more, which he seemed to enjoy.

The passport story had come alive once before when Naim had led me through the maze of Nasreen's passport story. Nasreen came to him because she needed a second passport; one which did not list her occupation as government doctor, and Naim had the connections to help her. The law requires anyone working for the Government to have their passport stamped 'NOC', shorthand for a no objection certificate. Even a weekend trip to Calcutta meant you needed your department head's permission in the form of an NOC, which you would then show to airport officials. And if your boss didn't like you, or was displeased with your work or attendance, he could easily refuse. The edict was originally introduced as a way of curtailing the massive brain drain of local doctors leaving for overseas positions. Many citizens, fed up with this bureaucratic hurdle, hold two passports as a matter of convenience. At the time Naim had been happy to oblige and declared that Nasreen was a columnist working on his paper a year before this actually happened. Nasreen travelled regularly to Calcutta, India, on her second passport for years, without any questions asked.

Four years later, the second passport listing her as a journalist landed her in trouble with the Government. In January 1993, on her way to Calcutta, she was stopped at the airport, where her passport was confiscated and she found herself accused of breaking the law by making a false declaration. All of this took place just a few weeks before the release of her controversial book in mid-February. Technically and legally she was in the wrong as she was still working as a government doctor at the time, but the incident was used as a means to harass her and reflected badly on the Government.

The international human rights movement began noticing her name on their lists of writers in trouble, and soon mounted a campaign, which caught the Bangladeshi Government on the back foot as they tried to explain, with no success, that she had broken the law.

There were times when I found it hard to fathom if Fazlul Alum was a man who pretended to know more than he actually did, but after careful consideration I came down on his side. Alum was held in high regard by his colleagues, had watched the reception of the novella and at the time was a confidante of Taslima's.

'When *Lajja* first came out in Bangladesh,' he said, 'it sold well; after all, she was a popular writer, but there was no public controversy, nothing like the impact it created later. Not a single reviewer in Bangladesh gave a damn. It was just a book, a novel on the Babri Mosque and the effect that had on Bangladesh.'

He sounded too offhand for my liking, yet the book he was talking about sold more than sixty thousand copies in the author's homeland before it was banned three months later, in June 1993, on the grounds that it 'contained substance prejudicial to the State which might create misunderstanding and mistrust among different communities living in exemplary harmony in the country'.

According to Fazlul Alum, the climate changed only after several articles appeared in Calcutta magazines; he hinted that there was someone behind the explosion of publicity around *Lajja*. It was Alum at his best, leading me further into the jungle and then leaving me to find my way. I concluded that the finger pointed to her Indian publishers, Ananda Bazar. Alum declined to discuss the background to *Lajja* any further. He seemed sad that he was no longer a part of Nasreen's circle and I wondered why she'd cut him out of her life. Later I encountered others who also felt cast aside; Nasreen has a habit of moving on if something displeases her, as I knew only too well.

The pro-Taslima camp included her publishers Ananda Bazaar, who made a lot of money out of Nasreen from Indian editions of *Lajja* and her earlier books. *Lajja* was serialised in magazines and papers around India and translated into a number of Indian regional languages.

Senior Ananda executive Nikhil Sarkar was sometimes called 'the master puppeteer' in Taslima's life, never to his face, of course, for he was a powerful man with a long memory and a long reach. After she moved overseas many from her old Calcutta circle complained about his Svengali influence; they felt neglected and blamed Nikhil.

Three years after visiting him at his home in Calcutta, in early 1997, I still have trouble accepting Nikhil Sarkar's avowal that Ananda was completely unaware *Lajja* was in the pipeline—time has not made it any easier to swallow his story. Nikhil was curious about the kind of book I was writing and set a few traps for me. I left feeling I'd been manipulated by a clever man who gave nothing away and enjoyed his little games. The next day I found myself refused access to the company's library where they housed the newspaper archives on Taslima. I was given a sequence of lame excuses by the Chairman's secretary, Rachel McBehan, who was loyal but unconvincing.

Given the history and strength of the Ananda relationship, why would Nasreen have left her publishing friends in the dark? It makes sense that she discussed her new book with them before she began writing—any other conclusion is naive. Even allowing for the fact that this book was written in seven days (sic), it was incubating for a longer period. Ananda had a sense of ownership about Taslima: they felt they'd discovered her and their reputation is second to none for selecting talented writers and marketing them aggressively. The Ananda culture relies on personal relationships with its writers, rather than contracts. Bangladesh's writing community, almost to a man (and woman), believed that Ananda had been grooming Taslima at least a year before *Lajja* came out.

❀

'*Ananda Bazar Patrika* is to Bengal what *The Times* is to Britain,' wrote *The Times, of London* in 1983 about the group's popular Bengali daily.

Founded in 1922, the Ananda Bazar Publishing Group is the most powerful publishing empire in West Bengal, if not India. Its stable incudes a Bengali daily, an English daily, *The Telegraph*, the famous literary journal *Desh*, an English-language weekly and a cluster of highly profitable magazines for film fans, children, sports fans, business men and women. Added to this list, a book publishing arm caters to literary and popular tastes, producing high quality educational texts which are marketed throughout India and Bangladesh. The latter defends itself against the flood of Indian publications but faces a losing battle because of the quality of the Ananda product.

In Nasreen, Ananda Bazar found the perfect commodity: a controversial Bangladeshi woman, a professed atheist from a Muslim family, writing in their language, Bengali, about topics which infuriated her Muslim readership—the stuff that publishers' dreams are made of and just the right material for a carefully orchestrated marketing campaign—Ananda knew how to make money. Nasreen was in the hands of a powerful commercial force which helped mould her into the woman writer she'd always dreamt of becoming.

Indian women activists were less enthusiastic about Nasreen, who by now was the darling of the Calcutta set. 'What is she saying that's any different to what we've been saying for the past twenty years?' they complained to their male colleagues.

In 1992 Taslima won India's major literary prize, the Ananda Purashkar, for her best-selling book *Selected Columns*; her essays were all about male cruelty and Islamic oppression of women. This annual literary event was organised, sponsored and judged by the Ananda group. Back home in Dhaka her award created enormous controversy. She was the first Bangladeshi ever to be honoured with this award and Dhaka's literary establishment now had another reason to dislike her. The more she was feted in Calcutta, the more she was frowned on in Dhaka. I became convinced that she was both 'made' and 'unmade' through her close association with the Indian publishing empire.

Calcutta loved Nasreen, and Nasreen loved Calcutta. Calcutta was heaven on earth compared to Dhaka, she wrote in a poem. She asked her Indian writer friend Sunil Gangopadhyaya to publish her poem in the famous magazine he edited, but for once he refused. 'I warned her,' he said. "You'll get into trouble in Dhaka, if I publish it." But Taslima wouldn't listen and, in the end, published the poem herself in Dhaka.

'Writers must be very careful about what they write in Dhaka,' Sunil told me. 'Years ago I wrote in a poem that Indira Gandhi's lips were dry because she had not been kissed for many years. My Bangladeshi friends were shocked. "We couldn't get away with this in Bangladesh—we'd be killed!" they told me. But here, even Indira Gandhi laughed and told her friends, "he is very naughty."

All Bangladeshi writers long for acceptance from the West Bengali literati—you haven't made it as a writer until you've been published in *Desh*, or had your books published and sold across India. Everyone knows this in Bangladesh and everyone resents it. 'If a third-rate Indian Bengali writer says you are good you feel flattered,' a local writer complained to me.

It was common knowledge inside the writing fraternity that the Indian judges first offered the literary award to the illustrious Bangla Academy, the country's national symbol of the liberation struggle. Senior directors of the Academy told me that the Academy's council was reluctant to accept the award because it was a commercial prize being offered by a multi-national concern and they, let us not forget, were a national institution—the implication being that they would be compromised; the official Bangladeshi version recalls that the honour was refused out of hand, politely but firmly, on ideological, patriotic grounds.

But there was more than one version in circulation I found out as I made the rounds in Dhaka and Calcutta: one story insists that the Indian jury moved on to the next candidate before the Bangladeshi Government's permission came through; while another Indian version has the Academy wanting to accept the prize, but their Government refusing permission.

Stir the pot and another reason surfaces: the Bangla Academy was anti-President Ershad's rule in 1992, and it seems that Ananda Bazar enjoyed a good relationship with Ershad, who at the time, was being brought down by the pro-democracy movement led by the arts community. Then came the whispers insinuating that the Calcutta publishers wanted to expand, open a newspaper in Dhaka and were wooing the esteemed Academy, which they knew would oppose any such move.

Inside Bangladesh there is at times a strong anti-Indian feeling. Big Brother, India, is always seen as trying to dominate its smaller neighbour, culturally and economically. Even though India helped her East Bengali neighbours against West Pakistan in 1971, the anti-Indian feeling often surfaces; and carries over into in the world of books. Since 1997 books from India—even the Bengali-language books from West Bengal—are neither displayed nor sold at the annual Spring Book Fair held on the grounds of the Bangla Academy.

The President of the Academy Council, venerated poet Shamsur Rahman, informed me that the book fair celebrated Bangladeshi writing only. 'There are other book fairs during the year for foreign [Indian] books,' he said.

Many in Dhaka believed that in order to teach the Bangla Academy a lesson for snubbing their award, Ananda offered the prize to Nasreen instead; that this was a deliberate slap in the face to more established writers of Bangladesh, especially to Shamsur Rahman, a major poet.

Leading Calcutta writer and a judge on the award panel that year, Sunil Gangopadhaya, favoured the senior poet and knew what a stir it would cause if Nasreen won. Although Sunil was a good friend to Nasreen, he voted against her and argued against the chairman's decision. But the owner of the Ananda holdings, Avark Sarkar, had his way.

The true story behind the award and why Taslima was finally selected may never be known, but in Indian circles it was also believed that Ananda saw a wonderful opportunity to promote a new, exciting writer onto the Indian scene and make money through her controversial writing. This was the Ananda style, left-wing Indian critics said, and in the State of Bengal there has always been tension between the socialist government and the multinational company with its giant stable of writers—a publishing dynasty certainly, and almost a monopoly.

Dhaka's literary establishment was outraged when the news broke that Taslima Nasreen was to receive one of India's highest literary awards. It's true she was a popular young writer, but was she writing literature, they asked. And to add insult to injury, they claimed sections of her prize-winning book proved she was a cunning plagiarist.

The charges of plagiarism certainly had substance. It is generally believed that Nasreen cited several pages, in her usual careless style, from a scholarly book by Dr Sukumari Bhattacharji, an Indian woman writer, giving the impression that she had done the research herself and could read Sanskrit.

Indian freelance journalist Maitryee Chatterjee counted twenty-two lifted pages. 'How can anybody get away with this and win such a prestigious prize?' she wondered as she sat trying to write her review. She told Sunil Gangopadhaya, who was also editor of the *Desh* book section, that her review made mention of the lack of acknowledgment, leaving it in his hands as to whether he would cut it or not—he left it in. Other papers ran with the story and finally Ananda countered their accusations with an entire supplement devoted to Nasreen. Maitryee believes that senior executive Nikhil Sarkar was angry with her; for a while Maitryee was persona non grata: one of her finished articles was put on hold and she received no commissions from the Ananda-owned publications for six months.

Letters of complaint, many of them anonymous, flowed from Dhaka to Calcutta and the debate raged for a few weeks. Only one or two Bangladeshi papers gave any coverage to Taslima's triumph. Dr Bhattacharji made no formal complaint but everyone suspected that was only because she too belonged to the Ananda Bazar stable of writers; indeed she'd won the same prize a few years earlier. Subsequent editions of Nasreen's prize-winning book acknowledged the source and Nasreen learnt a valuable lesson: the old scissors-and-paste trick worked when writing a column, but not in book form. *Selected Columns* remains one of her most popular works and was translated by Ananda into numerous Indian languages.

Two years later a devout Muslim would claim that his religious sentiments were hurt by certain passages in the book and would file a complaint against the author, landing her in court a second time.

Taslima was the star at the *Ananda Bazar Patrika* literary award presentation in Calcutta, which was followed by a flurry of promotional interviews. Then a few months later, just a month before her new book came out, the passport trouble started. A new round of sensational publicity was unleashed and this time it was picked up in the West. After the book was banned in June 1993, the Ananda machinery swung into action: the book ban sent sales of their Indian Bengali edition and the later English edition, from Penguin India, soaring.

The *Lajja* campaign, orchestrated by Ananda, was commercially motivated, although the embarrassment of their Bengali-speaking cousins across the border must have caused them some amusement at the time. In the dark world of Hindu–Muslim tensions, Hindus were usually cast as villains. On this occasion the tables were turned. But it is a nonsense to suggest, as some critics do, that Ananda were in cahoots with the BJP, the Hindu communal party in India, and that this was an anti-Bangladesh move. This is an extreme conspiracy theory with no evidence to support it. Ananda Bazar is a business empire and Bangladesh represents a huge market which the Indian publishing firm is keen to exploit and Bangladeshis are just as keen to resist. Politically, Ananda is regarded to the right of centre and is not popular with the Calcutta socialist government, but more cannot be inferred.

The West Bengal press, in Ananda's home city of Calcutta, first drew the attention of the national Indian press and later the Western media to the Taslima Nasreen story through newspaper interviews and magazine articles they ran in late 1993. Taslima, who was never known to turn down the opportunity for an interview or a photo session, was in her element. The Indian press went overboard: one journalist compared her to Naguib Mahfouz, the Egyptian Nobel Laureate, and Socrates, in the same breath—the others were content to keep drawing the Salman Rushdie analogy.

After *Lajja* was banned in mid-1993, even Indian journalists began calling Nasreen a 'media princess', the passport saga dragged on, there was always a story popping up for the tabloids. In February 1993 an incident occurred at the Bangla Academy Book Fair, where *Lajja* was being launched. The author claimed that she was attacked by hundreds of Muslim extremists—in her interviews over the years, numbers have varied between five hundred and fifty thousand. She claimed that the fanatics burnt her books and physically attacked her.

This was manna from heaven for the Indian media and Ananda publishers. Local eyewitnesses, including journalists and Bangla Academy staff, argue that the incident was blown up out of all proportion, but nevertheless it remains one of the more enduring ancillary tales of the Taslima mythology.

Six eyewitnesses I spoke to affirmed that the book fair hooligans were not Muslim extremists: they were either anti-Taslima student agitators or a mob of fans tired of waiting for her autograph. The latter version is the one that journalists and senior Academy staff favoured as they showed me around the grounds of the Academy where the book fair is held each Spring. Crowds become unruly in Bangladesh almost at will, tempers ignite; trouble makers find it easy to incite bored, ill-tempered crowds, especially during the fasting month of Ramadan when everyone is dehydrated. The 1993 event is also confused by some bystanders with another anti-Taslima demonstration the year before when twenty students or so, some of them *madrassah* boys, set out that day to harass the author for her 'pornographic' writing.

Taslima later told me in Sweden that she and her publisher met with the ring leaders, that same night, to try to resolve the conflict—this part of her story was also confirmed by Fazlul Alum, but they refused out of hand to let her return to the 1992 Book Fair. Keep away or they would make more trouble, they promised. When word of this 'secret' meeting leaked out in Dhaka, it led to rumours that Taslima had organised the attack as a publicity stunt and was meeting the students that night to pay them off. These stories are based on hearsay, are unreliable and spread by *madrassah* students and their teachers; Taslima's Dhaka publisher at Pearl Publications denies the attacks were a publicity stunt. Nevertheless, the stories reinforce how unpopular the writer was becoming amongst people who were ready to believe anything of Taslima Nasreen.

There is no question that Taslima was shaken by these incidents. On both occasions she was rescued by the Deputy Director and other members of the Bangla Academy with their guards, who escorted her to an office and then to her home, where they advised her not to return to the Book Fair. The signs were there: Taslima was in danger of becoming a target.

The image of books being burnt reeks of Nazi fascism and is forever sealed inside the psyche of the fifty-plus generation; it is seen as a direct blow against Enlightenment. But my eye witnesses, some of whom even called themselves 'Taslima supporters', were adamant: there were no book burnings, neither was the author beaten and stripped of her sari as one foreign news agency claimed. The tiny bamboo stall was wrecked; she was jostled and verbally abused and needed protection—this was frightening enough without the embellishments.

❀

There are over five thousand journalists in Bangladesh working on five hundred and more Bangla and English-language dailies and weeklies, most aligned with one or the other political party. Close to eighteen hundred journalists work in Dhaka. They are a close-knit crew and the Dhaka Press Club is their fortress.

Local city journalists are always suspicious of foreign and district correspondents. Out in the districts, far away from Dhaka, the correspondents employed by the national dailies want their news items published, so on occasion, if there is no news they make news—they must earn a living after all.

In the same way, Bangladeshi journalists stringing for the foreign press have been known to exaggerate, even fabricate stories to have them noticed by Western editors. There is a well-known story about an Associated Press (AP) journalist who filed a report that fifty people had been killed in a storm in Jessore. Fortunately before the story was run, the news agency discovered it was false. When one of the editors rang the journalist to learn why he had filed the report, he replied that he'd been sitting at his computer that night trying to think of a story. He went out on the balcony for a cigarette and noticed that some cloud had gathered in front of the full moon. Whenever there were clouds in that direction, he said, there was a storm in Jessore—whenever there was a storm in Jessore, around fifty people died.

Death tolls will be doubled or even trebled to make the news—that is an accepted practice. Smaller events are made to seem bigger by quoting large crowd sizes to grab the attention of the foreign media. Many a journalist has filed a story where he quotes that five hundred people died only to be told that unless it's five thousand nobody is interested. Journalists are quick to learn. Figures of numbers attending rallies are notoriously rubbery. In a country of 140 million and a mega capital of ten million, a rally of five thousand people is not considered large, if the number is even commented on at all. Even a small political party can assemble a crowd for small amounts of money, while a large party like the Islam-based Jamaati is always owed favours and money from small traders and shopkeepers who will close their shops and join a rally whenever called on—and, of course, when *madrassah* students are summoned, they come running like children eager to join the circus parade.

It is easier for fabricated reports to go to print because unidentified sources are the norm in Bangladeshi reporting. On sensitive issues few are willing to put their name to a quote, unless they live overseas, or their reputations make them sacrosanct and beyond reach; so where Australian newspapers are loath to use an unidentified source because of legal complications, here it is a common practice.

Farid Hossain realised how important Taslima Nasreen had become only when *Time* magazine printed his story in 1993. Farid is the Dhaka-based Bangladesh correspondent for the Associated Press (AP) world news agency service. Journalists like Farid work according to the interests of world readers outside the country they cover: national disasters like cyclones, floods, political riots and the like make up the news menu foreign readers like to peruse, but social stories, especially religious riots and women versus Muslim radicals, are also favourites.

When asked who determines his readers' interests, Farid shrugs philosophically. 'After fifteen years, you know what kind of stories your organisation wants from you. If I'm working for AP, my attention's focused on what interests American readers; that becomes the overall profile of my readership.'

Ideas for stories usually come from reading the local papers; story ideas are then pursued with the man on the spot covering his own interview. Newsagency correspondents are viewed as being in a class above local reporters, in terms of status and remuneration.

The Taslima story was the biggest story of Farid's life, 'an opportunity of a lifetime,' as he put it, which he made the most of like any professional journalist. 'The Taslima saga, in 1994, had all the ingredients which American and European readers seemed to want.'

What were these 'ingredients' in the years before September 11, 2001?

'I believe,' he said, 'that Western readers are paranoid about Islam, about what they call "fundamentalism". They feel very insecure about what happens in countries where their development aid is invested, either through the American dollar or through their volunteers. They are interested because they have an involvement; otherwise they wouldn't care. I've been working for AP since 1986.' Farid was a busy man for he also filed stories for the English-language *Telegraph* paper in Calcutta that belonged to the Ananda group, friendly to Taslima.

In early June 1993, Farid read about the banning of *Lajja* in local Dhaka papers but did nothing about it at first, thinking it wasn't of great importance. Only a few papers reported it in Dhaka; small pieces and, as Farid summed it up, there was no formal announcement from the Government, so he didn't think it newsworthy, until his colleagues across the border started plaguing him for a story on Taslima.

At about the same time the New Delhi–based AP bureau also made enquires. The bureau in Delhi is the controlling office for distributing assignments and requests copy and edits whatever comes across their wires. Whenever Farid filed an AP story it would be sent to Delhi first, for they acted like a regional headquarters and a filter.

He responded to the AP request by telling them that he'd keep in touch. 'But I don't think it's a big story,' he told them frankly. Up till then he had only met Taslima twice: once in his office when Naim introduced her, and asked him to review one of her books, and on another occasion; he remembered being miffed because she never bothered to thank him for writing a good review. 'You could say I wasn't a fan,' he said.

Soon after, Farid received a call from *The Telegraph,* the Ananda-owned English-language daily, telling him they were doing a special *puja* festival edition and wanted to put Taslima on the cover. *Puja*, or holiday, anthologies are big business in West Bengal and earn their writers large sums of money.

'Can you do the cover story?' they asked. A special edition all about Taslima Nasreen and how Calcutta writers saw her was being drawn together with pieces supplied by writers on the Ananda payroll. Ananda was organising advance publicity for a brand new Bengali version of *Lajja*. All of this interest was being shown after the Government's ban in June 1993. Farid knew that one never refuses assignments like this, so reluctantly he agreed.

The first time he met Nasreen, as he knew her then, for any length of time was after the Soldiers of Islam made their first death threats in September 1993. She was very nervous, he said, and wanted police protection, which the authorities took nine days to provide. He ended up doing a small story for the AP; nothing big, but he could tell that interest was mounting by the way it was received in New York, via New Delhi, of course, and they wanted more and more, especially *Time* magazine, which picked up his small item on Nasreen from the AP news wire. Farid was astonished because he'd filed his story on a Friday afternoon and the next morning these requests came flooding in for more details and confirmation of names and dates. He was simply amazed: for a story from Dhaka to get in the day before the magazine came out was rare indeed from his experience.

'This only happens with something like a military coup or a big cyclone,' he said. Only then did he realise how potentially important this story was going to be for AP, for *Time* magazine—and for Farid Hossain. His story also ended up being published on the front page of *The New York Times*; 'a small story, without my name, but on the front page,' he said. He and Taslima became friends.

'The Americans thought it was going to be another Rushdie story; again they were showing their paranoia against Islam.' All of this happened, according to Farid, before international groups like PEN discovered her. Before then Nasreen had never received any international coverage, beyond India. Farid did his best to explain to a bewildered Taslima what was unfolding, but she was unable to comprehend the enormity of it all.

Following *The New York Times* article, Taslima made what was probably the most important connection of her life, and from this moment, in early October 1993 on, she started receiving messages from a woman in New York called Meredith Tax. By then Farid had finished his special cover assignment for the Calcutta paper and began doing regular stories for AP on the beleaguered writer.

'Gradually the international campaign forcing the Bangladeshi Government to return her passport started to build up,' said Farid, 'and the local religious hardliners also began their moves.'

Farid started to become drawn inside the Taslima labyrinth; he translated a few of her poems for the benefit of Meredith Tax in New York and took care of the faxes from overseas, as Taslima's English was limited.

Time passed, everything started to die down, the demonstrations fizzled out and Taslima began moving around town again. By now she was quite the celebrity, holding court and granting interviews to senior journalists and camera crews.

And then, in late April 1994, she went to France after her passport was finally returned to her the month before and, on her way back, stopped in at Calcutta and gave the now-famous interview to Sujata Sen of *The Statesman* which the Government used against her. Everything went downhill from then on, Farid said. He was on his way to meet her the day the Government issued a warrant for her arrest. She reached him by mobile and told him that she was leaving the house, so once again he was the man on the spot, the first journalist to get this story.

❀

Lajja brought Taslima fame, money and Indian critical accolades, but also alienated her from the people who mattered in progressive circles in her own country. She had exhausted the limits of their tolerance and although they would write letters of support in favour of free speech, assuaging their consciences and keeping their foreign donors happy, this was as far as the majority were prepared to go. She became an invisible part of their agenda: while their banners demanded freedom of speech, they rarely mentioned her by name. It was the Greybeards who targeted her by name on their banners, demanding that she be brought to trial and hanged.

'She is another Daud Haider,' people told me. I knew the name but not much else about the man who'd been forced to leave Bangladesh many years ago and now lived in Germany.

By mid-1993 when her book was proscribed in Bangladesh and flaunted in India, liberal opinion started to turn away: her actions were seen as foolish and self-serving. But it was after the Indian press began treating Taslima like a tabloid star that public opinion really swung against her. Bangladeshis felt they were being shamed in the eyes of their neighbour and that the enfant terrible was telling the Indian and the Western media what they wanted to hear. They began to draw the line at how she promoted herself and maligned Bangladesh 'in those interviews', as they called them.

A member of *Naripokkho*, a leading feminist group, was furious as she recalled this. 'Another disservice, was to erase us,' she said. 'It's taken us twenty years to get women's issues on the agenda here—and she called us "housewives" to her Indian friends and to the rest of the world!'

If at the time you confined your reading to Indian papers and maga-zines, and the foreign media, you could be forgiven for thinking that there was only one person in Bangladesh who battled Muslim extremists, just one person who understood women's oppression, that only Taslima spoke out against Hindu discrimination. Nasreen willingly allowed herself to be moulded into the Joan of Arc of the Indian subcontinent, and the Indian media—who did know better of course—were happy for once that it was neighbouring Muslim Bangladesh making world headlines. The more left-leaning members of the Indian intelligentsia, however, chose to remain silent and were criticised for this by Indian journalists.

Nevertheless, Taslima was enjoying herself. She was a prize-winning author, lionised by her Ananda friends across the border, she was among the top three authors at the Bangla Academy Book Fairs from 1991 to 1993, she wrote for the Indian literary magazine *Desh*; she was making enough money now to be independent.

Liberal Muslims, however, were dismayed by what they saw as a lethal combination: a lack of knowledge and a loud mouth. Taslima was well and truly running with the enemy, they believed. The woman was a liability. The whole communal debate was being dragged in false directions, they feared. Trust was breaking down, with people in denial rather than focussing on what needed to be done to avoid any further outbreaks between Hindus and Muslims. Most activists wanted nothing to do with her in this tense situation but still stopped short of criticising her publicly. Well-known writer and social commentator Ahmed Sofa (now deceased) was a notable exception and rounded on her in fury. But most of the leading lights who called themselves progressive held back not wanting to strengthen the hand of the religious fanatics. Their silence was punishing and it was this silence which had first drawn me to the story of Taslima.

Activist Nasreen Huq was not proud that *Lajja* was written. 'I would have preferred a broader canvas, a more balanced picture,' she said, 'but we can't blame *Lajja*, because if any of our famous writers had written about the plight of Hindus earlier, then the reaction [to Nasreen's book] would have been inconsequential and *Lajja* would have been irrelevant.'

Finally the Government moved against the rebel author, using her as a pawn in their manoeuvres to accommodate the religious extremists. Who would care? Here they made their big mistake, because people and movements outside Bangladesh, especially amongst the giant freedom of expression groups, cared very much.

❊

Indian journalists were the first to use the Salman Rushdie analogy after Taslima's book was banned. Her minders at Ananda Bazar began to polish her new persona, as the female Rushdie, and she bloomed. The Western media quickly seized on the comparisons because Rushdie was a household word, but the original campaign which brought her to the attention of the world press emanated from India, through their stringers working in Bangladesh. After this the Western media was hooked.

International PEN in London was also drawn in by Indian sources. This came about when Sri Ananda Shankar Roy, the grand old man of Indian literature, was approached in about late September 1993 by a journalist called Ghose, who was well known to him and who worked for the *Ananda Bazar Patrika*.

When I visited Shankar Roy in Calcutta he was happy to reprise his role in drawing Taslima to the attention of the outside world. A ninety-two-year-old man of great intellectual curiosity and little ego, he was a marvellous storyteller. We sat together on his balcony while he told me the romantic love story of how he met his Texas-born wife, Lila Ray, to whom he'd been married for sixty-two years before she died.

Shankar Roy was overwhelmingly sympathetic to Taslima's predicament. He remembers the Ananda journalist telling him that they must help Taslima, because she was going to be killed and that it was the Rushdie case all over again. Shankar Roy was, at the time, President of All India PEN as well as Chairman of the PEN Calcutta Branch.

Shankar Roy, who had met Taslima two years before, and always thought of her as a 'woman born fifty years too soon', was persuaded to take action and came up with the idea of appealing outside India. He sent faxes to PEN centres in London, Paris, Berlin and Tokyo alerting them to Taslima's case. The Ananda Bazar journalist suggested they inform the BBC's India Office and Ananda Shankar Roy agreed to sign the press statement. All of this was happening in late September–early October 1993, at about the same time that Farid Hossain was introducing Taslima's name to the outside world, mainly at the behest of Ananda-owned papers.

Nineteen ninety-four was a cliffhanger of a year for the young, inexperienced BNP Government in Bangladesh, a party in power for less than three years. Politically, everything was going wrong and they badly needed a distraction which would help them regain the upper hand, a strategy which would deal their main opposition, the Awami League, a blow and simultaneously woo back their former electoral Islamist ally, Jamaat-i-Islami. Conservative, pro-Islam factions inside the Government began to examine the Taslima syndrome and interpret the omens, wondering how to use the religious card to trump their opposition.

At the time there were signs that a new election alliance was being worked out between the Awami League, associated with independence and secularism, and Jamaat-i-Islami the country's largest religious party. Politics makes for strange bedfellows, but both major parties, BNP and Awami, need electoral support from religious minor parties. The next election was only two years away—sooner if the opposition parties forced an early election. The ten-month-old boycott of Parliament by all the opposition parties was taking its toll; it was becoming impossible to govern.

By using the religious card, the Government could remind voters that they were prepared to defend Islam. The figures they targeted as un-Islamic, with the exception of Taslima, were linked to Awami and the very strong, populist, anti-fundamentalist movement led by the Nirumul Committee which had been gaining ground over the last two years.

The Government hoped that their action might send the main religious party, Jamaat, scurrying back to their side and also quieten the smaller religious groups congregated around certain populist mullah figures in Dhaka.

The cry of 'Islam in danger!' usually worked like magic, and here Taslima Nasreen could be useful. Taslima and the NGOs became linked, as a way of tapping into any dormant anti-Western feeling, although they had nothing to do with each other. The fact that outsiders were calling her the female Rushdie also played into the Government's hands, for *The Satanic Verses* was banned in Bangladesh.

The Government's failure to take steps against demonstrators who were breaking the law by making death threats against the writer sent the message to smaller Islamist groups that it was open season on Nasreen; open season on NGOs and tally ho on any journalists or editors who criticised the mullah-minded. In June 1994 the Government also arrested four editors from the *Janakantha* paper, which had been running stories on certain mullahs who lined their pockets by deceiving poor, rural villagers.

In early 1994 these small groups outside of Dhaka led by *pirs* (revered, saint-like figures) and self-styled *maulanas* (religious scholars) became bolder and began a spate of organized attacks against NGOs in remote villages. These attacks were at the time quite serious but fortunately short-lived, and they were always precipitated by fiery sermons at the mosques and speeches at the *madrassahs*, which were widely published in pro-Islamist papers.

For years the foreign-donor-funded NGOs had been threatening certain traditional livelihoods by providing, health, educational and micro credit services to needy people, especially women. The rural elites—the landlords, moneylenders, schoolteachers and the mullahs—were losing money and influence. NGOs were blamed for supposedly encouraging women to deviate from their Islamic lifestyle. A spate of illegal fatwas, or religious decrees, and barbaric punishments against 'disobedient' women ordered by village councils in remote areas was also happening at this time. Neither the Government nor the main opposition party, the Awami League, condemned these attacks. Both sides were seen to be wooing the religious vote.

Even central bureaucrats in Dhaka were working hard to convince the prime minister, Khaleda Zia, that the NGOs were trying to convert villagers to Christianity. The services administered by the bureaucracy in health and education usually looked bad in comparison to NGOs—here was another resentful group, not overly religious, but very threatened.

By 1994 the attacks against the NGOs suddenly ceased and the whole anti – NGO movement collapsed within a few months, through the intervention of the donor countries and the work of some progressive bureaucrats at the top. But for a few months, health clinics and schools in remote villages, especially in the religiously conservative district of Sylhet, and more significantly their female workers, were under attack. More than eighty incidents were recorded by ADAB (Association of Development Agencies in Bangladesh) and over 110 BRAC (Bangladesh Rural Advancement Council) schools and other NGOs were set on fire; even the high-profile Grameen Bank was attacked. Witnesses to these attacks say the placards were anti-NGO but also targeted Nasreen by name. The police took no action. To express their anger at this inaction two thousand women marched through Dhaka on 20 April protesting against the Islamists' calls to ban NGOs.

❉

But in the end the Government played the religious card too well. By mid-1994 the scene was set in Dhaka and in other cities for violent confrontations between the religious parties and the progressive–secular forces. Both sides were out in the streets fighting each other. Each contingent was holding its own rallies: the religious side demanding punishment for apostates, the banning of NGOs and a Blasphemy Law—the secular side demanding and end to religiously based politics and calling for freedom of speech in the Liberation tradition of 1971.

The major religious political party, Jamaat, had their own reasons for wanting a smokescreen at the time. The trial of their emir leader, Gholam Azam, widely reviled as an Anti-liberation traitor, had been dragging on for eighteen months. At the time the Supreme Court was hearing a highly controversial case dealing with his citizenship status. He held a Pakistani passport when he fled the country in 1971, returning years later after a general amnesty was granted and most of the 'traitors', as they were known, returned. The decision on his future was expected in mid-1994 and the whole country was caught up in the debate of whether his citizenship should be returned to him or not, could he stand for election or should he be tried as a murderer? Jamaat needed a distraction just as much as the Government.

Players on both sides of this surrealistic theatre piece were tough, experienced campaigners willing enough to take to the streets at any moment for violent confrontations. When viewed against this backdrop, Taslima was a political ingenue with no idea of the forces ranged on either side.

The political culture of Bangladesh is complex and violent. The only thing which brings it temporarily to a halt is if some terrible natural disaster like a cyclone or flood unites traditional opponents. Agitation-style politics weaken democratic institutions like parliament, the constitution, free-and-fair elections and the principle that when a Government is elected it has the right to govern or to see out its term.

Hartals, or political disturbances combining the characteristics of a general strike and a boycott, are a feature of politics; the whole country grinds to a halt. When the *hartal* is called, no one goes to work or to school; bus, rail and train services are cancelled; trucks and taxis disappear from sight, unless they want to risk being overturned and burnt, factories and shops are closed and the city is barricaded so that transport cannot leave or enter. It is tantamount to an act of national defiance which everyone is forced to participate in—whether they agree with it or not!

The aim is to show the Government the might of the opposition and to force its hand. In 1995, a year after Taslima left, at least one hundred forty-four such *hartals* were recorded, ranging from six to ninety-six hours at a time, held during a ten-month period—they had nothing to do with Taslima or any individual and were meant to force the BNP to agree to a caretaker government and elections, which were announced the next year. Street politics then are a way of life.

Judging what is an expression of true outrage by the people or what is political manipulation is hard. Newspaper figures on numbers of people that attend rallies are mainly non-existent or, when they do exist, hardly accurate. Newspapers of different political persuasions will inflate numbers that attend their chosen party's events, or deflate the opposition's numbers. This was one of the problems in trying to assess crowd sizes for the anti-Taslima Nasreen rallies, but the same conditions are likely to have applied. One thing is clear, however: those who demonstrated against Taslima came from the *madrassahs*, a minority who knew how to play the shouting game and win at street politics; they came from nowhere else at the beginning, although towards the end they were joined by disciplined Jamaat activists.

The events which led to the warrant for her arrest issued by the Government and the manoeuvres to get her out of the spotlight, and Bangladesh, had everything to do with Bangladesh politics and little to do with her individually. Taslima Nasreen had been criticising Islam for years; and other than the odd demonstration or two and the spate of nasty letters to her editors, nothing of any consequence ever happened.

But the climate towards her changed in the twelve months between mid-1993 and her departure in 1994. There is a demarcation line between the events of these two years which the Government was quick to seize on. In 1993 Taslima cried wolf too often in her interviews in what one might call the period of her 'high profile seclusion' or 'open hiding'. Although she told everyone and sundry that her life was in danger, her social activities were barely curtailed and she gave one exclusive interview after the other. Inevitably, one interview too many would lead to a sequence of events that would force her to leave the country.

In May came that fateful Calcutta interview, and the pro-Islamist parties, large and small, regained the upper hand. Taslima, returning from her first trip overseas, stopped in at Calcutta on her way home from Paris. She gave an interview on 6 May to a senior journalist from *The Statesman*, Sujuta Sen, published on 9 May, where she was quoted as saying that the Qur'an should be thoroughly revised. In Taslima's denial published two days later, her attempts to clarify her statements were unhelpful:

'I hold the Koran, the Vedas, the Bible and all such relevant texts determining the lives of their followers as "out of place and time".... We have to move beyond these ancient texts if we want to progress ... let humanism be our new faith.'

Taslima insisted, as she does to this day, that the non-Muslim, female reporter, as she called Sen, had confused the Qur'an with the Shariah or Personal Laws, which govern Muslims' lives. Taslima maintained that she was referring to Shariah Law in her interview. Unfortunately, the conversation was not taped, but Sen stood by her article; she continued to do so when we met in Calcutta in late January 1997. Sen described to me the context of the interview and the regal style in which it was given, with Taslima lying on a couch as she made her pronouncements. A third party who witnessed this interview, and who knows full well what was said, has chosen to remain silent, although reliable sources indicate that he is prone to giving conflicting versions of what took place when he talks about this privately.

When parts of the article were translated and published in Bangladesh, this set off another round of rallies and counter rallies and led to the Government issuing a warrant for her arrest, in spite of Taslima's public denials and letter of explanation to the Bangladesh Parliament.

The Calcutta Statesman interview was in reality no more than an excuse used by the Government and her religious enemies to provide them with the opportunity they'd been waiting for. The backlash from the interview was used to regain the control that was gradually being eroded by the popular anti-Islamist, anti-communal movement, then sweeping the country. Caught on the back foot, these progressive men and women still continued to fight. The national *hartal* called for June 30 by the fundamentalists was quickly countered by a progressive student group calling for a *hartal* on the same day. *The Daily Star* described the day as an 'unusually tense' situation.

But the Awami League stayed silent over Taslima: they neither supported nor criticised her. I know this was a great disappointment to the author, who had every right to expect some signal of support from the secularist party.

However, avoiding any entanglement in the Taslima controversy probably helpcd Awami to win the 1996 election two years later.

Taslima's few remaining allies who acted as her conduit to the outside world were in an impossible position. They might, or might not, like her personally, but she was the battleground, she was the cause—they had to support her, like it or not. They did their best to conceal her unpopularity because it was awkward trying to explain to the foreign governments, and human rights groups, that the author's actions had alienated so many natural allies. Her supporters, a core of dedicated human rights activists, worked hard to rally some vestiges of public support for her. This was another part of the story which was never told.

Violence broke out in the city and around the districts outside of Dhaka. A police barricade of barbed wire at the Purana Paltan intersection, famous for its violent confrontations, could not halt the fighting. Neither could 6,000 policemen posted around the city stop the clashes. Attacks on NGOs, and newspaper and political parties' offices, were reported from outside the city. A school student was killed and more than 250 people were injured in the fighting which broke out throughout Dhaka.

Several female activists told me that, for the first time in their lives, they were afraid to go out and join the picket lines as they'd always done before—they could not get through and there was a smell of violence in the air. Jamaat announced an eleven-point program of agitation and from July on, the demonstrations against Taslima and other leading apostates continued almost on a daily basis. Many Bangladeshi citizens watched helplessly as the image of their country was tarnished. They blamed Taslima.

But Taslima saw none of this because she was in hiding. The Government's failure to investigate the charge against her gives credence to my theory that they were not serious about the warrant in the first place, but used it tactically. This failure to investigate an incident alleged to have taken place outside of Bangladesh has been one of the main weaknesses in the Government's case against her. The effect was to silence her and give the BNP a breathing space while it faced domestic unrest and international pressure.

Finally on 29 June, after nine months' delay, the Government issued a press note saying that it was a punishable offence to issue death threats against people and to offer rewards for their killing. It threatened to take action against the lawbreakers, although this was never carried out and seemed more like an attempt to curry international favour.

Reports started to appear that the European Union had offered to help Taslima and had made an official appeal to the Government to allow her to leave the country. The Bangladeshi Government was completely surrounded. And so a deal was struck, and she left for Sweden in August 1994.

To many onlookers the Taslima Nasreen story ended there. She had been rescued by the good people and was now safely ensconced among an audience who understood her better than her own society. These forces rescued the princess and carried her away to a land where she *never* quite lived happily ever after.

But that was another story which I could only discover if I re-entered the Taslima maze and returned once again to Sweden and to her other places of asylum in Europe: a course of action I undertook in 1998.

Standing in the wings, I watched an intriguing story unfold; the characters and sub-plots I stumbled across engrossed me. I began to look at the Taslima narrative through the eyes of an investigative writer, rather than as a human rights activist; my point of view was often uncomfortable. This would sometimes lead to problems whenever I interacted with freedom of expression idealists in London, Cologne and wherever else I went in the summer of 1998. The book I was writing was not the book they would have written in my place, just as Taslima's *Lajja* was not the book that Bangladeshis wanted others to read.

Part II

Taslima and the Dragon Slayers

Exile is a dream of glorious return. Exile is a vision of revolution: Elba, not St Helena. It is an endless paradox: looking forward by always looking back.

Salman Rushdie, *The Satanic Verses*

Chapter 5

The Summer of Taslima

A myth does not take hold without expressing many truths—misleading truths, usually, but important ones: truth, for one thing, to the needs of those who elaborate and accept the myth.... Even the myths that simplify are not, in themselves, simple.

Michael Wood, *The New York Review of Books*,
April 24 1997

The summer of Taslima is how Swedish PEN remembers the months between June and August 1994: three intense months of lobbying and speculation—adventure on their doorstep. Would she choose Sweden as her destination or would their Norwegian neighbours to the west outbid them and snare the author-in-distress? The Swedes carried the day and although the relationship eventually wore itself out, there are only one or two souls who might openly regret their involvement—Gabi Gleichmann is one of them. But then we need to remember that Gabi has long since severed his links with PEN, resolutely turning his back on dragon slaying pastimes.

Swedish PEN, if given the chance, would gladly throw themselves into the Taslima fray all over again, or so they're inclined to say. Certainly their commitment to the PEN cause has never faltered and they continue working to free writers in prison and provide support, financial and moral, to others living in exile. As a post-script, and in the privacy of their homes, however, they will admit to disappointment that the fairy tale ending their self-driven plot had demanded slipped through their fingers. They soon discovered that the Taslima Nasreen they'd been committed to 'saving' was largely a fiction of their collective imagination. Piece by piece, the Swedish tale of rescue and retribution started to dissolve a few months after Taslima's arrival. The story unfolds much like a morality play for toiling literary pilgrims, and the Swedes have tried to apply the lessons they've learnt.

There are self-appointed guardians of the Taslima mythology scattered around the world: in Stockholm, Copenhagen, Berlin, London, Paris and New York. In 1998, beginning in late July and ending three months later in October, I met many free speech radicals as I moved from city to city. Listening to their stories, I became aware of the nature and limitations of 'eyewitness accounts' and how we are driven to create myths in an attempt to make sense of our lives. A myth is like a spell, conjured up to answer the needs of the believer, to deal with their secret angst. These are the times when manipulation becomes acceptable if your need is strong enough.

The Gabi Gleichmann episode illustrated the art of self-deception more than any other story about *Taslima and the Dragon Slayers*. Gabi was more than an eyewitness: he'd been part of a network of unofficial mythmakers who helped create the story of Taslima and introduced her persona to Western Europe. For a short intense period, Gabi and Taslima had even shared the spotlight.

The tale of Taslima's reception in Sweden, which I'd started to unravel in the winter of 1997, had left me vaguely disturbed. Parts of the story were brushed aside by the author and her Swedish allies: a pattern emerged of hints, innuendoes and blunt refusals to go any further. Gabi's entrance the following year changed everything. The man who had warned me over the telephone, in late 1997, that nothing personal about Taslima would ever cross his lips, had changed his mind ten months later. He never explained his reasons and I never asked him why.

Before keeping my rendezvous with Gabi, there remained one sortie left to face and so I made a detour and braved the 65th Annual PEN Congress in Helsinki, September 1998. Arriving from Stockholm on board a Viking cruiser full of inebriated, mainly Swedish, passengers who revelled in the cheap liquor and tobacco prices, and seemed to puff and scholl the night away, I settled in at the Hotel Marina on the harbour and took my bearings.

This was my first PEN Congress. As an acolyte of the lower ranks, I had the luxury of observing, rather than performing, in the Wagnerian opera over the next five days: intrigue, palace coups, assassinations by the truckload, romance, tragedy and back-stabbing of grand and bloody proportions—even lemming-like 'suicides'. A gathering of three hundred or more wordsmiths was always destined to hang itself with its own hyperbole, or drown in its own onomatopoeia. *The plethora of poets present added a pleasing poignancy to proceedings.* Debates rang with a passion which belonged on the written page of a romance or in the polemical tradition of the pamphleteer—Ah! But they had style aplenty, this gathering of the writer clans.

Over the next few days a long wave of international delegates, all of whom remembered Taslima's case, fell within my range: Meredith Tax, American writer and leading feminist arrived. Eugene Schoulgin waved hello as he passed by with his colleagues from the Swedish delegation, working the room with the ease of an experienced diplomat; he was once more, in 1998, helping Taslima overcome visa difficulties with the Swedish Government. Eugene cleared up the Swedish end while Meredith looked after the United States.

Meredith broke the news that Taslima was living in New York on a tourist visa with her parents while her mother was receiving hospital treatment for cancer. Her parents' visa would soon run out and a worried Taslima was trying, with the help of Meredith and her London-based lawyer Sara Hossain, to negotiate the conditions necessary for her return to Bangladesh to be with her dying mother. All her old companions-in-arms, from the 1994 campaign, were rallying to help her—old quarrels faded into the background.

The PEN congress was a literary caravanserai where PEN writers fought the dragons of censorship and obscurantism. The presence of Iranian writer Faraj Sarkoohi, living in exile in Germany, showed PEN at its strongest. Faraj had come in person to thank PEN: he owed his life and his freedom to the international movement initiated by the organisation, he said. His speech was a sober reminder of the PEN's charter and the importance of its Writers In Prison Committees. For the first time in twenty years, the Iranian Government had been forced, through the sheer weight of international pressure, to release someone they had wanted to kill. Those left behind in prison, Faraj said, now feel that they are not alone.

'Words make magic,' he said from the dais to a standing ovation. 'And that is why the authorities in Teheran think writers are dangerous, because we work with words; we try to discover and express through words, aspects of the truth.'

Iranian writers who fall foul of the authorities face two deaths, he told us. 'They kill you mentally by forcing you to deny yourself: deny the words and the ideas that you have written; so that your power of creation dies; they do this through mental and physical torture. And if you don't recant, then they kill you physically.'

PEN tried to save lives: it made a difference and you could forgive the organisation many of its peccadillos for what it achieved through slow, patient work in its defence of freedom of expression and linguistic rights.

PEN was founded in London in 1921 by English novelist Mrs C. A. Dawson Scotland, to foster understanding among writers throughout the world; today there are some 14,000 members in approximately 130 centres in 94 countries. Originally the letters P-E-N stood for Poets, Playwrights, Essayists, Editors and Novelists. Today membership is open to scriptwriters of radio and TV, journalists, translators, historians and other writers engaged in any other branch of literature. Famous presidents and executive committee members from the past have included John Galsworthy, HG Wells, Jules Romain, Alberto Moravia, Arthur Miller, Heinrich Böll, V. S. Pritchett and Mario Vargas Llosa. In 1998 the president was Mexican poet Homero Aridjis.

PEN's culture is influenced by linguistic rights exponents and by women's activists, but the fiercest of all warriors in the late nineties were the Kurds, the Iranians, and the Cubans from the various Writers-In-Exile centres. The Cubans have honed themselves into professional lobbyists: unrelenting soldier ants, they will march over anyone.

'It is impossible to have a dialogue with Castro,' the leader of the Cuban writers' brigade shouted interrupting the President as he tried, in vain, to depoliticise the discussion. I was left wondering if there was life after Castro for these men.

⁂

One day followed the next: The assembly room filled to the sound of clashing egos: amongst the three hundred or more delegates were at least one hundred PEN El Presidentes and their entourages, predominantly male, predominantly European, many of them gallant cavaliers of a bygone generation. PEN's culture remained as flamboyantly male as a flock of peacocks—albeit aging birds—strutting on manicured lawns, and women followed in their wake, as handmaidens, to smooth out the quarrels, propose compromises while doing much of the behind-the-scenes work. In many ways it was almost a domestic scene.

Important business was to be settled in a do-or-die effort in 1998. The Helsinki Congress would set in place the reform agenda and elect a new International Secretary, the patient Dr Terry Carlboom, who seemed as stoic and calm as Swedes are expected to be. Alexandre Blokh, of Russian–French descent, and a grand Renaissance man of yesteryear, was gone. New office bearers would replace the old European warrior caste entrenched for most of the Cold War. The new message preached by the reformers was Regionalism and Greater Gender Parity; it sounded like the 'Second Coming'. But organisational cultures resist change: PEN was strong on rhetoric, but the favoured Dragon Slayers from the past would continue guerrilla action for years to come. The influence of the former 'Captive Nations' remained strong; they seemed determined to keep the loaves and fishes for themselves and not lose anything to the newer Asian and African countries. One could only wait and see how Terry Carlboom handled the poisoned chalice he'd inherited.

The freedom of expression domain is packed with contenders: Amnesty International is a giant and there is also stiff competition from Reporters sans frontières and the French-based International Parliament of Writers. In spite of this competition, PEN stands tall in the freedom of expression forest as an NGO, with Status A classification in the eyes of UNESCO. PEN was busily carving out a new role for itself in the world which had emerged post–Soviet Union and post–Berlin Wall. The rapid rise of Islamist extremism had provided it with many new cases, and PEN had willingly taken up Taslima Nasreen's cause. But PEN had neither the resources nor the many full-time professionals of groups like Amnesty International and Reporters sans frontières. The Amnesty empire is enormous, with a membership base of more than one million and its modus operandi carefully negotiated step by step. Amnesty International is less inclined to mount campaigns through newspapers, unlike PEN, which is writer-rich, with good media links.

Taslima attended her first PEN congress in Prague in November 1994, year one of her self-exile. The audience stood and applauded and very soon PEN's new star found herself adopted as an honorary member by eight PEN centres. Meredith Tax remembers the Prague annual congress and so does Gabi Gleichmann, but by then he and Taslima were no longer on speaking terms. Gabi and Meredith's versions of their brief encounter at the congress differ markedly, although the New Yorker does remember that the Swede made it clear that he wanted nothing more to do with the Bangladeshi writer. Considering the stories she was hearing from Taslima and Swedish friends about the Frankfurt Book Fair and other incidents, Meredith is adamant that she would never have attempted to play peacemaker. She and Gabi had stopped working together months earlier, after he involved Salman Rushdie in Taslima's case. Meredith left Gabi in no doubt that she was unhappy with his paternalistic attitude and they stopped communicating.

Gabi's version is certainly more dramatic. 'This woman means nothing to me; she is not my enemy; she's nothing,' he purportedly said to Meredith, ignoring Taslima standing by her side. 'There is no animosity, but one day she'll get back what she does in the world.' He made it sound like a cosmic curse of some kind.

As he re-enacted this scene to me four years on, I was only half convinced, although I applauded his dignity. I could swallow his insistence that he was no longer bitter, I could believe that he no longer brooded over this period of his life, but when the pair fell out in October 1994, it is difficult to accept that Gabi, at the time, did not feel embittered or at least overwhelmed by disappointment. He may have had good reason to feel aggrieved. In Gabi's mind, Taslima was the woman who, in the end, did not come to his defence. On the return flight to Stockholm at the end of the Prague Congress that year, they boarded the same plane; Taslima sat two rows in front of him. No words passed between them and he has never ever met her again. The Gabi Gleichmann I'd first glimpsed smiling at the world as he stood side by side with Taslima, in a photo taken at the award ceremony in Stockholm, was long gone. What had happened?

❈

Leaving the Helsinki meeting behind me, I returned in late summer to Stockholm. The somersaulting of seasons turned Sweden into a delight and the memories of my last winter odyssey faded. Again the elusive Gabi had gone missing on a hurried trip to New York. As it happened, Gabi's absence hardly mattered because an Iranian woman who knew and admired Taslima crossed my path.

Mitra was a petite woman in her mid-forties with short reddish brown hair and nervous mannerisms. Because of her refugee background she identified closely with the Bangladeshi author, perhaps more than she ever realised. At an intellectual level she understood that Iran and Bangladesh were two different countries, but when she talked of Bangladesh, in her mind's eye, she was thinking of Iran; when she empathised with Taslima she was reliving the traumatic times of her own escape from Iran sixteen years before.

'I was following her case from the time I heard about her on TV, while she was in hiding and calling on the women of the world to help her. I was very worried, which is only natural because I am a woman from a Muslim land. This was the second fatwa after Rushdie, so it was very important,' she told me. Her voice had a breathy quality, which made everything she said sound like a secret.

The word *fatwa* entered the English language in the wake of the Ayatollah Khomeini's edict on Salman Rushdie. There are many—Muslims and non-Muslims alike—who mistakenly believe that a fatwa is a death threat. Ain O Salish Kendra (ASK), a human rights group located in Dhaka, Bangladesh, has this to say about fatwas: 'A fatwa is an opinion given by a jurist, learned in Islamic law, in response to a question involving a point of law. . . . It is being pronounced by people who have no authority or scholarship. . . . So fatwas are being given by the wrong person, in the wrong circumstances and for the wrong purposes.'

Mitra was waiting for me to give her some sign of agreement, something that she could take comfort from after each of her observations. A nod of the head, a few words, were not enough—she needed overt, symbolically loud utterances in total support of Taslima or else in her eyes I was also denying Mitra's pain. To talk to me in English, she was crossing two languages: her mother tongue of Farsee and Swedish, and this may have compounded our communication difficulties.

'I thought to myself,' said Mitra, "This woman's life is in danger." I remember hearing about the demonstrations against her in Dhaka, especially the rally where they announced they would release thousands of snakes and everybody would be killed.' These were ignorant people, she said, illiterate people who, if provoked, could do anything. 'I know because of my bitter experience in Iran. All you have to do is say that someone is insulting God and then . . . ,' she grimaced.

The snake infestation in Dhaka, which so alarmed Mitra, never eventuated. But the street rally, where a handful of snake charmers cavorted in the front ranks of a large noisy march wearing reptiles slung around their necks and grins on their faces—for they were the centre of attention and it was a great day's outing for all and sundry—drew international headlines; news wires hummed and television cameras recorded the colourful *tamasha* orchestrated by a powerful mullah who called himself a mufti and knew all the snake charmers and traders from the bazaars of old Dhaka—a man I'd met a year before, it so happened. He was the kind of man Nasreen often accused of using religion to enslave women.

> They have written up their religion
> sitting in Jerusalem, the Himalays
> and the Hera Mountains.
> They have declared this religion sacred.
> They have tied you up in knots in the name
> of this sacredness. . . .
> (Taslima Nasreen, circa 1992)

But he was not sitting high up in the Hera hills of Mecca. He sat behind his desk, in the heart of the *madrassah* he controlled, conveniently located next door to a mosque in Old Dhaka. He was a populist mullah-type figure, capable of holding large crowds entranced with his fiery oratory and leading them on rallies with banners unfurled and blood in their eyes; the kind of religious leader whose impassioned sermons were recorded on cassette and sold well at the many stalls around bus stops and train stations. I came to behold him as a political sorcerer who with a wave of his hand, a puff of smoke and a crash of cymbals could conjure up a *tamasha* at will and then, with another wave of the hand, make everything vanish into thin air as if it had never happened.

Mufti Fazlul Huq Amini was a jolly looking man, younger than I expected, with a thick black beard, flowing down to his chest in the style of a Santa Claus (without meaning to be ecumenically confusing). It wasn't often that I found myself so close to a white-capped mullah, but journalist friends had worked hard to organise this meeting. Amini was the Secretary General of Islami Okiyya Jote (IOJ), a coalition of ten smaller Islamically or mullah-based parties. Their demands were fairly simple it's true—simple but alarming: they wanted Shariah (Religious Law) to dominate over the secular laws of the land, they wanted the Constitution changed to include a Blasphemy Law, and they hated Taslima Nasreen and anyone else like her.

Amini was jovial and avuncular, a man given to smiling and laughing when the mood took him. He understood more English than he admitted, but we used an interpreter, which allowed Amini to preserve his image in front of an admiring crowd of older *madrassah* students, who stood shoulder-to-shoulder listening to their leader joust with this strange woman who didn't look like the foreigners they were used to seeing. I wore a *dupatta*, or scarf, out of respect for his religious sensibilities, but that was the only concession I was prepared to make.

I asked Amini why he mobilised his forces against Nasreen.

'We also believe in freedom of speech,' he said, 'but there are limitations.' His voice was husky and very loud, the voice of a man used to exhorting crowds. 'She spoke against Muslim women and dared to say that the Qur'an should be changed; that is deplorable, for the Holy Qur'an is unchanging.'

'But she denied *The Calcutta Statesman* article,' I said, 'she insisted she was misquoted.'

'She's been saying these kind of things for a long time. Patience has a limit,' Mufti Amini answered. 'She is a *murtaad* [an apostate], and if you disagree with holy words then the punishment under Islamic law is hanging.'

❖

Earlier that same day I'd spoken to another man whose patience with Taslima also ran out in the end—but he had nothing to do with mullahs or their cohorts. Shafik Rehman was educated, urbane, and well read; a man who favoured suits and ties, who'd lived in self-exile in the United Kingdom for six years after his paper was twice banned and he was detained three times by the Ershad government.

'Tone it down,' he begged the writer. Shafik Rehman was the editor of *Jai Jai Din*, a national weekly with a liberal reputation and a huge mass circulation. Between 1992 and 1994, Nasreen, as he used to call her, wrote a weekly column for his paper, which became one of the most talked about columns in the city. 'Noshta Column' it was called, using the word to imply a ruined or loose woman—in English, 'The Fallen Prose of a Fallen Woman.' Shafik's graphic artist drew a sketch of a bosomy woman, like Nasreen, the editor murmured, which helped boost sales as well. The editor had discovered a sure-fire way to shock and draw in his readers at the same time and his circulation increased, for which he paid her top dollar—for the moment he was a happy man.

'She was original: her metaphors, her imagery went right to the heart of the matter,' he said. 'What she wrote could certainly make you angry, but it got your attention. This is why she clicked.'

He had to keep a sharp watch, however, because Taslima would try slipping in certain words and phrases; sneak them past him, and if he wasn't careful his paper would land in serious trouble. He began to tire of the abusive, irate calls from husbands and fathers from Tokyo to New York. Bangladesh has an avid culture of readers who write letters of criticism and complaint for the sake of having a good argument and seeing their names in print—it's like live theatre. A vocal minority of *Jai Jai Din* readers complained, but kept on reading his paper.

'Why are you doing this to me?' he would ask Taslima. 'You can fight against dictators and hope to win at the end of the day, but fighting against Islam or religion is impossible—don't do it! Just write about women's lib.' He told me in an aside that his father had been an atheist, which had caused his family enormous difficulty.

'But she always wanted to go for "the women chained by religion bit"— she believed in it,' he said, and they argued constantly. 'She never cared about the consequences,' Shafik said, 'she wasn't even aware of what might happen.'

'I have a standing instruction,' he told me, 'that anything written on religion must be combed through four or five times . . . we are here to educate people, make them liberated so that they can make their own challenge against religion: it is not my business to challenge religion,' he finished off.

At the time I thought he sounded defensive. Scholars and writers were aghast at Taslima's critique of Islam, not only because of what she said, but because her views lacked any scholarly approach, neither had she done much reading beyond the basic, crude books written by populist, mainly uneducated, mullahs in Bangladesh. Rustic mullahs, as they are called, have

a crude understanding of Islam and are notorious for twisting the sayings of
the Prophet Muhammad, basing their quotations on extracts which genuine
scholars regard as forged. In Bangladesh, for instance, I heard that 'Heaven
lies under the feet of the husband,' as nasty a piece of Hadith perjury as
ever there was, for the original lines say, 'Heaven lies under the feet of the
Mother.' But illiterate people have small hope of finding out the truth.
Even literate middle-class men and women don't read beyond Bengali texts
to learn for themselves.

'Now as far as religion and Nasreen went,' continued Shafik Rehman,
'there was a credibility gap, for she was never known to be a philosopher
or a learned scholar—she never even practised Islam. But what she used
to do, and I saw it a number of times, she'd go to the library and get
particular books, not good books but third-rate commentaries written by
uneducated mullahs; we've got thousands of books like that in Bengali
which are explanations of the Qur'an and the Hadith. These books spend
an awful amount of time on sexual matters. Off she'd go, take these books
out, which had no context at all, flick through them until she found what
she wanted and if you wanted to bash Islam, well, this was the way to do it.
Naturally it upset a lot of people.'

But men more than women, I thought to myself, and not only the ultra
orthodox. Nasreen's articles attacked the crude mullah-Islam, the folk Islam
which shapes women's lives in Bangladesh; that is what she took aim at—the
prevailing social reality: the superstitious, ignorant beliefs that she had seen
played out in her own extended family. It wasn't only orthodox Muslims
she attacked—so-called progressive men also felt her sting. She was also
not the woman to enter into scholarly debates about Islam, or theological
arguments that rarely touch women's lives in her country. But hardly anyone
appreciated this.

Although sympathetic, Shafik worried that his writer was going overboard. 'In one of her articles she wrote about an old man taking his grand-
daughter out in a rickshaw and molesting her. Now this would have been
all right, but then she added that he had a beard and a cap and beads . . .
We all know that an old man can have sexual cravings, but she had to make
the old man a religious mullah!'

'But I always found her a modest, quiet woman, very decent in the way
she dressed, and the vile rumours circulating about her were wrong—people
had the wrong idea because of what she wrote.'

Nasreen continued writing her articles until 1994, but, gradually, she
began to run out of ideas and was having trouble reaching her quota of a
thousand words. Shafik Rehman continued to receive the abusive calls and
letters until, in 1994, hoods, or *goondahs*, as they are called, started throwing

baby bombs over the wall of his house. The organised anti-Nasreen agitation was beginning to ignite; the mullahs and the *madrassahs* were on the march.

❀

Could Nasreen ever return to Dhaka? I asked Mufti Amini that day as we sat talking in his *madrassah* office.

'Unless she says "*Tauba*" [I repent]—and it must be genuine and she must do it publicly—then there will be fire!' answered the cleric.

Had he no compassion for her parents, I pressed him for an answer.

Yes, the mullah answered, she was their daughter and he regretted their sadness, but the whole nation had suffered because of this woman, and the nation was more important than a single family.

We left the subject of Nasreen and began talking about non-government organisations, or NGOs. He was not opposed to education for women, but it must be segregated. Some NGOs did good welfare work but those which were against Islam and taught women to go without purdah and dared to interfere in politics, he said, should be banned.

And then he drew an interesting analogy. 'The East India Company first came to India to trade, but in the end they became the owners of the country. The NGOs and their foreign donors are just the same.'

I had heard this anti-Western argument before and not from the mouths of religiously orthodox Muslims either. Left-leaning Bangladeshis also saw the larger NGOs transforming themselves into alternative governments, especially in local government services, education and health, which ultimately weakened the Government.

The time had come to test what latitude Mullah Amini would allow his female inquisitor. 'Is a female prime minister permissible under Islam?' I asked. It was a litmus test I often used when talking to mullahs and religious scholars to gauge how liberal they were in their interpretations of Islam, for not all mullahs are reactionary or misogynist and play an important role in the lives of ordinary believers. The village mullah or imam going about his normal business is essential to the important life-cycle rituals of birth, marriage, death and in major religious festivals.

'No, it is not permissible,' he answered, wasting few words.

'But Ayesha [the Prophet Muhammad's youngest wife] led soldiers in battle,' I pointed out, trying to set a trap.

Like a good mullah who never leaves his followers in doubt, Amini had an answer for every occasion. 'The circumstances in those days were completely different and she was compelled to do this. She did not lead for the sake of power!' He looked around at his audience of students and teachers— everyone showed their approval by laughing out loud: their leader had not been bested by the foreign woman—I should have known better, still I thought it worth a try even if I'd been outfoxed in the end. I asked myself was I becoming mullah-phobic? Bangladesh is not a society riddled with 'mad mullahs' handing down fatwas arbitrarily. That image is as mistaken as assuming that all orthodox Muslims are Islamists, that Islam is a monolithic, backward and violent religion—an image offensive to Muslims, of whatever persuasion, around the world.

Amini was no run-of-the-mill mullah. Hiding behind the garb of the devout Muslim scholar was a small-time local politician who excelled at using religion as a tool and who in less than an hour could organise a mass demonstration with the help of his *madrassah* followers and local hawkers and traders who lived in crowded old Dhaka and idolised their charismatic leader.

The portrait of Amini as a pious mufti I found ludicrous—he was a man tempted by politics and power, someone who liked showing governments of either side his might: how he and his followers could control the streets with their own violent brand of politics as they did at the height of the Taslima crisis in 1994. Religiously based political parties are unscrupulous in using violence and religion to reach their goals. Their willingness to go outside the law, to let loose their terrorist student wings made it hard to counteract their influence—at least without imitating the *fatwabaaz*, as religious extremists are called derisively by their opponents, and meeting violence with violence. Amini's coalition of ten or more Islamic-based groups was not the largest religious political party, that honour was held by Jamaat-i-Islami. But he was still dangerous.

It must be difficult, I thought to myself, for a mullah like Amini to live in a land where there is not only a female prime minister, but a female leader of the opposition as well.

In early February 2001, I read with interest that my jolly-looking mullah acquaintance, Amini, has been arrested under the Public Safety Act for inciting violence in Dhaka after a rally where he declared two High Court Judges murtaad for delivering a verdict against a fatwa. The High Court had made a ruling that fatwas were illegal. Islamist parties, and the then opposition party BNP, cited the ruling as an example of the Awami League Government's anti-Islam stance. Amini was sentenced to one month's detention by the Chief Metropolitan Magistrate's Court. Amini's esteemed chairman and fellow IOJ bigwig, was also under arrest, at the same time, in connection with the murder of a policeman beaten to death by Muslim zealots inside a mosque. The High Court eventually dismissed all charges against the IOJ Chairman.

⊞

Although the snake theatre was nothing more than a confidence trick to snare media attention, a few reptilian images slithered their way onto television screens, which certainly brought the Dhaka fanatics to the attention of the world. Short–sighted men, I thought at first, with no idea that their *tamasha* had garnered Taslima enormous support world-wide from sympathisers like Mitra who actually believed that ten thousand venomous snakes were going to be released in the streets of Dhaka, unless the Government arrested Taslima Nasreen. Later I came to understand that the Islamists were not performing for Western cameras: their television audiences were in Pakistan, Iran, Libya, Saudi Arabia, Yemen and the Arab Emirates, places where their patrons and spectators looked at the mass demonstrations through different eyes. Their antics were like a public relations exercise—showing their control of the streets, how they defended Islam under attack from the ungodly; they could dine out on these staged rallies for a long time and become heroic figures to their peers and *madrassah* students around the world. At the end of the day their funding also came from foreign governments, like any NGO—not Western governments, of course, but governments eager to make a show of a pan-Islamic brotherhood. And of course many European audiences were taken in by the orchestrated show of menace, aided by wide camera angles which never accurately portrayed the crowd numbers or the fact that behind the marchers traffic flowed smoothly—or as smoothly as possible on crowded Dhaka roads.

✜

Mitra remembers clearly the first time she saw her hero in real life. Taslima was undergoing the ordeal of her first public meeting at the Tucholsky award ceremony, the grand event where Carola had first glimpsed her. Mitra recognised the problems the author was having with English and wondered why Taslima was not using an interpreter because she knew Bengali interpreters were available.

'If you use an interpreter you have time to think about your answers,' she said. 'Poor Taslima, she did not have the vocabulary to discuss human rights topics. People on the dais were trying their best to help, but it only made matters worse. Perhaps she didn't want them to know she needed help with her English.' It was an insightful comment from a woman who'd survived her own language nightmares. 'After some months,' Mitra continued, 'the stories started.'

Around the time Taslima received the prestigious Sakharov Prize for Human Rights, from the European Parliament (EP) in December 1994, she fell out of favour with some sectors of the French media who criticised the quality of her writing and accused her of opportunism. There was talk about a certain female politician involved in the publishing world who happened to be sitting on the right EP committee and had pushed her protégé forward.

Mitra became agitated as she remembered this storm in a teacup. Clench-ing her fists, she accused "them" of double standards. 'A lot of men get prizes they don't deserve and nobody says a word! A person doesn't risk their life just to become famous. If you put anyone under a microscope,' she pleaded, 'you are bound to find some mistakes. If we are to truly show solidarity with someone then we need to be more generous than criticising them for coming late or not turning up to events.' The question for Mitra was simple. 'Is there a fatwa against her or not?' she demanded, glaring at me as if I was on the side of the mullahs.

It served no purpose trying to explain to Mitra that the fatwa pronounced by a rural mullah belonging to the Soldiers of Islam—a group nobody had ever heard of before—was unauthorised, illegal and later denied by the culprit. The media had rushed headfirst into a complex situation with their headlines in their holsters. Mitra had read the papers like everyone else and compared her friend's situation to Rushdie's fatwa, with the full weight of the Ayatollah and the Iranian Government standing behind it.

Mitra saw Taslima as a refugee, a mirror image of herself. Now on safer ground, I allowed myself to enter the conversation. A refugee, I said, is an ordinary person without money, fame, or connections. 'If you are famous, you are not a refugee, you are a dissident.'

She agreed, for at about the same time that Taslima was in the papers, the Swedish authorities were deporting a group of less famous Bangladeshis who'd tried unsuccessfully to claim asylum.

'Being a refugee in Sweden, even after sixteen years,' Mitra said, 'has coloured my thinking. The way I'm treated depends on which day of the week it is. Swedish society had changed,' she said, and it seemed to be a generational change, a shift away from the older Swedes who, many years ago, in their young adulthood, had voted in their social welfare state, supporting the Sweden of the seventies that gave asylum to American anti–Vietnam War draftees, activists and homosexuals.

'You can be abused as you sit in the underground waiting for your train. "Go home!" they yell and so I go home and cry.' Her shoulders slumped. 'Sweden has been good to me, but I never have a chance to settle down; the wound is still there.'

In 1982 when she first arrived in Sweden alone, there were only 500 Iranians. Today there are more than 65,000. Over time the generosity of the Swedes has been tested.

'Sweden is so isolated,' she said with a sad laugh, 'and they never had colonies, you know, so they are not used to difference.'

Sweden was her second home, but she sorely missed the spontaneity of Iran, where people hugged each other and where the group was paramount.

I could understand that a noisy, bustling society given to mass demonstrations and the hysteria of some Shi'a rituals was far removed from the Lutheran background of a restrained Swedish society.

'In Sweden you have too much time to yourself,' she said.

Through an old friend, Mitra was able to organise a meeting with Taslima. They did ordinary things together, visiting one another's houses, eating out, going to a swimming pool. She advised Taslima to learn Swedish and improve her English.

For the third or fourth time she emphasised that she was not hostile to Sweden and I began to wonder if it is the fate of refugees everywhere to continue reassuring their hosts, until their dying day, that they are eternally grateful.

Mitra has learnt many things from the Swedes, but the lesson she values most of all is the art of compromise. 'Different voices will give you different viewpoints and you must be willing to listen and make concessions. Sweden is a country of compromise,' she said, smiling at her private joke. 'It is in their nature to compromise. They always want the middle road, and if you sit and argue with them, as one would do in my society, if you raise your voice, they think you are hostile. Sometimes I hate it, but when you come from a country where your neighbour can denounce you—' she raised her hands to the sky, 'this has been a great lesson in democracy for me.' Her bright eyes glittered.

The picture Mitra painted of Taslima was in many ways a self-portrait of the archetypal portrait of a refugee, but Taslima was a celebrity, not a rank-and-filer. This must have added to Taslima's burden, because by now she was beginning to act out her own mythology. Her needs were multiplying: she needed to retain her feeling of significance in this strange world and draw comfort and protection from her own legend.

'One day she is raised to the heavens and months later they complain that she is nothing!' Mitra said before she left that day. I walked with her to the railway station; somehow the idea of her walking alone troubled me.

Taslima had started to slide off her literary pedestal, but this time there was nobody left willing to catch her. Within a short passage of time she began to make new enemies. Nobody in Bangladesh would have found this at all surprising had they been asked: Taslima was a woman who confused people wherever she went.

By now there was a small coterie of critics in France, Sweden and, later, Germany who welcomed her slide and for the first time her reputation as an icon was threatened. There were occasions when the mythology was dented, but at this stage, the summer of 1994, it was never truly shattered or beyond repair. Taslima could always give another interview punching out the clichés, which aroused sympathy, for her story was still fresh; only in mid-1995 did it start sounding tired. At first it worked to her advantage that her critics were people with strong social consciences, who hated Islamist extremism. An unofficial code of silence protected her for a long time, although English activists, especially those involved in the anti-racist movement, have always been more open to discussing the dilemma she presented them with.

Gabi Gleichmann broke this self-imposed code when we met in late summer 1998. Four years had passed since he last saw Taslima on that return flight from PEN's congress in November 1994.

Chapter 6

The Dragon Slayer

Don't trust anyone, don't believe anyone. Run for cover!
French writer Philippe Sollers in an open letter to Taslima
Nasreen, July 1994

'We were enchanted by the goodness of our motives,' said Gabi, explaining how it all began. His introduction read like the opening line of a modern fairy story. Gabi was a romantic at heart and like many of his fellow activists this raised them above other mortals. At the time they were drawn to Taslima because she represented an ideal which shaped their perceptions of her as a person. Any insinuation that by helping Taslima they were also feeding, even fulfilling, their own dreams would have offended. There are others less romantic who might have used harsher language than Gabi's to describe how it all fell apart in the end.

Meeting Gabi for the first time was not the anti-climax I'd half expected. The man who opened the door surprised me and, for a moment, I wondered if I'd come to the wrong apartment. There's not a lot you can glean from a grainy newspaper photo, but the man in front of me was nothing like his image and only four years had passed. The Gleichmann in the photograph looked older and rather conservative in suit and tie. His receding hairline and spectacles added to a mental portrait of a prosperous citizen who dined well and rubbed shoulders with the famous.

The Gleichmann who opened the door reminded me of a grey, velvety Weimaraner dog, sleek of coat and sharp of mind. He wore jeans and a navy blue designer T-shirt and seemed muscular and fit. Still tanned from his holidays in the West Indies, his forearms were well developed like a tennis player's, and if he was given to long literary lunches, there were no signs of a sabotaged waistline. Adding to his air of 'hipness' was a shaven head and modern, rimless glasses from which friendly grey-green eyes peered out. He looked to be in his mid-thirties but was ten years older. Here was the man who'd put all of his energy towards getting Taslima to Sweden.

The story of Taslima's Swedish connection covers two phases. There is the pre-arrival phase, when she was just a name on paper, a time when the International PEN engine in London and in New York first took up the running and drew Sweden into the Taslima web. Phase two relates to the period following her arrival in Sweden in August 1994 and ended in mid-1999, when she finally left Sweden, along with her friend Gunnar, for Paris, where she lived for a few years before returning once again to Sweden.

We sit in Gabi's simple, uncluttered lounge room, a temple lined with books. Gabi is as serious as a novice monk. He tells me that he believes in Karmic law: that events don't just happen by themselves. 'Life is the Master Puppeteer,' he says.

I am not sure how to respond. Is this a test? His journey into Buddhist philosophy has taken me by surprise. 'Be that as it may,' I remind myself, 'there must be times when Life just cuts the strings, and we fall flat on our backsides!'

Gabi painted a picture of Swedish PEN as an organisation of altruism and good will, but whose members, like most artists, lacked the organisational or administrative skills to handle the tasks confronting them. There were 600 members and most of them were busy writers with guilty consciences: creative people who drifted in and out of the PEN Board, leaving two or three to do most of the work. There were always too many cases to monitor and, in the long run, it seemed that only the most spectacular cases grabbed their attention. Salman Rushdie was a case in point.

Gabi was president from 1990 to 1994 and during his reign his PEN activities came to dominate everything else in his life; it was almost a full-time job, an unpaid job, because, like everybody else, he was a volunteer.

Writers often join PEN because they are conscious of their own good fortune. Aside from the daily angst of filling an empty page, there are few consequences flowing out of their writing which places them at risk. They may wonder idly about crossing the thin line leading to libel or defamation, but this can always be disguised by straying into fiction or taking a detour into self-censorship of a kind that can be shrugged off, if it is even noticed.

Imprisonment, torture, and exile are words they comprehend, but they can never fully understand the experience of the victims, or the perversions of the perpetrators—there are limits to empathy. But because of their fertile imaginations and their compulsion to explore the human condition, they can find no peace. Always in the back of one's mind is the question posed by the Iranian writer Faraj Sarkoohi: Would you deny yourself by denying your words?

There is a long line of writers stretching as far as the eye can see and beyond: an anonymous line of faceless authors and journalists, publishers, poets and dramatists: people who have had to answer the question. Many remain in prison or are dead; many face a new prison—exile. Nigerian writer Ken Saro-Wiwa hanged in 1995, Nobel Prize winner Wole Soyinka in exile and women writers Dan San San Nue imprisoned for ten years in Burma and Alina Vitukhnovskaya in Russia. This adds to the moral discomfort of the 'lucky writers'. And this is why we so readily admire dissenters who have answered the question we will never be asked.

✺

At first Swedish PEN did nothing officially about Taslima, but her name kept reappearing. Carola Hansson as International Secretary started receiving faxes in early 1994 from London and from Meredith Tax in New York. The name emerged at an opportune time for many people who were united under PEN's banner but also had their own barrows to push. Taslima Nasreen was a high priestess who attracted many causes: humanism, atheism, feminism, anti-fundamentalism, racism, communalism and anti-communalism.

Gabi needed convincing at first. He felt that Taslima wasn't as urgent as other cases on their books, but he soon changed his mind. After it became apparent that this had all the hallmarks of a high profile case for PEN, Gabi's conscience, he said, began troubling him. Realising at last that women writers were being neglected and that perhaps his friendship with Salman Rushdie had allowed this case to dominate Swedish PEN efforts, he began to have second thoughts about the Bangladeshi author and started to think that the time had come for a woman to receive the Tucholsky prize.

'My conversion came from the head and not the heart,' he said. 'I was being politically correct.'

Accordingly, these and other factors worked in Taslima's favour, turning her into an immensely suitable candidate for Swedish backing. In Gabi's words, they could all feel enchanted by the goodness of their motives. The influences that swayed them were either never spoken aloud or buried in their subconscious.

'There was no personal risk in supporting her. You could easily say bad things about her country, Bangladesh, knowing that they wouldn't send out death patrols to kill you,' he said.

With the Rushdie–Iran stand off, the stakes were higher: the element of danger was always present. Rushdie's Norwegian publisher, William

Nygaard, had been shot in 1993, his Japanese translator, Professor Hitoshi Igarashi, murdered two years earlier and his Italian translator, Ettore Capriolo, seriously injured. Death threats were by now a nightmarish way of life for Rushdie and his circle of friends.

Secondly, said Gabi, Taslima Nasreen was a medical doctor, which to her supporters represented reason, rationality and Western science: everything that mattered to the high priests of the Post-Enlightenment Movement. 'She was not a sorceress, not a woman devoting herself to witchcraft, but a serious person,' he said.

Finally, he confessed, 'We had not read any of her writing and this worked in her favour.' If they'd read her work, he added, they might have been more cautious.

'We associated her with this tremendous feeling of purity: we saw somebody devoting herself to literature and, through her writing, trying to change things for the poor people in her country.' In summary, 'Mother Taslima' represented a good case for a good cause.

These were just some of the expectations Taslima faced after her arrival. Her hosts wanted a perfect dissident; they'd been seduced by the mythology they'd helped create. They found, instead, a difficult woman.

Fortunately for Taslima, Swedish PEN had the ear of its Government. 'PEN is supportable, it's nice and respectable,' Gabi revealed.

In Sweden, PEN was known as an organisation free of ideology and economic interests. The President of PEN could call a press conference and be supported by any number of famous writers. It certainly helped that Gabi Gleichmann worked as a deputy editor for Sweden's leading paper at the time, *Expressen*, and could always call on his journalistic colleagues. Swedish PEN, like all centres, is autonomous from International PEN in London and can act swiftly once its mind is made up or, as others would have it, 'Once Gabi made up his mind, what Gabi wanted, happened!'

But, there was one something Gabi lacked: he had absolutely no experience at all of working in a community-based organisation, where decisions are made through consensus, and was totally unsuited for such work—Gabi was not a team player.

※

Why was Gabi Gleichmann driven to tell his story to a stranger in a bruising account which made no attempt to hide his 'personal shortcomings' as he called them? Redemption? Revenge? I prefer to think that Gabi was indulging in some modern soul searching: a mixture of confessionality, sentimentality and spirituality. I think the need to have his role in the Taslima affair understood caused him to break his silence after four years. In spite of all his denials that the episode was behind him, he wanted his version of the truth recorded while it still mattered and the door finally closed. A neutral chronicler served this purpose quite adequately. Deep inside Gabi, the feeling lingered that he'd been treated unjustly. This was the only reason I could find to explain his amazing candour and his discovery that there were times when he was blinded by his own importance. Gabi personified the high-flying individualist who liked to do things on his own; an energetic man who only paid lip service to the ideal of cooperation. Now he knows better, he said as he made his confession. I was beginning to see how disarming it could be, to hold your shortcomings up for the world to see.

His greatest problem, he joked, was his faith in 'collective telepathy'. He didn't consult with his Board members. He believed they all thought the same way as he did and of course they were busy writing, so that after a number of disappointments he stopped asking most of them for assistance and 'took charge' going ahead and doing the job himself.

The paper he worked for, however, was certainly understanding and turned a blind eye to the time he spent on PEN work. They probably saw his PEN activities as complementary to his work on the cultural pages and Gabi certainly had access to many famous international writers and intellectuals. One hand washed the other, but later this led to accusations of a conflict of interests.

As PEN's profile increased so did that of its president. As Gabi liked to boast to himself, he knew the name of the game: he knew how to get publicity for PEN and if some of it rubbed off on Gabi Gleichmann, President of PEN, then that wasn't such a bad thing, was it? 'I didn't mind being in the newspapers with my name lent to good causes.'

Many inside Swedish PEN may have grumbled, yet they still kept re-electing Gabi. Not on his own merits, he said quickly, but simply because once you were elected as president, there you remained, automatically re-elected, until you chose to stand down.

A strange code, but perhaps fragile egos could never bear the ignominy of contesting an election, yet having seen the cut and thrust of PEN politics at an international level I found this 'curiouser and curiouser', as Alice would say. Perhaps Mitra might have explained this as another example of the Swedes' love of compromise, their way of avoiding conflict.

Now Gabi was also a member of the Defence of Rushdie Committee, and Sweden was one of the first countries to invite the author when he was at last able to travel outside the UK, in 1992. This took place at a time when other nations were still reluctant to receive him formally in case of economic or political repercussions, but Rushdie was Sweden's favourite embattled literary son and they adored him.

During Gabi's presidency, almost everything that PEN undertook led to big publicity: large important articles on Rushdie, especially when the Swedish Deputy Prime Minister handed him their beloved Tucholsky prize in 1992, although it was a shame that the Prime Minister couldn't present the award personally as planned. Coincidentally, an Iranian trade delegation was in town and not long after their visit, Sweden moved up the trade partner ladder with Iran from 50th to 15th. Still the Salman Rushdie evening was a great success and reminded the world that he was a writer and not the political figure he was being turned into.

These were champagne and caviar nights for Gabi, who started to believe that he had engineered this single-handedly. 'I think now that I was more and more intoxicated by how quickly everything was moving.'

Gabi was exercising a kind of power that came very rarely to a PEN President. Sitting in the heart of Sweden's largest daily newspaper as Deputy Editor of the Cultural Pages, he was able to manipulate events, to print the articles that he wanted printed, simply to make things happen by reaching out. Of course, he told himself, he wasn't doing this for himself, but for PEN and all the writers who needed his help. And the cynical among us need to remember that writers in life-threatening situations were helped by Gabi and his colleagues—self-aggrandisement and compassion are not an incompatible mix.

So when Taslima needed their help, in the summer of 1994, it was Gabi who made the decisions. 'Gabi had his way,' said Eugene Schoulgin. Carola was on vacation and Eugene—who was Vice President that year—well, according to Gabi, 'Eugene shared something in common with God—his absence, his total absence': for Eugene was focused on his latest novel.

By March 1994, Taslima and Swedish PEN were starting to correspond, and by the time of her Paris trip in May of that year, they were suggesting that she visit Sweden sometime in the future, hinting of ways to make this happen. By early June when the other Board members had gone on vacation, Gabi was left alone to carry on liaising and to see if she could come to Sweden to receive the prize. The affair began to move more swiftly once Meredith Tax intervened and moved the two sides resolutely towards each other—the embattled writer and the eager Swedes.

Meredith had pioneered PEN's International Women's Committee in 1986 against enormous, often vicious, opposition from the old guard and had won and lost some fierce battles at PEN congresses over the years. She always remembered with gratitude Rushdie's support for the concept of a Women's Committee at the height of its unpopularity. 'For while many men had signed our petition, only Salman Rushdie had cared enough to speak up when we were denounced from the chair [Norman Mailer]. "You should listen to the women; they're right," he said.'

Gabi and others inside PEN believed that, in 1994, Meredith was looking for a case that would raise the profile of the new Women's Committee, proving once and for all, the raison d'être for its existence. He was not alone in thinking that Meredith wanted, as he put it, 'to turn the PEN brotherhood into a sisterhood'. There were many men and women who felt threatened by Meredith and the ideals she represented.

In an organisation devoted to human rights, at the time, women's rights had a surprisingly low profile and participation in PEN's grandiose speaker panels was confined to white males in their sixties. 'We are not taken seriously as writers and thinkers,' Tax argued in a PEN 1986 newsletter. The answer from one of the organisers of that fateful 1986 New York Congress amplified this. Grilled as to why there were so few women speakers, he answered, 'We wanted to have the greatest minds in the world.'

There was certainly a widespread feeling throughout PEN circles, in 1994, that Meredith had an agenda, like everybody else, it seemed.

Gabi described Meredith Tax as a woman of enormous energy and commitment, with a great heart, who felt a strong sisterly engagement with Taslima. Meredith understood that being an American was not to her advantage in this delicate international matter and so she willingly swung her support and information networks towards the more neutral Northern European countries like Sweden, Denmark, Finland and Norway, helping them take a lead role in the Taslima affair while she concentrated on involving the women's movement.

The story of Taslima Nasreen made good copy for Gabi in June of that year. Summer time is usually quiet and filling the cultural pages becomes difficult. He felt full of energy, the cause was good and he held the story in the palm of his hand. Taslima received far more coverage than would normally be the case outside of summer. Everyone on the Board was going on their annual holidays except Gabi. His newspaper decided to run with the Taslima Nasreen case and there was a lot of space to be filled, a perfect opportunity to publish the faxes that Taslima was sending out of Dhaka, in July 1994, to Meredith calling for help.

Meredith passed them on to Gabi and Taslima knew they were being published. The author would later receive payment for the publication of these faxes and other materials and extracts from Gabi's paper, *Expressen*.

Five thousand kilometres away in Bangladesh, the object of all this activity waited impatiently. For some time now Taslima had been actively collaborating in her 'rescue'. Foreign journalists, who interviewed her in Dhaka in early 1994, confirmed this. French journalist Antoine de Guademar, from the Paris newspaper *Liberation* made a three-day visit to Dhaka in February

1994, three months before Taslima went into hiding and eventually fell into Gabi's orbit.

'It was very obvious that Taslima wanted her story told to the West,' he told me. 'She was very keen for this to happen. She felt isolated,' he said, 'and she needed the publicity.' He did not know who was advising Taslima inside Dhaka, but he found it plausible that she was being helped by a number of friends and supporters to map out a strategy. During his short visit he met only pro-Taslima locals, including her relatives, and journalist Farid Hossain.

Meanwhile Gabi was developing his own strategy to rescue Taslima. Around 10 June the Swedish Defence of Rushdie Committee, of which Gabi was a founding member, met with the Swedish Minister of Foreign Affairs, Margaretha af Ugglas. At the end of the meeting Gabi challenged the Minister by asking why she was doing nothing to help the woman called Taslima Nasreen. As it happened, a general election was only two months away. The foreign minister, like many ministers, was struggling to find an issue that she could use to out-gun the prime minister, who, as heads of government usually do, claimed the lead profile—and the headlines—in Swedish foreign affairs. The minister asked Gabi to remain behind after the meeting and called in her cabinet secretary. Gabi was in his element as he told them all about 'his' beleaguered writer.

Out of this informal meeting, a group was created in the foreign ministry, a group interested in very swift action. Three months were left to the election, and now the minister had a human issue to capture voters' hearts. Opinion polls indicated that the Government was going to lose this election. The three began working together and Gabi, although he had no political affiliations with the Government, seized the opportunity and was also given access to the Swedish Ambassador in Bangladesh. Sweden was enjoying its first year in the European Union and Taslima's case provided an opportunity to take a leadership role in human rights inside the EP. The political context in Sweden was ripe for inviting Taslima to come to Sweden. They could use her in a domestic political context and as a clarion call for human rights from inside the EP. Gabi began to feel more and more self-important.

'Self-righteousness, I had in abundance,' he said.

Gabi rubbing shoulders with ministers and senior diplomats; Gabi keeping secrets from his PEN Board colleagues, always 'because of security restrictions', he told them; everything added to the resentment which in the end would bring him down.

※

The curtain was about to rise on Act Two of the Taslima drama and it happened shortly after his meeting with the foreign ministry people. On

15 June 1994, Gabi happened to be in Paris for an important meeting with Reporters sans frontières (RSF) and other like-minded organisations interested in the Bosnian situation, 'An Evening in Bosnia', as they called it. The men at the top of these structures are quite capable of cooperating with each other one day, and ignoring each other the next, especially when chasing funding. Fortunately for the sake of human rights, their subalterns help one another across the board. Life at the bottom of the pyramid is less complicated: people have not tasted power and still hold most of their illusions.

Present at the meeting with Gabi were Henri-Bernard Levy, controversial French philosopher, writer and adventurer, a man sometimes accused of writing intemperately against Algerian Islamists—he would deny that such a thing is possible; Robert Menard, the strong-willed Executive Director of RSF; by his side sat Gil Gonzalez-Foerster and other French intellectuals.

Having finished with Bosnia, the men sat together informally, discussing, as Gabi put it, 'how to create a climate of opinion' to assist Taslima Nasreen: in other words, how to devise a campaign. These men were well versed in positioning audiences through the power of words. Now was the time to act. A week earlier Taslima had gone into hiding to avoid the warrant for her arrest. After much talking they decided it was a simple matter to pool their strategies and work collectively. RSF had journalists and editors stationed around the world, Gabi had Swedish PEN in his pocket and in the past had written for a number of Scandinavian and German papers. He knew many great writers and Henri-Bernard Levy was well known, and in certain intellectual quarters, well disliked, but who in the end could resist one of his passionate letters railing against injustice and rallying his fellow writers to the crusade.

This was the beginning of the Taslima Nasreen letter campaign in July 1994, almost identical to the one used years before for Rushdie. Leading newspapers in twenty-two countries would publish an open letter, every Wednesday, written by an internationally famous author to 'Cherie Taslima'. The aim of the campaign, Gabi said, was 'to get her out'; for this to happen they needed to engage the media—to start the media talking about this unknown female writer. Personally, he thought it an excellent opportunity to also show PEN's power. Gabi was juggling a lot of slippery balls: PEN, his newspaper in Stockholm, the letter campaign, his talks with the Swedish Government—he was enjoying himself immensely.

Years later he freely admits that, as a group, they acted without thinking—victims of their imaginations. 'I think we overestimated the threat and maybe in a way we destroyed her life, because I'm no longer sure that it was the right move to make at that moment.'

They were running the show and it never crossed their minds that Bangladeshi law might play a role. The letter campaign created a climate of opinion where diplomatic missions were able to work together to remove Taslima from any possible danger. To achieve their goal, the human rights activists and the media painted a picture of Bangladesh as a rabid Islamic fundamentalist country. Bangladeshi national pride was shattered—this rebounded on Taslima. Even those who'd felt sympathy found it hard to forgive her.

Gabi finds it hard to forgive himself and now admits, 'I supported this betrayal. I didn't ask the questions I should have. I didn't seek the information.'

❀

Salman Rushdie was the first writer to be approached for a letter and it was left to Gabi, who knew him personally, to woo him. None of the other authors knew anything about Taslima, nor had read any of her work, unavailable in any Western language. The absurdity of writing a letter to an unknown writer escaped them at the time; the magical word 'solidarity' has a way of blinding people and as Gabi knew, 'each big name guarantees another big name writer.' Rushdie agreed to cooperate and then it became easier to attract the other big fish they needed: Nadine Gordimer, Susan Sontag, Martin Walser, and Philippe Sollers. Sollers wrote his letter with more than a touch of prophecy; it was a cynical letter warning Taslima of the morbid fascination which people, 'even the most enlightened ones', feel for martyrdom.

Sollers wanted her to hear something different, he said, to the smooth talk of justice and freedom and the basket loads of pious words. 'You don't have to die for one or the other god,' he said, 'and even less for human rights and women's rights and you don't have to become a heroine of the Western world, where a wave of conformist thinking encounters a media storm.'

Gil Gonzalez-Foerster knew all about the letter crusade. Gil is a journalist who has the look of a person at home anywhere in the world. Once upon a time, he would have described himself as a professional activist. At the time he became embroiled in the Taslima affair, Gil worked for RSF in Paris and was in charge of its Asia Desk. It fell to Gil to coordinate the campaign: the others were 'men of vision', and he was the workhorse. He has since become disillusioned and no longer works for RSF or the International Parliament of Writers, another French invention protecting freedom of speech. Today he is a freelance journalist with a special interest in Chinese minorities, human rights and environmental issues.

Gil's responsibility as an RSF employee was to collect all the texts from the writers and liaise with the press. The month before, he'd acted as Taslima's escort travelling from Paris to Dhaka and back again, accompanying her on an RSF-sponsored conference. They had become friends and stayed in touch. On this first trip Gil noticed how the French media were ready to snap her up without knowing anything at all about her. Politicians and publishers alike followed her around like hungry sharks. At the time, he said, she was still regarded as a writer by the media; later they would see her as a symbol and 'play with her, taking pieces of her life, and running away,' he said.

Gil was one of many foreigners who received a midnight fax, from Taslima, calling for help when she was in hiding in mid-1994. Secret messages were starting to pour out of Dhaka like an overflowing drain during the monsoon. Most people were flattered, believing they were the only ones she trusted, but she and her friends were taking no risks and cast their nets wide. She was well aware that some would be published, with or without her express permission and polished them for dramatic effect—she is a writer.

The letter by Salman Rushdie was published in more than twenty-two papers around the world, including *The New York Times* in mid-July 1994. The campaign lasted for about five weeks, but was regarded as a great success even though it was cut short after Taslima left Dhaka in early August. Still nothing went to waste and Gil later collated all of the letters, including those not published by the press, into a book *Cherie Taslima*, published in France by Stock, with the money being donated to a good RSF cause. The German rights were also sold to a small German publishing house with an activist reputation who also wanted to sell Taslima T-shirts at the forthcoming Frankfurt Book Fair in October. Gil strongly objected to this kind of commercialisation of Taslima.

Gil, while disillusioned, is less cynical than Gabi about the campaign and the harvest it yielded. He would like to think that the letter campaign forced the hand of the Bangladeshi Government, but knows that there is always a range of other complex factors at work, not always visible. Although he doesn't discount the diplomatic pressure applied to a Bangladesh heavily dependent on foreign aid, he thinks internal politics was the main reason, but he is not sure. 'How can you be sure,' he wants to know? It was a question I would try to answer by the end of my journey.

Not everyone on Taslima's side agreed with the famous letter campaign. And it seems that men and women often disagreed over tactics and responded differently. Meredith Tax from her New York base and Sara Whyatt and friends from PEN's London office were completely opposed to the campaign, when they finally heard the news in July 1994. The women's sphere of influence moved between Dhaka, New York and London; the men initiated events from their Paris and Stockholm bases. The women activists tried hard to stop Salman Rushdie from publishing his letter.

Linking Taslima's name to Rushdie was not a clever thing to do, they believed: tensions would only be exacerbated by associating Taslima with Rushdie, whose book was banned in Bangladesh; for in 1994, his name was still an abomination amongst the ultra orthodox in most Muslim societies. A high profile campaign led by Rushdie was certainly not in the best interests of Taslima, they believed, and could stall negotiations under way in Dhaka. Letters were faxed to Gil and Gabi in Paris and Stockholm; Gabi transmitted the text of the letter to Salman Rushdie, who in his response on 13 July 1994 was none too pleased to be asked to gag himself. He pointed out the irony of being asked to remain silent on a matter of free speech. He was only writing in her defence, he protested. They were blaming the wrong side. 'We simply must not allow the men of violence to determine what are "good" and "bad" times for us to speak.'

Gil was not convinced by London's arguments either. 'Bangladesh is not Iran,' he thought to himself, so he told them in no uncertain terms that if Taslima had known about the letter campaign, she would have given her approval. 'She always told me that I must talk in her name and organise things in Paris.' She was in hiding anyway, and how could they get in touch with her?

Through her lawyers was the obvious answer, but at this stage Gabi and co. showed a tendency to ignore Taslima's lawyers as if they were of little importance in the grand scheme of things.

The men believed in their letter campaign and could not understand the women's objections. Shortly afterwards, Gil received a handwritten ten-line fax from Dhaka with much the same content as the call from London; it was signed by 'The Anonymous Supporters of Taslima Nasreen'. Gil did not know that Sara Hossain was in Dhaka at the time, or he might have speculated that some of her local friends rose to the occasion. However, he resisted the pressure, seeing it as an indication of the competitiveness inherent in the 'human rights market', as he called it, rather than the rights and wrongs of the letter campaign: some organisations, he believed, were far too territorial with their star authors.

The women's lobby wanted what was best for Taslima and they were prepared to listen to her lawyers and stay in the background, something which Gabi could never do. Later they were horrified to learn there was also some talk of Gabi and Henri-Bernard Levy going off together on a 'boys' adventure'-style rescue mission where they would secretly land in Dhaka and smuggle Taslima out! Levy was no stranger to Dhaka and was very attached to the Bangladesh he remembered from twenty-three years earlier. According to Gabi, this was just a passing thought never seriously entertained, and he was embarrassed for the first time that day to hear that I knew about this Quixotic scheme.

Gil felt he was doing what Taslima would have wanted; Gabi believed it could only benefit Taslima's cause to be associated with renowned writers, some of them Nobel Prize winners. Meredith Tax, Siobhan Dowd and Sara Whyatt were taking their cues from the Hossains and were sensitive to Bangladeshi politics. Negotiations with the Government were at a crucial stage. The key negotiators must have been frustrated to have their efforts undermined by the prospect of unwelcome publicity. However, in the end, the letter campaign was not picked up by the Bangladeshi media and was a storm in a teacup.

Who owned Taslima Nasreen? Who really rescued her? There were any number of claimants, people of goodwill, energy and commitment, and along with that came a feeling of proprietorship.

Gabi is prepared to answer the question. 'Yes, I was intoxicated by a feeling of ownership as well: we all wanted to be the "good" people.'

Gil eventually stopped working as a professional activist. The giants he knew in the freedom-of-speech world, with their lofty ideals, had lost the capacity for self-criticism, he believed. Gil learnt the hard way, that if you tried to criticise the less-than-democratic processes within an organisation like the RSF or criticised the famous director's opportunism, or fought for industrial democracy within the organisation, it was like daring to question human rights.

Certain taboos were not to be broken. The RSF liked to be first with a story, and the way to attract money was to run dramatic stories and there were always plenty of reporters in life-threatening situations around the world. It was never a question of fictionalising events, just now and then altering the balance, or adding a dramatic touch that 'might' have happened. The director never allowed the West European media to be criticised. How could you criticise a major European daily one day and then call on them the next day to publish your story?

During the campaign, Gil shed more of his illusions. An Israeli writer whose letter was due to be published the week the campaign came to a halt had a new book coming out. Someone close to the author called, asking if they could continue the campaign for another week as this would help promote the new book.

❀

By the end of the campaign, the Bangladeshi author was the toast of Europe—her supporters also knew how to throw a Western-style *tamasha*.

The giant public relations machine had done its job well. If the secular image of Bangladesh was tarnished, there were few to notice, few to care. If facts were invented or bent, then it was all for a good cause.

Taslima Nasreen became a political talking point within the European Union, which in July 1994 released a statement criticising the Republic of Bangladesh and calling for economic sanctions to punish Bangladesh, questioning the morality of supporting a country with such a poor human rights record. Gabi went on air arguing that applying sanctions to a struggling country like Bangladesh would affect the very people that Taslima was trying to support through her writing. Scandinavian countries like Sweden, Norway and Denmark took the lead in diplomatic negotiations and PEN, RSF, Article 19 and others organised their rapid action messages which rained down on the heads of Bangladeshi senior diplomats in Washington, London and other parts of the world—the intensive campaign calling for her protection and the dropping of the charges against her intensified during July. Because of their perceived neutrality and because by comparison with France, Britain and the USA, there were few expatriates from the Subcontinent living there, the Nordic countries became engaged in a bidding war for Taslima and it was mainly through the efforts of Gabi that Sweden won out in the end. During July he carried out negotiations with the senior lawyer leading Taslima's defence in Dhaka, Dr Kamal Hossain, who began meeting with the Swedish Ambassador in Dhaka sometime between late June and the mid-July European Union statement.

Gradually Sweden edged ahead in the Taslima stakes and after Gabi told Hossain, sometime in mid- or late July, that the Tucholsky prize money would be increased, Sweden surged ahead. Gabi successfully promoted Sweden as a safe place and with the increased prize money, doubled from 75,000 to 150,000 Kronen (about US$23,000), Kamal Hossain, whom Gabi understood to be the chief negotiator on her behalf, became pro-Sweden. Gabi's idea was to involve the minister of culture and immigration in the rescue mission. This would enable the Swedish minister to counter the negative stories appearing in the press about poor Bangladeshi asylum seekers being deported. In return, the immigration ministry would have to provide ministry funds to help 'up the ante'.

The Taslima story held enormous appeal for a Swedish Government in the middle of an election campaign. Oppressed women, raving mullahs and Muslim zealots releasing snakes in the streets and burning books—all of these images made for dramatic news stories, and like all mythologies there is always that element of truth tucked in beside the exaggerations, embellishments, and plain untruths. The women were oppressed, yes; the fanatics were raving and calling for her blood and, by July, they organised demonstrations almost at will inside Bangladesh. But there was no burning of books, no attack by the killer snakes, and the Bangladeshis closely following Taslima's story were divided as to whether her life was really at risk—most were sceptical over these claims. They knew that Bangladesh had not turned overnight into a theocracy.

What the mythmakers ignored was the organised opposition to the religious fanatics from inside Bangladesh and the rule of law sustained by a secular constitution and a legal system modelled on the British system. And if the political situation had been more stable, perhaps the Bangladeshi Government might have protected her and not used her, along with everyone else at the time.

⊞

After she arrived in Sweden, Taslima accepted invitations to speak at a number of Europe's great cities: London, Prague, Copenhagen, Oslo and Lisbon, where she attended the prestigious International Parliament of Writers conference. Life outside Stockholm was one enormous Taslima party where she was feted and adored by some of the most critical brains of the Western intellectual world. Politicians, statesmen, and philosophers hung on her every word. Gabi described it as a kind of hysteria which affected the French in particular.

But in Gabi's eyes, 'the emperor was naked' and to him it was more than a language problem. He watched everybody swallow whatever Taslima said. He expected her to mention women in Bangladesh, their suffering and their struggle, but she talked only about herself, Gabi complained.

But when Taslima talked about her own struggle against family, and religion, wasn't she breaking the silence for other women? Didn't the "I" stand for "We"? Was Gabi being unfair?

'These good people,' he said, 'were sitting there saying, "How wonderful, how fantastic!" standing in line to honour her and shake her hand.'

Gabi was not slow to observe the effect Taslima had on men: how she brought out the cavalier in middle-aged and elderly men in particular and he told funny stories about famous elderly writers puffed up like fighting cocks, as they struggled to sit next to her.

⊞

There is a mythology and glamour around dissident writers; they seem like romantic figures out of a Russian novel, expected to be perfect in every way. Living at close quarters with Taslima eventually affected Gabi: he still believed in the cause but was fast becoming disenchanted. His next story explained how truth is often subdued by our own psychological needs: our intellect tells us one thing, while our emotions say something else.

Many years ago Gabi attended a PEN Congress where a very sweet man from South Africa was mouthing a number of really awful platitudes about how grateful he was to be safe in Sweden. Sitting next to Gabi was a distinguished man, an elderly Swedish poet, who'd travelled and seen much of the outside world. 'This great poet began to cry,' said Gabi. 'At first I wasn't sure if it was because the platitudes were so dreadful or what exactly! But I remember him whispering to me, "These are the most touching words I have ever heard." I was stunned. I don't believe he ever really heard what the South African had said,' Gabi said, 'but his heart was touched by what he imagined the man had gone through.'

'And this for me,' he continued, 'symbolises the attitude that many people feel: that someone else's suffering is always deeper, much more profound, always more full of wisdom than anything else you yourself have experienced. Because after all what do we know in this God forsaken country which has never even suffered from a world war! So, yes, we have this romanticised ideal, where nobody who has ever been persecuted can be criticised ever again. "How dare we judge?" we say to ourselves. And we gag our own critical judgment in the name of creating harmony.'

The role of the intellectual was not to create harmony, but to create questions. 'If you don't dare to ask questions out aloud then you may lapse into a kind of cynicism,' he said at the end of his story. Already he was having doubts about Taslima's integrity, but because she was an untouchable icon, he could never voice his concerns.

Gabi's early romanticism is shared by all of us who want our dissidents to be superior in every way. Dissidents may be willing to face imprisonment and exile rather than recant and yet, at a personal level, when it comes to a moral code, they are neither saints nor fonts of ultimate wisdom. They are flawed and no different to anyone else, including the very people prepared to worship them. When the truth emerges there are always followers who will feel a sense of betrayal that their hero is not a perfect human being. Taslima is an imperfect woman; this dismayed many of her close supporters.

Sweden and Taslima were not a good match. The Swedes were welcoming, as we know from Eugene's and Carola's stories, but the Swedes were also very formal; there was no sign of the intensity and the passion of Bangladesh. A coolness developed between the author and her hosts.

People who come from third world countries are expected to be beholden for the moral commitment and concrete assistance they receive from the 'good people'. Surely if the West is morally committed to helping the poor, then the poor should at least be damn well grateful! And if they don't act appreciatively as you expect, then they must be arrogant and ungrateful.

Svante Wyler, Taslima's Swedish publisher, quickly pointed out that Taslima was never the problem. 'We were the problem,' he said, 'the way we received her and tried to turn her into something she wasn't.' He became so upset by what was happening, the gossip and the way that everything was being taken up in the German papers, that he wrote in an article for the *Frankfurter Allgemeine*, 'Does she have to have an opinion on Swedish and German political life? Can't we stop asking her these questions and let her rest? All of these tremendous honours and the nonsense of treating her the same as Gorbachev, the way she was met by presidents and prime ministers wherever she went.'

Wyler never doubted that eventually she would find her way. He saw her problems compounded by her shyness, her anger, and her problems with the language. 'You and I are talking now, but you are only getting a part of me because in English I don't have the right words, or the nuances. I am only me when I am speaking Swedish,' he said. 'Why can't people in her own country cope with her?' At the time I thought it a naive question.

Gabi knew better. 'Bangladesh is not Sweden,' he said. 'Sweden is not a jungle where you must watch out and everybody fights everybody else. You can trust people here in Sweden: they may not love you, or hug you, but you can trust them.'

He didn't mean to sound condescending, he said, but he imagined Bangladesh was not a country where the Swedish ideal of 'correctness', in their understanding of the word, played much of a role. How could they expect Taslima to know what correctness was then?

At first it sounded as if Gabi was indulging in a form of self-flattery, delivering a sermon on Western morality and a condemnation of 'the other'. But I came to see that the Lutheran foundations were still powerful in Sweden and Swedes prided themselves on being correct, formal and straight dealing, with strong links between the law and ethical business practices. Later I had good cause to wonder how these values affected journalists' ethics.

Taslima and Gabi were bound to clash; it was only a question of when. Observers, like Eugene, felt that there came a time when she started to transfer her rage to Gabi.

Christianne Besse, Nasreen's French publisher, who has a motherly engagement with her author as well as a business relationship, visited her shortly after her arrival. Besse believes that Gabi's role has been misunderstood. 'Gabi did his best to protect her from the media frenzy, to give her time to settle in, to recover from her terrible experiences. He was only carrying out her lawyers' wishes,' said Besse. 'People have been unkind.'

Gabi soon learnt to his discomfort that if there was one thing this difficult woman author hated, it was being told what to do. She found his attitude just as stifling as the Swedish security arrangements imprisoning her. There was nothing normal in her life; she had no chance to form friendships. Instead, she found herself relating to hordes of journalists from all parts of the world, fighting to get to her and facing restrictions from their journalist brother-in-arms Gabi Gleichmann.

Gabi's roles were starting to multiply: he was the president of PEN, the organisation which had helped 'save' her; he belonged to the Swedish literary establishment, which was beginning to wonder what on earth was wrong with 'their author'; he'd been a foot soldier and part of the giant press relations machine, waiting in the shadows, to unleash the 'Save Taslima' letter campaign. On top of this he was the journalist whose paper had mounted a Swedish campaign to assist her, and naturally enough was rewarded with exclusive interviews on her arrival, while other Swedish media outlets were quarantined. Gabi was her press agent, her personal secretary, and a permanent feature in the Nasreen entourage. Gabi was everything but a close personal friend, it seemed.

Gabi, and his wife, tried hard to provide a surrogate family for the lonely woman and at one stage Taslima lived with them, for four weeks, although it was a far from pleasant experience for his wife Lee. She felt that her guest never saw her as 'anything but thin air to look through. I've been washing her clothes, feeding her, up from early morning to late at night and not even a smile. I didn't expect a "thank you," but just a smile; in her eyes I must have been lower than a servant! I was a *bhakti yogi*, there to serve others,' she told her husband.

He tried to be a friend. Gabi wanted Taslima to like him; he is that sort of person. Unfortunately, however, he was becoming more her agent and at times her censor, as he had promised her lawyers, monitoring what she was saying in her speeches and articles, watching for slips in political correctness. She had an unfortunate habit of blurting out the most intolerant thoughts, sounding as fanatical and dogmatic as those obscurantists who opposed her—it made her listeners blanch, to hear her say out loud, 'the books of the fundamentalists should be burnt,' and that, 'all religions should be banned.' She grew to resent his attempts to curb her. What he saw as kindly paternal guidance she probably saw as a policy of containment, another male trying to dominate her. Eugene was right; in Gabi, Taslima found a temporary surrogate object for her rage.

Slowly the edifice started to crumble. There are many versions of what took place. The pieces are difficult to put together; the cast of characters involved are intelligent, creative writers used to exploiting their imaginations, but it is still possible, at some level, to clarify the conflicts which sprang up like spiky cacti.

The house that Gabi built came tumbling down at the Frankfurt Book Fair in 1994, the world's greatest book market, which publishers around the world consider de rigueur to attend. Some Taslima watchers point to earlier signs that the partnership was breaking up. Taslima was travelling more and moving away from Gabi's influence, listening to alternative advice, making a few friends of her own.

Trying to make sense of what took place is not easy and depends on how one looked at Gabi Gleichmann, because there was a clear line separating friend from foe. People well disposed towards him accepted his version of events; his enemies believed the worst of him. The truth hovers somewhere in between, but there is no doubt that many Swedish journalists used the incident to even scores with Gabi—out of envy, pique, frustration or perhaps because some of them smelt a good story.

The Frankfurt Book Fair scandal all began some time in late September 1994, when Gabi received a call from a small German publishing company with an activist reputation which wanted to bring out a book drawing together the letters to Taslima from the July letter campaign. The letters had already been published in France, but now a German edition was to be launched at that year's Book Fair.

Gabi was asked to write a short piece for the book outlining the Swedish campaign to save Taslima. The women editors told him that the Swedish experience would be a useful lesson for activists wanting to help women writers in Algeria. Gabi found this gratifying. Funds from the book sales would go towards a solidarity fund for Algerian writers.

Taslima and Gabi were both invited, but Taslima, Gabi says, told him that she could see no reason for attending because there was no publication of hers appearing at the festival. The Swedish version of *Lajja* was coming out the following month and Gabi knew that she wanted maximum publicity for this launch. He also recalls her wanting to be somewhere else at around the date of the Frankfurt event. At the time all invitations, business correspondence, requests for interviews, faxes and so on passed through Gabi's hands and he relayed them to Taslima. In Gabi's eyes he was acting more like her secretary—to others he was the gatekeeper who barred the way.

Gabi replied to the publishers telling them that Taslima was unavailable and that he might also have to decline. According to Gabi, they started to plead with him and because he always had a weak spot for small publishing enterprises, he eventually accepted.

Gabi says he tried to persuade Taslima to write something, a special foreword, but she refused. He didn't outline the reasons why. So in the end, Gabi wrote the foreword and went to Frankfurt while Taslima stayed behind—she had never accepted the invitation, that much is clear. At the time the author was inundated with requests for public appearances. Gabi couldn't resist telling me that if she'd known about the prestige and history of the famous Frankfurt Book Fair, she would have paid her own way!

At the time I smile. Later I ask myself why Gabi never explained how prestigious the event was, or at least inform her Swedish publishers that Taslima had been invited to the Frankfurt Book Fair. They surely would have jumped at the opportunity even if their author knew no better. This is the only question which unsettles me in his account. And it leads me to wonder if Gabi was only human after all, and he'd simply had enough, so he decided to let her cut off her own nose and somewhere along the line decided to fly solo?

So Gabi went alone. 'At least one day without Taslima,' he thought.

Arriving at Frankfurt Airport, he saw police cars and two women standing there with large bouquets and larger smiles. Suddenly he realised that something was amiss.

'Are you expecting Taslima Nasreen?' he asked.

'Yes,'

'But you know she's not coming!'

They seemed surprised—surprised and horrified.

'You invited her; she declined, and besides,' he reminded them, 'you never sent Taslima any plane tickets. You sent me tickets and here I am.'

Both parties were bewildered. If one puts the most likely interpretation on the debacle, it was probably caused by poor communication between Gabi and the organisers and between Gabi and Taslima—the clues are there that the two had already started to fall out. The women were not dealing with Taslima directly, but through Gabi Gleichmann. Taslima at this time was still receiving round-the-clock protection and her address was a secret. In the aftermath of it all, however, Gabi would be blamed because some people believed that he had deliberately engineered the whole fiasco.

The women organisers drove Gabi to a pre-arranged luncheon at an exclusive restaurant with the head of the Book Fair, who was also expecting to meet the Bangladeshi writer. Everyone was upset. Gabi, who could understand German perfectly and listened in to the German publisher's conversation, was at last beginning to appreciate that the press conference he'd thought was to launch the book to help raise funds for the Algerian women was, in fact, a press conference focussing on Taslima Nasreen the celebrity, an event planned as the major attraction of the day. He began to suspect that in order to entice Taslima to Frankfurt, the publishers may have used the Algerian women's issue as a lure. He went on to hint at some elaborate trap to garner publicity, which confused me, for it really seemed more a case of gross mismanagement, on somebody's part, than a Machiavellian plot.

If you are prepared to believe the best of Gabi then the most likely interpretation one can make is that relations between Taslima and Gabi were becoming tense anyway; that he tried to persuade Taslima to accept the invitation which she didn't want to do for her own reasons; that he kept things on hold for too long while he tried to persuade her to change her mind—because he certainly wanted to go—and that the Germans were left in the dark.

Two months later, Kore Verlag, the German publishers, issued a press release giving their version of events, which added to the tangle of ex-planations. They argued that Gabi had insisted their invitation be sent to him via German PEN (to give it extra weight, he had explained); that he had confirmed his and Taslima's participation, and then turned up without her, telling them a story of Taslima being refused permission to disembark at Frankfurt Airport, the previous Friday, as an 'undesirable' person. After talking to Taslima, much later, they chose to believe that their correspon-dence and invitations had been deliberately kept from her by Gabi. People kindly disposed to Gabi find this incomprehensible.

Whatever lay behind the fiasco, the Germans must really have expected Taslima: why else would they have gone to such elaborate lengths as waiting for her at the airport with security police and bouquets; and arranging an expensive lunch with the director of the Book Fair to their mutual chagrin, and why of all things would they set themselves up for such a devastating backlash with the impatiently waiting members of the media.

A crowd of more than two hundred journalists from around the world were expecting to see Nasreen in the huge main hall at the Frankfurt Book Fair. Gabi insists to this day that he tried to persuade the German publishers to cancel the event. They refused, and so he let himself be persuaded to play a role for which he was totally unsuited. He gave the impression that he was representing the author and may even have been introduced by the embarrassed organisers in this role.

'Of course Taslima was completely innocent,' Gabi told me. 'In the end they persuaded me to talk [in her place] and to try to explain what had happened.'

This was a huge miscalculation on his part and, in thinking that he would be able to carry this off successfully, Gabi had misjudged the moment, the mood of the gathering—they had been waiting for two hours it seems—and well and truly overreached himself. He cast himself in the wrong role. To make matters worse, Gabi tried to cover up the debacle. His explanation for this is disconcerting, but if one is to believe the best of Gabi, then he was being soft hearted and trying to ease an embarrassing situation without laying the blame where it seemed to rest in his eyes: with the small publishing company. He must have believed that he could perform this trick without leaving any casualties behind. Gabi is a charming man from a family of diplomats who needs to please everyone, if he can.

And now the Swedish journalists, who'd been denied access to her in the past by Gabi, entered the picture. Gabi's explanation seemed to lay the blame at Taslima's door and in their eyes it looked like he was trying to give a press conference in her name. Gabi Gleichmann was full of his own importance, they thought, he'd forgotten he was a journalist. Gabi, while not disagreeing with this assessment, insists his intentions were the best.

Gabi wanted to be a hero and save the day. 'Where is she?' they all asked; the crowd was getting angry. Gabi then tripped himself and proceeded to drop one of the balls he'd been juggling so adroitly for so long. He told a lie—not a big one, but a white lie for the best of all possible reasons, which is usually what lies at the bottom of untruths of this kind.

'I was stupid,' he sighed. 'I mean there are times when you tell a little white lie. I didn't have the heart to say the blame lies with these women.' He made the mistake of playing the diplomat, which he admits he should never have done. 'I should have been very clear about it,' he now says. Instead he tried to keep everyone happy, to negotiate a compromise where nobody would lose face, or feel aggrieved, and it exploded right in his face.

'I thought it would be better if I said, "I'm sorry, but I don't know exactly the reason why she isn't here, she was invited, but she has other engagements and couldn't be here. I think there has been a misunderstanding but you must understand her position: at the moment she is being run over by interview requests."'

A member of the audience, sensing something was wrong, later told me, 'he seemed to be on her side, but you could tell he wasn't really.'

'And then,' continued Gabi, ' I started telling them all about our campaign and, while I was doing this, practically all of the journalists sitting there walked out and I was left alone.'

The audience was not interested in the Dragon Slayer—they wanted the Princess.

Gabi had only made matters worse 'I asked them to try to understand that we are all writers and literary people, and as journalists it is important not just to work for Taslima but for thousands of others who needed our help, particular those in Algiers.' They turned a deaf ear to Gabi, unimpressed by his moralising.

A few Swedish journalists were swift to spread the news on their return to Stockholm. One reporter, Gabi said, wrote a small mean article accusing him of trying to take Taslima's place and become a star. The tone of the article was harsh. It concluded by accusing Gabi of preventing the Swedish media from interviewing Taslima because he wanted exclusives for his own paper. There was certainly Schadenfreude aplenty, in Stockholm, the day the article appeared.

There were old scores to be settled; some of them dated back to the July letter campaign two months earlier where only a select group of international papers were involved and others bypassed. His colleagues accused him of a conflict of interest between his role as Swedish PEN president and as a professional journalist. Word soon reached Taslima and she reacted swiftly.

The night before the first article against Gabi appeared, he received a disturbing phone call from Taslima. 'Her father was terribly angry, she said, over something printed in the local fundamentalist paper far away in Dhaka.' There was no doubt in Gabi's mind that she was genuine. 'She was almost crying,' he said. 'They had written that Taslima Nasreen had married Gabi Gleichmann, an anti-Muslim Zionist and a Jew.' Her father was extremely upset.

'I asked her what was the bad part of the article for her father,' Gabi said. 'Without mincing any words, she replied that the bad part was marrying a Jew. And she said it without any sensitivity at all,' he remembered, 'as if I was now creating problems for her.' Gabi then reminded her that he was already happily married and asked why her father, of all people, would believe what the pro-Islamist papers printed.

'Listen Taslima,' he said. 'Many people who have helped you, including Meredith Tax, are Jewish; lots of intellectuals in the West are Jews! You'd better get used to it!'

Gabi was hurt and he'd had enough. Was Taslima beginning to think of him as a burden who might complicate negotiations for her return to Bangladesh? He may have been overly sensitive and events were moving forward at a rapid pace: on Wednesday he'd left for Frankfurt; on Friday she'd called very upset about her father and then on Saturday, the very next day, he was reading about himself in the papers. To this day he is still unsure if there was any connection.

Soon after, Taslima contacted him again. 'Please give my telephone number to any journalist who wants it,' she told him; it was an order, not a request.

Gabi rang every paper that had been lining up since September. Taslima started giving local interviews and when the reporters asked why she'd refused them before, she replied that Gabi had kept her in the dark. They pricked their ears sensing a good story and so for another ten days Gabi continued to take a battering in the Scandinavian press, helpless to stop the tide turning against him. The interviews were all about why Gabi Gleichmann, president of PEN, had kept the famous author hidden in Sweden for weeks in order to exploit the situation and refused to allow other papers in Sweden, Norway and Denmark to interview her.

'I helped get her out of Bangladesh,' he said in exasperation, 'only to lock her away in a hidden place to stop her from being interviewed by the Swedish press?'

Gabi thought he was carrying out her lawyers' wishes by curtailing interviews. The Hossains had sent messages requesting that Taslima be given time to rest and recover. Don't let her talk directly to the press, they said, because she is still in shock. Reading between the lines he knew that they were worried in case she said anything to jeopardise her case and, with it, her chances of returning home. Yet many of his colleagues believe that this quarantine period suited Gabi, the journalist, and that he let it continue for far too long.

The major article criticising him appeared on October 12 and included an interview with Taslima. Gabi tried his best to explain, and listed in great detail the dozens of menial tasks he'd performed, just like an unpaid secretary. His overly long rebuttal was passionate, at times difficult to follow, and had been written in the heat of the moment by a man who believed that he'd been wronged.

Yes, he might have influenced Taslima in her choice of interviews, he conceded, but she had asked him to identify the twenty European dailies which had been part of the July international campaign to save her. It took little imagination to read between the lines and understand that Gabi was making sure that these papers were on the "A list" when it came to getting interviews—those on the "B list" would have to wait.

Of course Gabi must have pointed out which was the main Swedish paper—his own—to which Taslima should feel indebted, but never did Gabi think that one day he'd stand accused of a conflict of interests between his role as PEN president (Taslima's chief guardian and protector), and his job as a journalist. I for one believed Gabi, for he'd been getting away with what appeared to me as a clear conflict of interest for as long as he'd been Swedish PEN president.

Gabi concluded his defence by listing all the international papers and TV networks which had received interviews from Taslima and it was an impressive list: approximately thirty-eight interviews within two months of her arrival. It was a full and frank defence but as the Romans knew, and Gabi would learn, *semper aliquid haeret,* 'something always sticks'. The Scandinavian papers were not concerned with the international coverage: they were angry that Gabi's paper appeared to have the front running while they'd been cut off.

A senior Swedish newspaper editor later told me that he saw nothing wrong in Gabi's own paper the *Expressen* getting the first exclusive with Taslima on her arrival and that the attack on Gabi had been petty and unwarranted.

Only after Taslima failed Gabi by stating, publicly, that he kept her isolated, did Gabi call her. 'You need to set the record straight,' he said. 'It affects your image, as the great freedom fighter for women's independence, if you let yourself be so exploited by the first man you met in the West!'

'She was making herself out to be a victim again and I had to defend myself,' he said, trying to explain his bitterness. She assured him that she would have the article corrected. '"I will make it up to you," she told me, "I will tell them you are innocent"', but nothing happened and the campaign against him continued for ten long days. Salman Rushdie defended him, in the end, by writing an article published in Sweden, reminding people of Gabi's contribution to human rights and calling on Taslima to come forward and to clarify the matter.

Taslima, like many an exiled writer before her, had learnt by now that in order to retain the interests of the freedom of expression organisations, she needed to use the media for her own ends and not anyone else's. Keep the media interested in you, or they move on.

She responded, Gabi said sarcastically, 'by writing a beautiful piece about herself, where she told the story, once again, of her persecution and her suffering and how so many wonderful people had helped her and worked hard for her. She mentioned a number of groups but she forgot that she was in Sweden and when she listed the groups which had helped her, she upset everybody by failing to mention Sweden—not one word about Sweden. We weren't after gratitude,' he said, 'but even New Zealand was mentioned,' he could laugh about it now, 'New Zealand, but not Sweden!'

The Gabi Gleichmann story at its peak crossed borders and appeared in Germany and France and all over Scandinavia. Gabi Gleichmann eventually left his newspaper and did not stand for re-election at the next PEN AGM.

I let Gabi know, that when I'd first met Taslima, the year before in 1997, she had told me quite unmistakably that when she first came to Sweden she did not want to give interviews and that he, Gabi Gleichmann, was acting on her instructions.

'Great,' he said, 'but a little late in the day.'

Gabi Gleichmann helped create the Taslima mystique and in the end it helped bring him down. Theirs was a strange duel, not unusual between exiled writers and those who 'rescue' them. Such relationships often depends on mutual needs being fulfilled: the needs of the writer who has suffered, and their rescuer who, perversely, needs them to suffer. Inevitably the day always comes when the writer wants to sprout wings; sometimes their 'saviours' have problems adapting to this.

By the end of 1994 it was clear that the Swedish monetary arrangements which had been supporting Taslima were drying up. So far she had been living off her prize money and her overseas royalties from *Lajja*, the Sakharov Prize and other awards, but her expenses were high. There is every reason to believe that she was also subsidising her family (parents, her three siblings and their families) at the time, although the extent of this is unclear. This is the only explanation for the amount of money she exhausted in less than six months.

Taslima thought of herself as Sweden's guest with all that this implies in the Indian subcontinent, where hospitality is an art form: a guest is looked after; their expenses are absorbed, they receive gifts, are cosseted, their every wish is attended to no matter how humble the home . . . and they are never expected to pay.

The Swedes expected Taslima to look after herself financially: to use her prize money, her royalties and the money she received for giving interviews. In handling her own affairs from everything to shopping, cooking, paying her own bills and dealing with the Western media, Taslima was an infant. Being responsible for herself was one aspect of emancipation that Taslima overlooked, and the adjustments she needed to make in the West were difficult.

She no longer wanted to live in Sweden: winter was looming, the hospitality seemed thinner and there were the bills. She wanted to travel and see the world; she was beginning to see herself as a writer with an international audience. Perhaps it was time for the guest to move on? By the middle of 1995, Taslima and the Swedes were more than happy to part company. Her next stop would be Germany, and three years later, so would mine.

Chapter 7

German Fairy Tales

There are those who believe that persecution is good for writers. This is false.
Salman Rushdie

The streets of Lichtenberg, Berlin, are lined with stories, and the stories are all about hard times. Small corner pubs, Turkish take-aways and dog-shit–littered pavements are common sights. Clang-ing trams shuttle people to and fro; drivers open and close doors like robots and look as morose as their passengers.

Nomadic bands of tribal youth with ill-kempt dogs, always of the large variety, by their sides, command the side streets of this eastern inner city suburb. Manacled to their owners by chain leashes, the animals look sullen, their wild-haired keepers, truculent. There is an unwritten law that dogs are never patted or acknowledged, or called by name: their master's image is paramount. I like to think that inside their four walls at least, the owners romp and play with their animals and give them doggie treats, but I'm sceptical. People make way for these Goth troopers striding along the pave-ments: androgynous bands of ragged young men and women with pierced bodies, reeking of an assertiveness that tempts you to pause and applaud as they stalk by, which of course you never do, as you scuttle to one side using as much space as they're willing to allocate.

In their own strange way they act as street police, and can usually be depended on to confront and drive off any Neo-Nazi skinheads they stumble across; it's a comforting thought. They form a maze of narcissistic youth tribes with their own laws and philosophies. They only have eyes for each other.

Other Berliners also lay claim to the locality. Dowdy, lumpy, women, with bent shoulders and heavy shopping bags struggle along the streets,

161

while elderly men with tired grey faces sit at their *Stammtisch*, their regular tables, with nicotine-stained fingers clutching their *Skat* cards as they drink their Pils. For the older generation, reunification is not the paradise they expected.

The year is 1998 and I have travelled to Berlin by train and ferry from Stockholm determined to meet a writer whose life Taslima has imitated without knowing. The part of former East Berlin where my modest hotel lies is overrun with derelict buildings and brown crumbling walls. Cranes and tractors are slow to enter this part of Berlin; they remain busy rebuilding other sectors of the capital, places where witty, hip Berliners with thicker wallets and BMWs abound: rich *Wessis* (former West Germans), who made it long before the Wall came tumbling down and continue to make their Marks—but the tractors will reach the old places in time.

Berlin is a city bent on accepting its history while moving ahead to forge a role as the born-again capital of the twenty-first century. Over the years, German leaders of various political shapes and sizes have shared the same vision of national redemption and laying to rest the ghosts of the past. Acts of repentance and reconciliation have been enacted: repentance for past wrongs and reconciliation through reunification with former East Germany. Today young Germans accept the past as their history, but a history which moves further away with each passing year. They are the first generation of Germans since the war not to be caught in a vice between remembrance and denial.

Berlin has become a city of non-believers. More than fifty-four per cent claim no organised religion. The demography shows an interesting mix of 1,340,000 Christians; 200,000 Muslims and 12,000 Jews. The older generation remains touched by the past, and the past is everywhere in Germany, despite attempts to bulldoze and rebuild.

Taslima Nasreen was not the first famous Bangladeshi writer to make her way to Berlin. Fifteen years earlier a man called Daud Haider, trapped in similar circumstances, found in Berlin a city of asylum. As I listen to the story of Daud's life in Germany, I am reminded of Taslima wandering from place to place, searching for ways to anchor her writing.

Daud Haider is tied to Germany and there are signs that he is almost reconciled to his life here in Berlin. Some days he wonders if he should become a German citizen; he says that he can never return to Bangladesh. I bide my time and defer asking Daud why, after a quarter of a century, he still believes he can never return: Daud, as far as I know, has never tested the idea of repatriation.

More than half his life has been spent in exile; twenty-five years in total: eleven years in Calcutta and fourteen in Germany. The young man who fled from Dhaka has passed from youth to middle age in foreign lands. Occasionally he flies to Calcutta for a reunion with his brothers. There have been women in his life, but he has never married.

The years have been kind to him physically and the small signs of vanity one detects are endearing: his thick head of smooth black hair and dark trimmed moustache look nothing like the Daud from his old newspaper photos, which reveal a young man prematurely greyed—through family genes or the traumas he's endured, is hard to tell. Although now in his late forties, he looks much younger. Behind black-rimmed glasses, dark brown eyes are watching impatiently; the genial manner is partly a facade.

His determination makes him seem taller than he really is, as he strides down the street with a 'make way for me' look in his eyes, and I begin to resent the man for making me hasten my steps on this humid summer's night. Stepping aside for no one, he leads the way along the pavements of Nollendorf Platz, across the busy roads down into the underground; five minutes later we emerge into the still night air of downtown Berlin. A cigarette in one hand, he noisily draws in large doses of nicotine through a clenched hand, the South Asian way, as he tries to spot an empty outside table in the streets off Kurfürstendamm, always the 'in place' to eat. But it's Saturday night, Berlin is at play, and every locale we enter is full; we must move on ... the search continues; there is a rhythm to the hunt which becomes more fulfilling than finding somewhere to eat.

On this night he chooses to wear a white embroidered *kurta*-pyjama and sandals. The gesture is more than symbolic. He is deliberately using his 'difference' to make a statement, and some people stare at his 'exotic' attire, others are taken aback by the confident strut of the peacock, someone so obviously non-German who walks 'their' streets as if he owns them.

There is something unutterably sad about Daud Haider, an emptiness he tries to fill with constant activity: writing, lecturing, broadcasting, reading, and walking the streets ... in search of? Behind the witticisms and the bravado, there's a loneliness. It requires little imagination to suppose that, even after nearly three decades, his sense of place remains fragmented. After reading an early poem, I begin to understand.

> The life I live today is not
> of my choosing, my home,
> is across the border.
>
> Half my youth has passed
> in exile, in an alien place. . . .

Daud Haider is called by some of his countrymen 'the great blasphemer.' Long before Taslima captured the spotlight, Daud Haider was vilified and turned into the most notorious poet in Bangladesh by pro-Pakistan religious factions who had everything to gain by targeting this young man, a favourite of their enemy, the Prime Minister, Sheikh Mujibur Rahman. Even today, if Daud's name is mentioned in Dhaka, people lower their voices; they are simply being discreet, but it's also the way we act when we speak of the dead.

The small-minded amongst the religiously orthodox judged him guilty, although he was never charged nor brought to trial. Many chose to see insult when there was none intended, just the unhappy existential thoughts of an angry young man of the seventies.

We sit together over a Bangladeshi meal he has prepared in the small kitchen of his crowded flat, which reeks of aromas found in spice markets far away. From behind the closed doors of the other flats in his building, schnitzels, *bratkartoffel* and sauerkraut lurk; the smells clash in the corridors, but the tenants are used to difference, it is built into the bricks and mortar around bohemian Nollendorf Platz.

The open living area of his flat is crammed full of books. His writing, he tells me, is influenced by Balzac and Proust, Alfred Döblin, Joyce and Hemingway. Our debates are loud and we disagree frequently. 'I get your point' becomes his catchcry as he interrupts me once again. I have the ghost of a feeling that he's been longing for a good stoush for days and decide not to disappoint him. He generously makes time for me on three separate days: I'm a messenger with news from home; we even know some of the same people. So for a few days at least, he allows me to interrupt his work.

Daud hails from a family of seven brothers and seven sisters. The Haider family name is an illustrious one, which exerted enormous influence on behalf of their erring young brother when he fell from grace. As they say in the Subcontinent, Daud comes from 'a good family'. All of Daud's brothers became writers, yet none of his seven sisters followed the way of the scribe. When this is gently pointed out to Daud, he reacts by arguing that this has nothing whatsoever to do with gender; it was because his sisters married, leaving their natal home to live with their husbands' families to become wives and mothers. I think it has everything to do with gender and that he has proven my point, but we are both stubborn, neither of us gives an inch.

Many famous writers visited the Haider home; his family members were a part of the literary establishment and doors were wide open to young Daud, who never had any difficulty getting his poems published because the top literary editors of the day often visited his house. The wonderful *adda*, as the Bangladeshis call the lively discussions and arguments on every topic imaginable that carry on half the night, were an important part of a writer's development, open to men, who lounged on sofas and large cushions, smoking, eating and talking up a storm as the *adda* meandered back and forth from politics to poetry, from great love affairs to petty jealousies.

⊞

On February 24, 1974, three years after Bangladesh's secession from Pakistan, Daud wrote a poem which changed his life. At the time he was literary editor of a paper, a young guru with followers, and life was promising.

'I Do Not Celebrate Eternity' was an anti-war, anti-religious poem which criticised all religions and all prophets of religion: Buddha, Jesus Christ, the Prophet Muhammad—Daud made no exceptions. The poem was immediately banned by the Awami League Government, because they knew it would cause trouble. Factions wanting to remain with Pakistan were still angry and resentful: the tension between religion and secular politics stems mainly from this time. A group of Anti-liberation mullahs used Daud's poem as an example of what could happen to Bangladesh under a secularist government, where young men were allowed to defame the Prophet Muhammad. Their followers began an agitation by pronouncing a fatwa and demanding his head. Daud was a prize: a convenient scapegoat in their larger war against Sheikh Mujib. My Bangladeshi friends had quietly insisted that I meet this man; now I could see why.

Sheikh Mujib reluctantly agreed to his arrest, for his own safety it was rumoured, which took place on 10 March 1974 and Daud was housed in Dhaka Central Gaol, where he stayed in safe custody for nearly two months. Eventually, through his family's connections with the home minister, he was released on 1 May 1974 under the condition that he leave the country immediately—there were no charges.

He arrived in Calcutta with a few cents in his pocket, his passport in his hand and a packet of sweets, which an official at the airport confiscated. His account of his early years in Calcutta are told in his evocative novella, *Calcutta Days*. He spent the first years moving, like a lost soul, from one acquaintance's house to the next, a few days here, a week there. There were periods when he lived with families and bleaker days and nights when he shared communal digs with poor students who befriended him and let him stay rent free for as long as they could. Other nights he slept in the streets, but as one of his characters says:

Calcutta doesn't know rejection. It will never shun you. It accepts crooks and clairvoyants alike; it has room enough for saints and angels too. It nurses arts and artists, encourages culture and literature . . . , it feeds you while you starve. It's neither communal nor secular. It weeps, smiles, grimaces and makes friends. It won't judge you, won't count your joys and woes . . .

He was fortunate to be adopted by some of Calcutta's literary salons. As the years passed, it is true that some of his benefactors became patronising and made jokes at his expense, but they always rallied round when another Daud crisis raised its head, as it often did. One of his patrons eventually helped him gain a university scholarship.

These were the not-so-rich days of what he called his 'bohemian life', where drink and an open lifestyle (he was a bit of a lady's man, was Daud, popular with female foreign students) helped him pretend he was on an extended holiday. In his day, Daud made university history for being the only student to ever fail in all eight papers of the Master of Arts exam—Calcutta academics tell me his record still stands. 'Excessive Bohemianism started taking its toll on my health,' he later said of his wayward life. He made it sound like a disease, and perhaps it was to a man who lived off his wits and the patronage of others and who needed to keep a steady head and a clean shirt ready for any occasion.

His life changed for the better through the friendship of Sri Ananda Shankar Roy, and his American wife. His new patron, who loved all things Bangladeshi, took the young man under his wing, providing a stability and family warmth which he badly needed, for Daud remained out of favour with the two governments which followed the assassination of Sheikh Mujib. From one acquaintance to another he was passed on like a piece of lost luggage, always under the patronage of Ananda Roy. 'I was his protégé,' Daud says simply, 'and he was my protector.'

His Indian scholarship terminated in 1979 and he became stateless when his passport was impounded by Bangladeshi authorities after he tried to have it renewed, and he was accused of being an apostate. This is a grievous crime for any Muslim to be accused of—better to be an infidel than an apostate! Someone born a Muslim who has abandoned their religion is beyond the pale, with many ultra orthodox Muslims arguing that the punishment is death, unless they repent. The charge of apostasy has also been levelled at Salman Rushdie, Taslima Nasreen and many others from Muslim backgrounds who dare to dissent either publicly or in their writings.

The President of PEN in India, and a great writer and scholar in his own right, Ananda Shankar Roy mounted a signature petition with other notables like film director Satyajit Ray and scores of other distinguished Indian intellectuals, in February 1985, to prevent Daud from being handed over to Ershad's military government, for he was in trouble again. The

Congress Central Government had changed and Daud was refused Indian citizenship and ordered to leave.

The campaign attracted front-page coverage, lauding Daud as the greatest poet of South Asia. It was successful in the end and bought him more time: he could stay in Calcutta on a year-to-year basis. Nine years later, a similar campaign would be launched to save Taslima Nasreen, with many of the same players, including the newspaper and publishing dynasty of Ananda Bazar, managing affairs in its usual style, always in the background, guiding, shaping, quietly urging. Nikhil Sarkar, Deputy Editor of *Ananda Bazar Patrika*, helped Daud as he would later help Taslima.

Daud has always possessed the singular talent of endearing himself to men of influence. His charm and good humor have made him a ready friend of famous authors, who saw their own rebellious youth when they looked at Daud. Writers like Nobel Prize winner Günter Grass have taken him under their wing, having met during the German author's sojourn in Calcutta in 1986. Grass' friendship and largesse would help Daud when he needed it most, a day not far away, for without a passport Daud was in trouble and he needed official asylum.

Grass, who greatly admired Daud's poetry, came to his rescue by writing a letter to the German Foreign Minister Genscher, and to the Academy of the Arts in Berlin, which awarded him a three months' scholarship and a Lufthansa plane ticket. He arrived in Berlin, in usual Daud style, without a *pfennig* in his pocket and lived with Grass for one year. He has been with Radio Deutsche Welle in the Asian Department since 1989, has a residency permit, speaks fluent German and continues to write plays and essays.

Daud first put Taslima's experiences into a context that German journalists could understand. By giving journalists like Jörg Lau insider information, Daud was useful in explaining her situation sympathetically to German readers. At the beginning, Lau (who was then with the *taz*, a paper sympathetic to the Green Party) and his colleagues relied heavily on Daud—too heavily it seems—and neglected other sources. But when reporters first heard about Taslima, everyone thought, 'Ah ha! Another fatwa!'

'It seemed so simple,' said Lau. 'We heard of the demonstrations, the snakes and the magic word "fatwa", it sounded just like Iran' (Lau's wife is Iranian and his paper had links with Reporter sans frontières and Article 19, which spearheaded the Rushdie case). 'It took some time before we learnt that it was only a small, unknown group of fanatics and neither the state, nor the head of state, like in Iran, was involved. Maybe we didn't want to know,' he confessed to me in Berlin.

Daud was an important link in the chain which introduced Taslima to the German public—it was a long chain. Lau's paper was a part of the Reporters sans frontières (RSF) brotherhood and had orchestrated the German chapter of the 1994 Taslima letter campaign; Lau drew her case to the attention of famous German writer Martin Walser, who, in turn, appealed to his good friend Minister Klaus Kinkel to help her leave Bangladesh. Walser's open letter was published and aroused the interest of the European Parliament. Herr Minister had his own agenda and there were some political observers who felt he wanted 'an understudy' for Salman Rushdie, someone easier to rescue, like Taslima.

Having heard the French and Swedish versions of how Taslima was 'saved', it was interesting to learn that the German campaigners also laid claim to having been the first to liberate Taslima.

That was the brilliance of it all! I marvelled again at the blueprint of the French-based solidarity campaign: RSF was the engine driving it along, but they shared their bounty with their 'affiliates' in every European country, and were not too greedy: they could enhance their reputation and at the same time provide a feast for everybody. *The New York Times* could run its article penned by Rushdie; the Germans could have their own Martin Walser letter published in *taz;* in Paris there were French writers galore, lining up: willing and able to come to the rescue of Cherie Taslima. At the end of the day all the letters of support would be published in French and German: best of all, a long queue of individuals and important news-papers could all claim to have 'saved Taslima' like a headline banner for universal human rights. An industry, with all the right moral credentials, had developed around Taslima Nasreen.

After she moved from Stockholm to Berlin in mid-1995, Taslima and Daud's paths were bound to cross one day, yet Taslima never sought contact with Daud. Months passed. Daud could offer no explanation, but I suspected that Taslima was taking advice from her lawyers, the Hossains. If they believed that Taslima's case would suffer by having her name associated with Salman Rushdie, the same veto could apply to Daud Haider—long gone, but not forgotten in Dhaka.

One evening, Daud recognised Taslima sitting in the audience at a reading by Günter Grass. She looked intimidated as he approached her, which surprised him, but to Taslima, Daud was a stranger, and might well be a dangerous stranger. The author was always uncomfortable when Muslims recognised her and reproached her, as sometimes happened. She appeared so vulnerable that onlookers were often moved to help her. This gives credence to Taslima watchers, like former BBC journalist Ali Riaz, who believes there is a great difference between the authorial voice of Taslima, which he and others call 'assumed', and her personal voice, or 'other voice', which hides an often shy, insecure figure.

'I introduced myself,' said Daud, 'and she laughed. "He is the man they say I've married!" she said turning to her friends.'

The pro-Islamist papers at home were up to their old tricks. They seemed obsessed with marrying Taslima off to a range of controversial men. Years before they'd spread the rumour that the rebellious author was willing to marry a certain mullah if only he would shave his beard and change his ways. As Taslima had explained to me in Sweden, protesting publicly, or even filing a case against them, was a waste of time and money. In late 1994, if we remember, Taslima had been 'married off' to Gabi Gleichmann, the 'wicked Zionist from the West' and now that she was in Berlin, they could sustain their attacks by uniting in wedlock Bangladesh's two most infamous 'blasphemers'.

At the time Daud had been furious rather than flattered, or at least pretended to be. He telephoned Sujata Sen at *The Statesman* on 14 June (the same journalist who had conducted that fateful interview with Taslima in May 1994) and thundered down the telephone line that this scurrilous news item had been reported by Reuters, no less, which had picked it up from the English-language Bangladeshi paper *The Independent*, which in turn had picked it from one of the Bangla-medium papers. Sen ran Daud's comments as a tongue-in-cheek article with the headline 'Haider Denies Marrying Taslima'.

The next day we continued talking about Taslima, but something about Daud's manner warned me that overnight he'd had a change of heart and was starting to edit his story. We sat around an old wooden table, the centre of all his activities: eating, writing, talking; its gouged surface was strewn with papers and clippings, the meat and bones of his personal history, reconstructed for my benefit. The candour which coloured his earlier reminiscences was being reined in as if I was no longer his partner-in-conversation and he'd suddenly become aware of me as a researcher. Daud was being careful.

Cocking his head to one side he looked at me with large round eyes. He couldn't understand, he said, why Taslima had never stayed in touch. I found that hard to believe. Somewhere along the line, I guessed that there had been a falling out.

He moved over this terrain swiftly. 'She was very busy. Really, I wasn't interested in calling her and she wasn't interested in calling me. People said she had other Bangladeshi friends here and I was busy with my girlfriend.'

Daud confessed at our next meeting that months later he came across Taslima in a Bengali restaurant in Berlin, but by then she wasn't talking to him, he said. 'Interesting that she has never tried to contact me any more,' he mused, once more playing the innocent. I took the bait, but not in the way he'd expected.

I laughed. In an interview in *taz* on 29 September 1995, Daud had spoken candidly about Taslima's writing and her sudden rise to fame—his comments were not flattering. Daud seemed to have changed sides at a time when sections of the German press were starting to ask questions. Aspersions were cast that Taslima was lying, or at best exaggerating her plight for publicity purposes.

'I wouldn't talk to you either,' I told him, looking him in the eye, 'not if you'd labelled my writing soft porn and told everyone I was a sensationalist at heart!'

❀

In an interview with Mariam Niroumand of *taz*, in September 1995, Daud was quoted as saying that Taslima's writing went unnoticed until she started writing juicy columns for a newspaper where her second husband was editor. Even then, he claimed, nobody was much interested until she started spicing it with what he called 'pornographic' fantasies: a syphilitic husband who frequented brothels; a woman who wanted to take off her shirt in public—like a man—who demanded to know why a woman couldn't visit brothels. Not wanting to dampen Daud's missionary mood, I held my tongue and refrained from telling him that my women friends in Dhaka thought parts of his own writing lascivious.

Daud's pièce de résistance came when he was finally asked by the reporter if he thought Taslima's life was ever in danger, his German reply '*Ach was!*' can be translated into English as meaning either 'Come on!' or 'Are you serious?' or if one puts the worst connotation of all on the phrase, it can also mean 'Not at all!'

But three years later, in 1998, when I met Daud face to face in Berlin, he had changed his mind again, and had no hesitation in affirming that he believed her life was in danger.

If we return to this earlier 1995 interview, then it was disingenuous of Daud to wonder why Taslima no longer gave him the time of day. She must have been furious. Why would Taslima want to build any fences with Daud Haider? There were other expatriates in Berlin, far less critical and certainly less piqued about the publicity she was receiving as Germany's new anti-Muslim hero.

There is little doubt in my mind that Daud's comments contributed to a climate where her standing in Germany was damaged—the tide turned and so did Daud. His motives are interesting, but remain elusive. By the time of my visit, however, he had learnt his lesson and was curbing his tongue. He almost stopped playing games.

The inevitable comparisons people made no doubt rekindled interest in his old case; after fifteen years people had lost interest in Daud, he was no longer topical. It's only natural that he'd enjoy being in the limelight again. He even wrote a letter to Taslima published in the German version of *Chère Taslima*, where he talked mostly about his own case. But while he continued to praise her stand against his old foes, his criticism was sharpening by 1995. His reason being, he says, he had time to read more of her work.

The last time I saw Daud was at the fashionable Cafe Einstein, where he took me for *Kaffee und Kuchen*. We talked about his return home. The coffee house is a meeting place for writers and other literary types and is housed in a gracious villa with well-tended grounds. We drank hot coffee and toyed with our strudel as we sat watching everyone else, who in turn watched us in between mouthfuls of torte. Daud felt at ease, he smiled and chatted away, happy to be seated in a crowded, smoky room alive with conversation, but I could tell what pleased him most was being on display.

He says he would love to return home; but he dares not, even though he likes the Awami party and they like him, as he neatly phrases it. In 1998 the Awami League was in government, with the daughter of Sheikh Mujib as Prime Minister. 'The trouble is, they can't give me any protection: they can't guarantee my safety. At any time an extremist can murder me.'

> The life I live today is not
> of my choosing

But in Bangladesh there are men and women, certainly not unfriendly to Daud, who believe that the life he lives today is of his own choosing: all he has to do, they say, is clear up the business with his passport and the Awami League Government has the goodwill to make that possible. A quarter of a century has passed since the young twenty-three-year-old left Dhaka; today a middle-aged man would be returning in his place. The personal threat to his life has faded with the passage of time, people say, with no animosity towards him, as if they're talking about a naughty boy. People admire his family and those who knew him personally seem fond of the rash young poet they remember. A few smile as they wonder aloud if the return of the wayward son would complicate life for his family. They hint that life is easier for everyone if Daud remains at a distance.

The real question to be answered, say the cognoscenti, is 'Why on earth would Daud want to return?' 'What would he do in Bangladesh?' There are hundreds of educated Bangladeshis lining up outside foreign embassies in Dhaka every day, hoping to emigrate, who would envy him. Daud has at his fingertips the resources and networks which other artists of the region long for, but never attain. He is also a well-known figure, not a celebrity in the Taslima mould, but a genuine intellectual who still receives his share of invitations to literary festivals; he has a well-paid, interesting job, and pursues his writing vigorously. He visits Calcutta, they point out, and he could easily slip into Dhaka if the Government gave him the nod—that's how things are done in Bangladesh.

Of course, he would have to behave himself. And he may not care to unravel his own personal mythology: Daud and his shadow are inseparable; even the tiny fabrications have become real.

Daud's and Taslima's lives have both come adrift from their moorings because of words they once put down on paper which were used by the mullah-minded to create havoc and unsettle the government of the day. A few lines in a poem sealed Daud's fate, and with Taslima? Ah, well with Taslima, the waters are always muddier; her audience always more unforgiving: there were her columns, her protest novel *Lajja*; her 'mirror, mirror on the wall' interviews she so loved to give and her own personal style.

Taslima and Daud also have Big Brother Ananda Bazar in common, for both writers have at one time or the other been clients of the publishing giant. The signature campaigns mounted on their behalf in Calcutta—in Taslima's case bringing her immediate international attention—have been orchestrated by prominent and respected intellectuals, with the same gener- ous figure of Professor Shankar Roy acting as a catalyst. Yet there is always an Ananda presence somewhere in the background ready to press the button which starts the magic lantern media show.

Unfortunately for Daud, he came to grief in a pre-Rushdie era, in the days of the Cold War, when Communism was the great foe and nobody outside the Muslim world knew the meaning of the word fatwa.

✥

The Taslima 'Carnival in Deutschland' lasted almost four months, before it began to implode. 'The man who ruined the party,' as my informants called him, came from within their own ranks—that was the pity of it all, they complained. When it all began, Burkhard Mueller-Ullrich was a freelance journalist, but when we met three years later, in September 1998, he had risen in the world and was now the director of *Kultur heute* at Deutschlandfunk (German Radio) in Cologne.

None of his colleagues seemed to bear him any grudges now that the Taslima affair was at an end. Initially, the reaction had been hostile, with many labelling him a conservative trouble maker, but then journalists have appalling long-term memories and over a beer, or a *Schnaps* or two, or three, are given to shaking their heads and laughing over matters that at the time had them manning the barricades. 'Just part of being a journalist,' they say with a shrug.

He was not an easy man to track down, but the train trip from Berlin to the famous cathedral city of Cologne gave me time to put together the disjointed pieces of Taslima's timetable in Germany. From her Swedish days, the author was an inveterate traveller moving from one invitation to the next: Berlin, Munich, Stuttgart and back to Berlin, the Taslima caravan kept moving ahead, never staying too long in one place.

Taslima left Sweden for Germany in early June 1995, hoping that she would not have to return. She arrived in Berlin with great fanfare for a twelve months' stay, invited by the Minister for Foreign Affairs, Dr Klaus Kinkel, as a guest of DAAD, the German Academic Exchange Service. Through DAAD, the Government co-sponsored a program conceptualised and partly funded by the International Parliament of Writers (IPW), whose inaugural president was Salman Rushdie and later president, Nobel Prize winner Wole Soyinka.

Taslima was granted a rent-free apartment and a monthly stipend of DM 3,100 (US$1,500); the State Police would watch over her. Fees for certain of her speaking engagements, which took her in and out of Germany, added substantially to her income. According to Gabi Gleichmann, she also received payment for many of her media interviews—while some people were shocked by this, others showed more understanding of the expenses faced by a writer in her position. For the time being at least, Taslima had shored up her finances.

Taslima and an Algerian writer were the first authors to come to Berlin, under the 'Cities of Asylum' concept supported by the IPW, but as the Algerian had visa problems, Taslima was the star of the evening at her first press conference, where she was introduced by the exuberant Frenchman Christian Salmon.

Her legal status was based on a German law which grants certain foreigners the right to enter and stay in Germany for reasons of international law or urgent humanitarian or political reasons. She was issued with a special permit giving her legal entitlement to reside in Germany as a foreigner for one year and also entitled her to enter any of the other member countries of the Schengen Agreement: France, Belgium, the Netherlands and Luxembourg, and Spain and Portugal. Taslima's residency permit was silver in her pocket and the German Government and the Berlin Senate appeared, at this stage, to have done everything to help the author.

A friendly letter, dated 27 December 1995, signed by the minister of external affairs tried to allay her concerns. Taslima, who was clearly edgy about her future in Germany, was reminded that the Minister had first welcomed her the previous summer in his role as President of the Council of the European Union. Her fears were groundless, he told her; an extension was possible at any time should she so desire. The minister assured her that he would always support her interests, as he soon proved by providing visas for her brothers to visit her in Germany. However, in less than two years, the welcome mat had vanished and Taslima's visa was not extended.

The German Government regarded Taslima's stay as an important benchmark in their cultural policy and were eager to do everything they could to promote her artistic well-being. But they were still faced with a grave security risk and although they refused to go overboard like the French, before she moved into her Berlin flat in Storwinkel Strasse, Halensee, two security experts and one public servant inspected her flat. Their report contained a detailed description of the apartment house: entrance doors, locks, a suspicious-looking pantry opening and the observation that the roof could be reached from the building next door. Recommendations were made to minimise any risk of rifle attacks from outside: fortified windows; alarm systems with emergency buttons in each room and an attack alarm connected to Police Emergency.

Taslima had other important allies inside Germany: Alice Schwarzer, editor and publisher of feminist *Emma* magazine; the Ahriman Verlag, a small prickly publisher given to exuberant campaign politics; Christian John from the Humanist German Organisation; Taslima's German publishers, Hoffmann and Campe, in Hamburg and, of course, PEN centres throughout Germany. Altogether they made up an impressive army and placed at her feet their national and international networks, and media contacts.

Significantly, the humanist and atheist cartel began to give Taslima the emotional support and understanding that she had seen very little of up till now. They welcomed her as one of their own and made few demands. Their expectations were different to the European writing communities, and they refrained from comparing her with Salman Rushdie. Taslima was at ease in their company and behaved naturally, they shared the same dialogue and she could always trust them; they eased her gently into the international rationalist movement and so began the rounding off of her humanist education.

Other groups, far less altruistic than the humanists, used her to further their own causes. There is no evidence showing that she objected to this, but then again, there is also no evidence indicating that she was ever aware that she was being used.

From the beginning she was flooded with invitations to give speeches and make appearances throughout Germany, her invitations were coordinated mainly by DAAD, who communicated with Taslima in English. DAAD provided the infrastructure support which the beleaguered Gabi Gleichmann and Swedish PEN had either lacked, or decided not to foster.

Taslima Nasreen was enjoying the sweet taste of celebrity status afresh. Sweden, she thought, was behind her and in Germany she could make a new beginning. Her German reception was tremendous and largely orchestrated by the *taz* newspaper. Everyone knew the name Taslima Nasreen in June 1995, yet by 13 December 1997, only two and a half years later, the *Frankfurter Allgemeine* (*FAZ*), the country's leading national paper, published an article by Uwe Schmitt stating bluntly that no one seemed interested in her any more. 'Old Courage Counts for Little, The Fate of a Dissident', subtitled 'Why hardly anyone wants to know anything about, or cares anything at all, about Taslima Nasreen.' By then Taslima was back in Stockholm, where we met a month before the *FAZ* article came out.

The carnival was over. It had started to wind down in the autumn of 1995, only four months after her arrival. There are as many different versions of what really happened as there are civil libertarians claiming to have rescued Taslima. The truth is buried somewhere, but digging just reveals more and more bodies. Was Mueller-Ullrich some kind of deadly print tarantula? Had Taslima choked on her own mythology? Was she brought down by her enemies, as she claimed? Or was there a more complicated morality tale, where Taslima had been complicit in her own downfall?

Before my arrival in Cologne, slowly, and with much dipping into my English–German dictionary, I'd read sections of Mueller-Ullrich's book *Media Fairy Tales: Perpetrators Out of Conviction in Journalism*. The book contained a full chapter on Nasreen entitled 'False Martyr—Taslima Nasreen and her friends.' Published in 1996, it was based on his newspaper articles of the year before. Most of his criticism focussed on her book *Lajja*, which was published in Germany in early 1995. *Lajja* was not a commercial success, he claimed, although it was well publicised in Germany. Later he told me in a typical Mueller-Ullrich aside, that 'in Germany you are never given the sales figures. In France they tell you the figures, but they are usually false!'

Mueller-Ullrich's critique went right to the heart of the matter. Her book's central argument, he said, gave a totally distorted image of Bangladesh as lying somewhere between Rwanda and Iran: a country of massacres, horror and corruption; a land fallen prey to Islamic extremism. This, he explained, was the reason for its grandiose reception in the West, by those who saw themselves 'as protagonists of the Good in an evil world.'

'Only by representing Bangladesh as a country of injustice was she able to become accredited in Europe as a persecuted writer.'

As journalists they had all been hoodwinked, he argued. Writers and intellectuals in Bangladesh had kept their distance and this should have suggested, at the very least, some caution on their part. This had never happened, he maintained, because the entire human rights machinery was in full swing to rescue the allegedly persecuted woman ... to save her from a Bangladesh not only terrorised but dominated by Islamist bogey men, which had little to do with reality and everything to do with a hysterical projection by 'Western do-gooders'. He called her 'a false martyr', accusing her of plagiarism, greed and a love of self-publicity.

Mueller-Ullrich's cynicism peaked when he wrote that if Nasreen's trial was ever completed, 'and she was sentenced to a quite insignificant fine, perhaps the world audience might sit up and take notice of the grandiose swindle they'd all been taken in by.' He accused her 'Occidental sponsors and business partners' of creating a 'Taslima *Taumel*' or frenzy. 'They ignore facts they must be aware of,' he insisted. He accused the German culture industry of manufacturing a shining, but largely fictitious, story of courage and morality. He asked DAAD embarrassing questions about their criteria for awarding scholarships, and when they replied that Taslima's grant was for humanitarian and not literary reasons, his tone grew sharper.

Mueller-Ullrich's attack posed a serious threat to Taslima's German supporters, because he was a maverick: a journalist who stood outside Taslima's circle of admirers. When other journalists laughed, and dubbed him 'the man who ruined the party', they were admitting that he was the first German who dared debunk the official Taslima mythology. Or as the postmodernists would have it, Mueller-Ullrich was deconstructing a fairy story of grand proportions.

Taslima and her publishers were incensed. Hoffmann and Campe's publicity department called his *SZ* article 'shameless', warning their author in a letter dated 27 September 1995 that the media discussion would continue for sure until the 1995 Frankfurt Book Fair the following month. Care was taken that her response to Mueller-Ullrich's article was widely circulated.

By the time I stepped off the train in Cologne, I knew what to expect. I hounded Burkhard Mueller-Ullrich by telephone until he gave in: when I slyly repeated the open sesame line of 'They tell me you're the man who spoilt the party', he finally agreed to see me. What transpired was well worth the price of a train ticket and three days' accommodation in a small hotel, on the outskirts of the city, full of technical salesmen with serious faces and modest expense accounts, gearing themselves for one of Cologne's massive trade conventions.

From the beginning we negotiated an odd-sounding but perfectly sensible way of communicating with one another. We used a bilingual format. My passive German was very good, which meant that I could understand German but had difficulties generating the vocabulary for anything more complex than a social conversation or securing my daily needs. Nothing is more frustrating or destructive of one's self-esteem than understanding a complex discourse but not being able to respond at a level commensurate with your native language facility. Floundering in a foreign language perjures your own identity. You end up sounding like a child—and not a very bright one at that.

Mueller-Ullrich's problem was exactly the same. He could understand English well, but was handicapped when it came to carrying on the kind of literary–political discussion we were both relishing. The solution was simple. He spoke to me in German, and I answered him in English. For two afternoons we held a discussion with subtitles; we introduced humour into our discourse, cracked jokes and understood one another perfectly well.

Mueller-Ullrich was a newspaper addict: *Figaro, The London Times, The Independent, The Guardian, Liberation, Le Monde,* and all the German dailies were stacked untidily on chairs, his desk was chaos, with files sprawled everywhere. Grey filing cabinets were crammed full of clippings and articles, and from their innards he pulled out more and more files, like a Levantine merchant showing off his silk carpets to a bedazzled customer. His archives had me gaping: an impressive El Dorado, all about Taslima Nasreen, and the reaction to his own articles—all placed at my disposal. Here was a man who enjoyed playing detective, who stored precious papers away for another day. He seemed pleased that the day had finally arrived and that he was meeting someone as addicted to the story of Taslima as he had once been. Although three years had passed, he still kept 'in touch' with Taslima, certainly not as vigilantly as in the past, but the Mueller-Ullrich eye was still watchful.

Against this background of organized mayhem sat Burkhard Mueller-Ullrich (I had started to think of him as BMU by then) elegantly clad in a charcoal-grey three-piece suit with a light grey white-dotted tie. Although he wore the uniform of an executive, he didn't look like a broadcast executive or the kind of man who'd been an inveterate suit wearer all his life.

BMU thought of himself as an investigative journalist in the field of culture. 'A man who digs for the truth,' was how he carefully described himself. He probably had all the tenacity of a pit bulldog, who, once he had a good grip on your leg, would not let go. For more than twenty years he'd been a freelance journalist, but two years ago, he moved into broadcasting journalism.

'Less money,' he said cryptically, 'but much more influence.'

He was a tall slim man at that mysterious time in some men's lives—which women know too well only lasts for a few years—when they defy their real age. He could easily have been in his mid-thirties, but was probably older. His straight dark brown hair was cut short with the kind of wispy fringe favoured by some German men—why I'm not exactly sure; perhaps there are a lot of Prince Valiant fans in Germany. Altogether he was a poised, engaging man, and underneath the surface one sensed a certain doggedness which might easily be mistaken for pigheadedness by his foes. Plainly, in his day, BMU had collected many foes.

Before he began his investigative journey, BMU knew nothing about Bangladesh; he was not an international traveller, like many of his colleagues, but more of a local European voyager. He first heard of Taslima indirectly through the French press, but had no direct links with RSF, the leading media human rights group.

French writer Jean-Edern Hallier (now deceased) was the first journalist to criticise Taslima in the French media in late 1994 and he was more than happy to share his materials with BMU. Mueller-Ullrich described his French colleague as 'a man with extreme views . . . always against mainstream opinion'. Others labelled him 'a professional polemicist', but Mueller-Ullrich always liked this 'scandal type', as the Frenchman was often called by his German detractors. Jean-Edern Hallier was also the owner of a French newspaper *L'Idiot International* and in 1989 had become embroiled in the Rushdie affair by publishing *Satanic Verses*, breaching French law, and incurring a fine of 500 francs for each unauthorised copy sold, after which he renounced his intention of selling more.

One day a thick pile of briefing papers and press clippings from Bangladeshi newspapers arrived on BMU's desk, passed on by Jean-Edern. His sources were excellent, especially the French diplomatic briefings which BMU had translated into German. BMU recognised at once that he was looking at original material that gave him a counter version to the orthodox Taslima story so far in circulation.

'The opinions were different; the voices were different and I started to think, that the people over there [in Bangladesh] must have a better idea of what is going on than we have here!' BMU checked Jean-Edern's facts for himself and was convinced. He adopted the same position and wrote his first critical article for the Swiss paper *Die Weltwoche* in December 1994.

At the outset Taslima and Bangladesh were of little interest to him. What fascinated him most was 'examining how the media; how my colleagues—indeed the entire culture industry—functioned. How journalists were sometimes carried away, acting out of conviction or a desire to prove their solidarity with a just cause.' He found himself under attack, and people started calling him a muck raker, but as he said with a gleam in his eye, '*das macht Spass*,' 'that's always fun; it goes with the job.'

But his troubles were just beginning. In early 1995, at the time of *Lajja's* release in Germany, he wrote a large feature article on Taslima but had trouble getting it printed. Although the article had been commissioned by *Die Zeit*, for whom he'd been writing as a freelancer for ten years, the new chief editor refused to print it because he didn't share Mueller-Ullrich's opinion. BMU was staggered. For fourteen years he'd written for the *Frankfurter Rundshau*, a left liberal paper, and his articles were always printed although they were not left-leaning.

'This had never happened to me before; in the past an editor might say to me, "Are you sure of your facts?" But if it was well written and well argued, they would print it. Now for the first time in my career,' he said, 'I had the feeling that I wouldn't get this article through.'

A long time passed before it was printed, he'd finished writing the piece in early summer but it was not published until early autumn in September 1995. By then *Lajja* had been out on the bookshelves for at least six months.

His second article was finally published in the *Badische Zeitung* on 24 August 1995 and a month later an extended version printed in the *Süddeutsche Zeitung* (*SZ*), one of Germany's leading regional papers, which also had a large readership in other parts of Germany. 'I was lucky,' Mueller-Ullrich said, 'that these papers had the courage to take a stand and protest.'

Mueller-Ullrich readily admitted that he had followed his French colleague's blueprint. 'Jean had the original idea and I was more the copyist,' he smiled. 'My critics called me a "revisionist",' he said. 'Jean was definitely more famous; he did it first and he did it much better!'

He was being modest, for BMU had gone beyond his colleague's sources and collected his own materials for the *SZ* article. By now he was also interested in Bangladesh and so he visited the Bangladesh Embassy thinking they'd be glad of the opportunity to tell their side to a German journalist. He found the embassy under-resourced and totally unprepared for any public relations opportunities.

'Month after month,' he said, 'Taslima was affecting what shaped people's opinions on Bangladesh. But never once were we telephoned by the embassy, who really should have been interested in feeding us something!'

'Imagine, for instance, if the same thing had happened to the USA,' he said. 'Suppose there'd been an anti-USA campaign like the anti-Bangladesh campaign, propaganda attacks, not against Christian fundamentalists but against the country. The US Embassy would have flooded journalists with materials; they'd have run a counter-campaign and distributed information specially prepared for the media: glossy, beautifully written and well-presented pieces, putting forward their claims.' Bangladesh, however, was not a public relations superpower. He visited the embassy to hear for himself and soon discovered that things work differently in Bangladesh.

Perhaps if BMU had ever travelled outside Europe, his expectations might have been more realistic. Yet he was the first to admit that his previous investigations, even his holidays, had been confined to European cities and resorts. He'd never been exposed to 'the third world', otherwise he might not have said so seriously, 'They are not good at PR,' forcing me to hide a smile because his disappointment was so earnest. In any public relations contest between Taslima, her supporters and the Bangladeshi Government, the Taslima coalition won hands down.

'It was hard to get anything out of them, ' he said. 'I was given some poor-quality fact sheets. This was an indicator for me that the information they had given me was likely to be accurate.'

He went there four times and on each occasion it was like pulling teeth: the usual information that journalists were handed ad nauseam was simply unavailable. 'Nothing glossy, nothing dressed up,' he repeated, shaking his head at the lack of spin doctoring.

'I thought to myself, that if they're so bad at PR, they're probably bad at lying too!' He grimaced, making it clear that he was serious even though it sounded comical. 'What they gave me was so primitive that it had to be the truth.'

The reaction to his articles was tremendous. Taslima responded with the help of the Freiburg-based Ahriman Publishers in the *Badische Zeitung* on 31 August 1995. Under German media legislation, conditions allow those holding opposing views to write a reply, which helps avoid further legal action. He wasn't sure if Taslima had written the article herself, but suspected that Ahriman may have had a hand in it. Why the German publishers of *Lajja*, Hoffmann and Campe, stayed in the background is curious.

Taslima's response was badly thought out and badly executed, with an air of desperation about the text: it swung wildly from one point to the next trying to find holes in BMU's arguments. And it's true that there were one or two factual errors and an occasional weak interpretation, which could have been focussed on to advance her case while weakening his attack. In trying to shoot down everything he said, the English version sounded garbled. An edited account was finally printed leaving out her references to how some Germans pretended that there were no atrocities against the Jews. Her rebuttal may have landed an occasional punch, but BMU remained standing at the end of the round.

From the time of his second and third articles, Mueller-Ullrich was delighted to note a change in the current Taslima discourse as reported in the print media. 'It shows what can happen when a prominent newspaper like the *SZ* takes a stand and says, "Hey, stop and listen!" From this moment on, you could notice how commentators adjusted their language in their reports.'

Words like 'exile' changed to 'self-exile'; Taslima was now and then described as a 'controversial author' no longer automatically 'the persecuted author'. 'There was a complete change in tone,' he said. The pattern of Taslima media stories was beginning to change.

What delighted him most of all, I think, was the *FAZ* article printed 26 September 1995 which followed on from Taslima's response. He couldn't disguise his pride that such a reputable paper had taken note of his arguments.

'What a nice surprise!' he said, like a man more used to being stood in the corner than ever being singled out as the teacher's pet. It was a good article.' A big paper like the *FAZ* did not usually comment on another story carried by a rival paper, especially in terms of agreeing with it rather than disagreeing. 'I made a lot of mileage out of that,' he remembered fondly.

✦

My question made me sound like a first-year student in journalism, all starry-eyed but not very knowledgeable. 'If journalists are the gatekeepers to reality, don't they have a duty to be absolutely positive about their facts?' I asked.

'With your historian's background, you'll find it sad, I know,' he began smoothly. I raised an eyebrow, waiting for the bad news; he sounded as if he was gearing up to pacify me. 'But we journalists don't have time to look back: every day, new things come in. It's always like that. We don't have time to check the news items we get over the telex. Who can do it? But what you do is use your nose and your commonsense to prevent you from getting carried away.'

Background knowledge must also be essential, I insisted, for it was becoming clear to me that the Western media's ignorance about Bangladesh was staggering. Yet their influence in shaping people's opinions about

Bangladesh had been deadly. The media relied on short-term memory, and many younger reporters had a woeful understanding of history and politics outside their own borders.

Burkhard Mueller-Ullrich protested once again that it was an impossible task: pressures of the job, constant deadlines, the solid mass of information coming through each hour. I remained half convinced, but I had a sober picture now of BMU, the journalist, trying to halt and think while afloat in the maelstrom of information and misinformation.

✧

BMU had turned his back on the Taslima cult, but glancing around the walls of his office the next day, the man behind the journalist seemed as vulnerable to mythology and fairy stories as anyone else: the intrepid reporter might well be a closet romantic. Not some shabby old affair to be hidden away in the dark, but a full-blown declaration of romantic love. Out in the open where everyone could see, was a montage of Princess Diana photos stuck to his cupboard door, turning it into a shrine of remembrance.

I tackled him ferociously thinking I might trip him, just once!

But Mueller-Ullrich stuck to his fantasy. 'I loved her a lot, but she was with the wrong man,' he said as he defended himself, staring back at me po-faced. 'She should have chosen me as her husband and she wouldn't have had all those problems. She wouldn't have had bulimia—I'm a very good cook and she would have loved my cooking. But I never had the chance to tell her and now it's too late.' His delivery was straight: droll humour at its best.

From Princess Di to Professor Annemarie Schimmel seemed a grand leap of the imagination. Once again Mueller-Ullrich found himself writing against the mainstream.

He knew all about 'the Schimmel affair', as it was called; he was a fan of the Frau Professor. The Peace Prize of the German Book Trade, awarded annually during the Frankfurt Book Fair by the Association of the German Book Trade (Book Sellers and Publishers), was the most prestigious event on the cultural calendar. The winner in 1995 was Professor Annemarie Schimmel, in honour of her life's work towards promoting a better understanding of Islam—at least that's what she believed. The award is more of a cultural honour than a literary award for a single book: it is given for a body of work and a life-time commitment towards humanitarian ideals.

The crux of the problem was that the award—essentially a very political cultural prize—was being given to a very apolitical scholar with Iranian connections, God help her!

I became drawn into examining the Schimmel affair because the debate fell into what I called 'Taslima territory'. The same players who ardently supported Taslima were the same people who attacked Annemarie Schimmel. The latter was hounded by fundamentalists of a different strain: Enlightenment Fundamentalists, with Taslima recruited to their ranks. Just as I had tried to explore the mindset of the Bearded Ones in Dhaka, I found it necessary to understand the thinking of Taslima's European allies.

⁂

Literary awards, and cultural honours, are a minefield: no matter how carefully one treads, a bomb will go off, leaving the battlefield strewn with literary carcasses. The judging panels, whose in-house politics and final choices are as ceremonial and secretive as a meeting of Freemasons, rarely satisfy everybody—rows of great passion surface. The keen nose of bloodhound dissenters will sniff through all the evidence if their favourite doesn't win—sometimes they strike pay dirt.

Taslima Nasreen was no stranger to this kind of brouhaha and knew what it felt like to be targeted as 'unworthy'. As the winner of the Sakharov Human Rights Award in 1994, and at the height of her popularity her triumph was howled down in certain quarters. Even Sakharov's widow was unhappy, it was reported. European protesters wrote to the judges calling for a review of the decision, others alleged some sleight of hand. Previous winners had included Nelson Mandela and Alexander Dubček, the former Czechoslovak leader. This was the second time in Taslima Nasreen's career that a public row of this kind occurred. In 1992 she won an important Indian literary award; but hometown critics in Dhaka denounced her as a plagiarist and the Bengali equivalent of a *homo novus*, an upstart.

In Germany a number of Taslima's allies mounted a campaign trying to prevent Schimmel from receiving the prize. Taslima, invited by her supporters to join in the anti-Schimmel campaign, jumped on board three months after she arrived in Germany. Her name and anti-fundamentalist credentials were used to validate the attack on Schimmel and she gave numerous interviews and addressed rallies.

'She [Schimmel] defends fundamentalists,' Taslima said. 'It is a shame to give her that prize. It's a shame for all of Germany. This was a terrible shock for those of us who fight fundamentalism.'

The time had come for Taslima to pay her dues, although I believe she needed no coaxing, for by now, she saw it as her mission-in-exile, to speak out against Muslim extremists and their fellow travellers whenever she could. Taslima needed a surrogate for her all-consuming rage.

'What does she do with all that rage now?' her Swedish publisher, Svante Wyler, had once asked me. Here lay part of the answer. Belonging to the international anti-Islamist movement is important to Taslima's psyche, providing a target for her pent-up fury and sense of injustice that she needs to propel her writing. (Only since the September 11 tragedy has the term *Islamist* come into wider usage. In the twentieth century the term *fundamentalist* was in vogue and was synonymous with militant extremist Muslims whom in the twenty-first century we now label *Islamists*.)

BMU confessed that he liked Professor Schimmel for reasons he found hard to explain; 'Because she's such a little woman, a stubborn little woman; she's over seventy, and very tough, with a good sense of humour and a wealth of funny stories.' (Frau Professor Schimmel died in 2003.)

A bit of a strange fish, the Mueller-Ullrich, I thought. . . . He was loyal to his favourites like Schimmel, and swore that he would do anything for Salman Rushdie, whom he eulogised as a magnificent man and writer, but as for Taslima . . . he remained unforgiving. He couldn't pardon her for not being a good writer. '*Sie ist einfach schlecht*', 'She's simply bad,' he said dismissively.

I thought he needed a lecture from PEN activists, who always emphasise that defending freedom of speech has nothing to do with the quality of a writer's work: in PEN's eyes there are no 'good' or 'bad' writers—only writers at risk.

But Professor Annemarie Schimmel brought out his sense of humour and a chivalry that took me by surprise. Yes, he agreed with all the reports which proved she was very naive and not at all political. And of course she was most likely an apologist for former Pakistani presidents, the late Zia ul-Huq and the man he had hanged, Zulifiqar Bhutto. No, it certainly wasn't fashionable, but he didn't give a damn and couldn't stop himself from liking this politically incorrect woman, the grand old lady of German orientalism.

'She wrote books about Zia and Bhutto and was friendly with both men: that's the kind of woman she is,' he said, pulling a funny face, as he handed me a thick file on "The Annemarie Schimmel Affair", 'and when I talked with her, she told me that it was so sad that one killed the other—and she meant it!' We both burst out laughing at Schimmel's lament and the incongruity of life.

The Frau Professor appeared to love all things Islamic and that was her undoing. For fifty years she'd been translating and writing about Persian and Urdu poetry, about Sufi mysticism and Islamic theology. But times had changed: the people she had empathised with for more than fifty years, and the cultures and the places she loved, had become highly politicised, almost, it seemed, without her even noticing. Her scholastic ideas belonged to an earlier generation and contained a strange mixture of romanticism and religiosity. As a Catholic she understood the meaning of faith, which bonded her to orthodox Muslims.

Her main crime was her criticism of Salman Rushdie and her failure to speak out publicly against Khomeini's fatwa. There were minor misdemeanours: a street named after her in Lahore; visits to Turkey and Iran and the honours she received; her habit of wearing traditional clothing when in Muslim countries, including the 'dreaded' headscarf. Benazir Bhutto had been one of her students at Harvard University, but perhaps that was not a crime.

BMU was not the only journalist who smelt trouble. Middle East foreign correspondent Gudrun Harrer stood back, watching everything with a growing feeling of unease. The Austrian-based journalist felt uncomfortable over the tactics used by some of the die hards on the anti-Schimmel side. In an article penned for the Rushdie International Defence Committee Newsletter, *Rushdie Alert*, October 1995, she outlined a critique of both sides. While there were some highly respectable individuals protesting the award, there were others involved—'people you just wouldn't want to fight the same cause with,' she said.

'In Germany we have a saying,' she wrote, 'if you lay down with dogs you get up with fleas. This is just what happened to Annemarie Schimmel. . . . [She is] the prototype of the German orientalist who thought it would be enough not to say anything. Talking with Zia ul-Huq, the late President of Pakistan, about the weather, food and his children was OK: after all, he was a nice person. But this is how you catch fleas.'

On the other hand, she argued, turning her attention to Rushdie, 'Can he who fights against sacrosanct beliefs be declared sacrosanct?'

Campaign journalism is all about taking to the barricades, but the barricades can be a dangerous place. Passion is overtaken by aggression and people make monsters of each other. The trouble begins when you raise your rifle, peer through the sights and see only a target: the person has disappeared.

After her nomination was made public, the Frau Professor gave an interview where the inevitable question arose about the Ayatollah Khomeini's state-sanctioned bounty on Rushdie. The interview turned out to be a disaster: sides were taken and the hostilities began.

She soon became the target of an unofficial, anti-fundamentalist, pro-Rushdie coalition. At the start, Ahriman publishers led the campaign; a long four months' crusade, starting from when the news leaked out until the award ceremony later that year; it was a dirty business, as campaigns claiming the high moral ground often become. It lasted long enough and was massive enough to make her life miserable, and the attacks clearly hurt Annemarie Schimmel.

'It was like a witch hunt,' she said in an interview. 'Like I was being flayed alive. . . . a no-win situation.' Ahriman eventually lost credibility because of their vigilante style; others distanced themselves and took over the cause.

Emma magazine assumed a lead role. The magazine's editor, leading feminist Alice Schwarzer, was a long-time exponent of campaign journalism, famous for her stand against pornography. *Emma* is the best-known feminist magazine in Germany, a feminist version of *Time Magazine*. Founded in January 1977, 'this magazine by women, for women' has a circulation of 100,000. Worldwide, it is the last autonomous feminist mass circulation periodical—and a unique publication.

One afternoon, after leaving BMU's office, I called in at *Emma's*' headquarters in Alteburger Strasse, Cologne. From there I made my way to the FrauenMediaTurm, founded in 1984 by Schwarzer as the 'The Feminist Archives and Documentation Centre'. Since 1994, the centre has been situated in Cologne's famous Bayentower, an ancient structure and famous landmark of the city for almost six centuries. There I met with a senior editor of the magazine, whom I shall call Elsa here.

Elsa was slim and serious, an overworked woman with short cropped hair and enormous commitment to her style of feminism. She looked like a tough campaign veteran, everything about her seemed intense, and she was clearly not going to be lulled into lowering the tower drawbridge to an unknown visitor by making any asides. She towed the official line, and Schwarzer would have been proud of her lieutenant; however, *Emma's* owner and editor was away on an author's tour promoting her recently published biography on actor Romy Schneider.

Today the FrauenMedienTurm holds the most comprehensive and technically best-equipped scientific archives on women's issues in German-speaking countries. It remains a great visionary achievement and covers the Early Women's Movement from the mid–nineteenth century, with its main emphasis on the New Women's Movement from 1971 onwards. More than 25,000 documents (books and essays), 333 clipping files, 2,000 leaflets and posters and 700 national/international titles of feminist press are held, with 2,000 new documents added to the data bank every year. 'The FrauenMediaTurm: A Place Where Women's History Makes History,' says the sign.

But *Emma* refused to let Professor Annemarie Schimmel make history, although it was only the third time in the award's annals that a German woman was honoured since it began in 1950.

Emma women have an opinion on most topics. One expects that from a leading feminist magazine; it would be disappointing if this were not the case, except there are times when their opinion is set in stone. Taslima must have felt at home with *Emma's* style: their audacity, their flair, their obstinacy. When the anti-fundamentalists circled Schimmel, ready to do battle with this running dog of regimes like Iran and Pakistan, Taslima smelt blood, like everyone else.

A year before the campaign against her began, Schimmel had commented on Taslima in a well-meant defence of Bangladesh and Islam, which included an injudicious and unscholarly mention of her three divorces. The letter to the editor published in *Die Zeit* in late August 1994, which called the author 'a brash young lady', was drawn to Taslima's attention. Reading Schimmel's letter three years after it was first written, her defence of Bangladesh sounds apologist, but it reflected the opinion of many Bangladeshis who, while they might be called conservative, were certainly not religious fanatics.

Out of the Schimmel debacle, some of the players who faced each other over the barricades emerged with their reputations and integrity intact: the German Humanists argued rationally as one would expect rationalists to do; Schimmel, who battled on with the support of the popular German president, Roman Herzog, kept her dignity; Taslima made a useful contribution without pillaring Schimmel—but some of the tactics employed by *Emma* magazine and the Ahriman guerillas, I thought, were shabby.

At the time, all of this was hidden from me. Only through meeting Elsa did some of the pieces come together. Normally these were women I would want on my side in any fight, yet there was an edge to their attack which concerned me. Schimmel was a nobody, they thought, plucked out of obscurity for political purposes, a signal that Germany wanted to be on good terms with trade delegations from Islamic countries. These accusations had some substance.

Emma and co. were shrewd fighters: on this occasion they publicly aligned themselves with Rushdie. While some called him privately the darling of the liberal right, this didn't prevent them from recruiting Rushdie's friends, like author Fay Weldon, to join the anti-Schimmel crush.

In that disastrous first interview which forced people to take sides, Schimmel voiced an understanding of the theological reasoning behind the Iranian fatwa and tried to convey how hurt most Muslims were by *The Satanic Verses*. In the eyes of many of her opponents, it was only a short move from understanding the fatwa to supporting the fatwa, and from this premise, they argued that she supported extremist (read terrorist) Islam.

The professor was her own worst enemy: her thoughtless criticism of Rushdie was her undoing. She was ridiculed by the press for saying that she had seen grown men in Iran crying over what he was supposed to have written in *The Satanic Verses*. Her attempts to explain the deep hurt many believing Muslims felt backfired. She missed the point that people had little sympathy for Muslims who could criticise Rushdie's book—even cry over the perceived insults—without ever having read it! *The Satanic Verses* is a book which may go down in history as more talked about than read. Salman Rushdie, on 8 May 1995, wondered aloud if she had ever read his book. 'It is interesting,' he said, in a German Press Agency news report, 'that I can insult a man who has been dead for almost fourteen hundred years.'

Schimmel's immediate apology to the British author, for any misunderstanding, carried little weight with Rushdie or her critics. She argued that the less overt pressure applied, the faster the problem would disappear, and that Iran was beginning to realise how isolated it was becoming in the international world. Her critics rejected this argument.

On looking back at this affair in years to come, a forum organised by the Humanist Association of Germany may stand out as one of the few occasions when reason prevailed. A majority of the panellists that night praised Schimmel's scholastic record, emphasising that she had never expressed any support for religious fundamentalism, but concluded the prize was not suited to her.

The Book Traders Association said she had been honoured because her explanations of Islam helped eliminate the sinister image of fanatical hordes. 'All well and good,' said panellist Sabina Kebir, 'but events like the Gulf War are not about religion—they are about oil and politics. It's absurd to try to understand Islamic societies only through the Qur'an.'

Taslima, also on the dais that night, was described as the star of the evening. She was puzzled, she said. Why had the German Government given the prize to Schimmel when they also gave protection to those persecuted by fundamentalists [like herself].

Jens Jessen, a reporter from the *FAZ* raised the most intriguing question of all: 'Can there be peace between Enlightenment fundamentalism and religious fundamentalism—between two such antagonistic fundamentalisms?' That, Jessen said, was the question of questions in the whole Schimmel debate.

I was about to explore some of the tensions Jessen was talking about.

Elsa and I were alone in the women's tower. I'd really come to *Emma* to talk about Taslima, not Schimmel; the Frau Professor had been an unexpected bonus. There were a few questions I hoped Elsa could answer, all to do with an exclusive interview her boss had done with Taslima in May 1995.

We sat drinking tea and I thanked her for sending me the *Emma* materials on Nasreen and their special edition against Schimmel. I was excited at the chance to talk to an *Emma* woman. As one feminist to another I expected that we would get along like a house on fire.

Ninety minutes later I left feeling disturbed: to be more precise, the hair on the back of my neck was standing up. In spite of BMU's comments, up to now I'd remained neutral about the Schimmel affair and was still feeling my way through papers and personalities. Yet when Elsa recounted how she and her friends had carefully examined every piece of writing, every single comment made by Schimmel—radio interview, or scholarly book or essay, it made no difference—looking for what, they never said exactly, but I imagined anything they could hang her with—my stomach turned. It sounded like the Inquisition. Was freedom of speech, in their eyes, only a one-way street?

Their rigour left nothing to chance. Team Elsa also examined her CV, and made a discovery. Schimmel, a brilliant student who had enrolled at university when she was sixteen, and completed her PhD at the age of nineteen, began working soon after as a translator of Middle Eastern languages at the ministry of foreign affairs in Berlin in 1943. Her critics hinted that this made her a Nazi sympathiser. 'It was better than being drafted into the army,' Schimmel answered back in an interview.

The atmosphere between Elsa and myself started to cool after I began asking questions about the famous Schwarzer–Taslima interview, published in *Emma*. I was amazed to hear that no interpreters were used and that German-speaking Alice Schwarzer spoke no English, but was fluent in French—while Taslima spoke Bengali, limited English, but no German or French. How on earth had they communicated? Elsa was very vague, but her boss, she said, was an experienced interviewer used to empathising and using body language to communicate—her interviews were famous for their special intimate quality (including mind-reading, I thought to myself).

In an effort to strike common ground, I started telling Elsa about the experiences of immigrant Muslim women in Australia, assuming that there must be parallels with Turkish women in Germany. As an international feminist, and a supporter of Taslima, I thought Elsa must be interested in all minority women. I was wrong, or else I misunderstood her. Elsa's response was strange: neither a flicker of the eyelashes nor a shake of the head, no sign of a '*Ja*' or '*Nein*', just a cold unblinking stare as if nothing I said registered.

I withdrew from the tower, feeling disturbed. Even in Pakistan, when I walked into the lion's den and talked to Islamist women's groups, I'd opened up a dialogue of sorts. They fiercely disagreed with me when I said there was nothing in the Qur'an about women covering their heads, or their arms, or their wrists, but at least they responded: we argued, we disagreed, we tried to convince each other but I was not shut out. 'Oh, sister, you are wrong!' they'd cry, shaking their heads. If they thought I was going to burn in hell, at least they were polite enough to keep it to themselves.

What did it feel like to be so absolutely sure about almost everything, just like the fundamentalist women? I bit my tongue—'Muslim fundamentalist women'—I told myself, for it was clear that the word 'fundamentalist' could be levelled at 'liberated' European women as well.

But *Emma* and I had not disagreed on everything. 'What interests stand behind Schimmel's nomination?' the magazine asked, first pointing the finger at what many feminists around the world called the 'unholy political alliance' between the Catholic Church and ultra-orthodox Islamic nations. There were other interests as well, they hinted, influencing the Schimmel nomination—political and economic interests.

The anti-Iranian feeling, which ignited the anti-Schimmel feeling, had a long history. This was no storm in a teacup, but at the time of my visit to Germany in 1998, I knew nothing of this. Two years later I stumbled across the missing pieces in a chronology put out by London-based Article 19, *Fiction, Fact and the Fatwa*, compiled by Carmel Bedford in August 1994.

In a nutshell, most of the German literary establishment and the bands of feminist and human rights activists were angry about the Iranian trade delegations traipsing in and out of Bonn, seeking closer trade ties with Germany, while their German hosts failed to confront the Iranians of the need to end the Rushdie–Iran stand-off. Although one can never be sure what was really being said in private meetings, it was seen as German duplicity at its worst, especially in light of what was happening on German soil.

On 27 May 1993, German officials in Karlsruhe confirmed that Iran was behind the killings in Berlin of four anti-Teheran Kurdish leaders. Five months later *Der Spiegel* magazine revealed that for the past two years Germany's intelligence services had sold Iran electronic equipment for es-pionage purposes and that an attempt to arrest a high-ranking intelligence chief connected to the Kurdish murders was prevented by the Government in Bonn.

Yet behind this background of terrorism, trade relations between Iran and Germany were never better. Germany's ongoing efforts to improve trade and diplomatic missions with Iran, Turkey and Middle East countries were paying dividends. In 1993 German exports to Iran reached DM 8 billion and by 1994 Germany had emerged as Iran's major trading partner. To help ease the way, in 1993, the Visiting Deputy Speaker of the Iran Parliament told his German counterpart in Bonn that Teheran was not sending any killer commando squad to carry out the death sentence on Salman Rushdie.

The ice had thawed since 26 September 1991, when the organisers of the Frankfurt Book Fair had withdrawn invitations to Iranian publishers after pressure from German publishers, authors and politicians in a show of symbolic politics. The Iranian presence was incompatible with the continuing death threats against Salman Rushdie. Günter Grass and two publishing houses objected to the insanity of punishing [censoring] authors in the name of freedom of speech and threatened to boycott the event, one assumes because of the futility of reacting to book bans by banning books from the 'other' side. Four days later—tit for tat—Iran banned German publishers from attending the Teheran International Book Fair. The Frankfurt ban continued for two years. But two years is a very long time in international relations and now it seemed that Germany and Iran were the best of friends.

This was the international, trade and diplomatic fog which incensed many Germans in May 1994. The rapprochement between the two countries explained part of the overall anger towards Schimmel a year later, although it would have been better directed at the German Government than at the shell-shocked professor of Oriental studies.

In the end her critics underestimated Schimmel's toughness and I began to understand why BMU admired the woman for refusing to recant. She withstood the jeering, the ridicule and the ageist and anti-intellectual comments. I was told by one activist that this high award had been given to a woman who, after all, 'only wrote books about dead languages'—citing Urdu and Persian. [sic].

The award ceremony went ahead as planned on 15 October 1995 in the famous St Paul's Church in Frankfurt, where, in spite of a number of people including publishers boycotting the ceremony and placard-waving demonstrators outside, the seats were filled and everything went off smoothly. I find it difficult to judge who won in the end. Nevertheless, with the support of popular president Roman Herzog, and a German media which became pro-Schimmel half way through the debate, the professor weathered the storm.

The awards which Nasreen, Schimmel and countless others receive are rarely ever just literary and human rights awards. Presenting the Sakharov Award to Taslima was meant as an act of political symbolism by the European Parliament to signal their disapproval of Islamic fundamentalism and their solidarity with public figures like Taslima. Ironically, because of the political climate in the early nineties, many European nations felt unable to acknowledge Rushdie—in effect giving awards and stipendiums to Taslima, symbolically made up for having to lower their heads over Salman Rushdie.

There are some observers who believe that presenting an award to Schimmel was also an act of political symbolism by a political establishment appalled at the effects of the Huntington Theory, named after the Harvard professor, which argues, amongst other things, that Islam has an inbuilt drive towards extremism. Huntington predicts an imminent clash of civilisations: it will come about because of an irreconcilable gulf of values and beliefs separating Islam from the Judaeo-Christian traditions of the liberal West. German politicians over decades had never seen Islam as the West's mortal foe and seized the chance to prove it. But as one commentator said, 'it's not so much the wrong prize winner as the wrong prize.'

Western societies in general have become increasingly worried about their Muslim minorities. Today they are uneasy about the association with terrorism that has, since September 11, become synonymous with the word Muslim. *One third of the world's Muslims, who number 1.2 billion now, live as minority members of secular countries; the prevailing narrative that Islam is violent and that Muslims have divided loyalties is growing in strength.*

After eighteen months in Germany, Taslima returned to Sweden. Her German visa was not renewed for reasons which are unclear, but it was evident that the friendly assurances of 1995 had melted away. Reading between the lines she was running into media criticism, bureaucratic intransigence and a waning of political will.

Added to this, a number of her stipendiums from regional German governments had dried up—money was a problem once again. During this period she also tried to enter the United States for an extended time, but had difficulties with the US Embassy in Berlin, which at first denied her a visa, she said, because they suspected her of wanting to work in the States.

'Now, it really surprises me when I see the door of the USA is not open for me,' she complained in a letter written in November 1995. The US Embassy in Bangladesh had been so helpful in the past and Taslima could not understand why there were suddenly problems. '[My] Swedish visa is already finished, my German visa will soon be finished—then where will I go?'

Back to Stockholm. And while she occasionally visited Berlin, Taslima found herself once more living in Sweden, through whose intervention is not known, but most likely with the help of the European Union. It was around this time that I first met Taslima in the winter of 1997.

Germany's leading national daily, the *FAZ*, attempted to find an answer to what had gone wrong in an article of 13 September 1997, by correspondent Uwe Schmitt, 'Fate of a Dissident'. She was written off in Germany, Schmitt reported, and was having trouble writing; she was depressed to be back in Sweden and wanted to return to Berlin. He told a story of a woman who had fallen out of fashion.

'For the time being she's worth only a few lines to Berlin newspapers,' Schmitt wrote. 'This is the woman who was virtually turned into a saint by some Western media. The image created was monstrous: half an atheist Mother Teresa, half a female Salman Rushdie. . . . When in autumn 1995 allegations of plagiarism and self promotion motivated by a desire for profit were made, some took bitter revenge and ostracised the "false martyr".'

What stopped her from returning home? Schmitt asked the author in his telephone interview. According to Taslima the Government of Bangladesh refused her entry, and would not agree to her conditions: to drop the allegations of hurting religious sentiment made against her in 1994 and to guarantee her safety.

'She is being punished,' Schmitt concluded in his article, 'for not being especially talented or charming, not excitingly beautiful, not even being remarkably endangered by Islamic obscurantists. Old courage holds no glamour.'

'Even Salman Rushdie cannot stand me any more since I criticised him because of his half apology,' Taslima told Schmitt, referring to the time when Rushdie tried to seek the support of liberal Muslim scholars in the UK. Yes, Rushdie was a great writer, but she had survived living for two months in the country which wanted to kill her. 'Rushdie has never lived in Iran,' she emphasised—soon this became one of her favourite refrains.

On my last visit to Deutsche Rundfunk, where I said goodbye to Mueller-Ullrich, the news was bad. The worst floods in Bangladesh's history were taking a terrible toll. The United Nations was calling for $22.5 million and food was already arriving from the World Food Program. To goad my curiosity even more, a Dhaka-based stringer confirmed to me by telephone (courtesy of BMU's connection) that, in the wake of the floods, Taslima Nasreen had returned to Bangladesh in mid-September 1998.

'It's on again, you know' BMU said, one conspirator to the other. I was headed for the Central Station to catch a train for Darmstadt and German PEN. 'There's a new Taslima story in the air,' he said, sounding like a prophet. 'I tell you I can smell it! It may not be like the one of four years ago, but remember, for a lot of journalists who weren't around then, it's a brand new story. Watch the style, look at the language and remember that newsagencies don't have long term memories.'

Taslima Nasreen was in the news again, if not exactly in the headlines. News flashes were coming across the wires that in spite of claims that she could never return home because of government intransigence, or because she would be murdered, Taslima had quietly slipped into Dhaka without telling anyone. Her lawyers, her publisher in Paris, Meredith Tax in New York and everyone else in Stockholm and London working behind the scenes on her behalf, trying to negotiate a deal for her return—the entire Taslima team—had been kept in the dark.

Chapter 8

The Land of Rushdie

No blasphemy does as much damage to Islam and to Muslims as the call for the murder of a writer.

Arab Association of Human Rights, 1989

A fly caught in a cobweb does not draw attention to itself; it lies motionless in the hope that the spider will find some other distraction.

Ziauddin Sardar, Independent article, 1991

The gatekeeper to the kingdom of Rushdie for nearly ten years was an Irish woman named Carmel Bedford. I'd met the former journalist, for the first time, in the winter of 1997 on route to Taslima in Stockholm. Bedford, as Secretary of the International Rushdie Defence Committee, was respected as one of the canniest networkers in Great Britain—it went with the job.

There is a certain building in Islington, inner London, which houses five or more autonomous freedom of expression organisations—almost like a supermarket of human rights. A stranger from the office of the Index of Censorship suggested I climb the stairs and talk to Bedford; 'Well worth your while,' she promised.

I found Carmel Bedford tucked away in an untidy, corner office on one of the well-secured floors, fossicking around in an old leather briefcase for a missing document. Her glasses were perched on the end of her nose, her greying hair escaping from an untidy chignon. She wore the look of a distracted headmistress. We had a hurried coffee together, but I knew I'd struck pay dirt, that spending a week in London had not been a waste of my time as I'd started to fear.

Meeting Carmel Bedford changed everything for me and a great weight was lifted from my shoulders. At the time I was going through a bad patch with my research. I knew nobody at all in the UK who could tell me about Taslima's reception there; I suspected her audiences were unlike the audiences she met in Sweden, Germany and France. I'd been playing literary sleuth for a long time now—perhaps too long. I was becoming troubled by my isolation and the single-mindedness of the pursuit. Was I becoming as fixated on my own version of Taslima's long journey into self-exile as her Dragon Slayer friends?

After one daunting, but mercifully brief, telephone conversation with Rana Kabani, activist, social commentator and author of the Penguin book *Letter to Christendom*, I felt like packing my tent and slipping away. I'd telephoned her hoping to set up a meeting to talk about Taslima. The woman almost took my head off and I was embarrassed by my gaucheness. She was fed up, she told me, with the preoccupation shown by the media and everyone [including me] in the Taslimas and Rushdies of the world, while the real problems facing the hundreds of millions of people struggling for survival in their societies went unnoticed. Red faced, I retreated, for I agreed with her view.

To many activists discussing free speech as if it were a self-contained absolute is trifling, for instance, when the race is on in Bangladesh to save between eighteen and twenty-four million people facing death by arsenic poisoning because forty per cent of the wells are contaminated by arsenic.

I accepted the futility of laying siege to Kabani, but after meeting Carmel Bedford, the tide turned; Bedford agreed to help me meet 'the right people'. I knew that I must return to London the next year on route to PEN's Helsinki Congress—I'd be a fool otherwise.

When I returned the following year, nothing had changed: her office was still as cramped as ever; Rushdie was still in hiding—but on this visit we made time to talk. Understanding that my interest in Taslima and the cause was not of the waning kind, Carmel opened up her vast treasury of 'who's who' in the hot house I was about to enter. London became my base that summer of 1998 as I spent three months travelling between Stockholm, Copenhagen, Helsinki, Berlin, Cologne, Paris, New York and Atlanta, and Carmel became my lightning rod.

The fortunes of her author, Salman Rushdie, remained the same: he continued to live a clandestine life. The tenth anniversary of Ayatollah Khomeini's decree would come to pass in less than a year. How did one mark this event without turning it into a maudlin celebration?

'He is still fighting to reclaim his life,' Carmel said.

A famous Rushdie quote of 1991 relayed some of the bitterness creeping into the British author's attempts to remain a writer and to stay alive. 'For many people, I've ceased to be a human being. I've become an issue, a bother, an "affair".'

Creating something positive out of this 'anniversary' would prove difficult, but if anyone could rise to the challenge, it would be tall, brave Carmel of the indomitable will, who bore an uncanny resemblance, I thought, to actor-politician Vanessa Redgrave.

Carmel was never directly involved with Taslima's case and described her experience with her as very minimal, but she knew most of the players in the northern hemisphere who, at some time or other, had become caught up in the troubled life of Taslima. If you supported Rushdie, you supported Nasreen: the same names, the same faces, the same cause.

Six years ago Carmel had begun setting up the National Rushdie Defence Committees in eight countries: Denmark, Finland, France, Germany, the Netherlands, Norway, Sweden and the USA. They were established under the auspices of an international centre against censorship called Article 19, which fought for the right to freedom of speech as embodied in Article 19 of the Universal Declaration of Human Rights.

The idea came to her one day as she was digging in her garden, 'reliving my Irish peasantry,' she called it. She realised that her organisation and its supporters needed to go beyond the world of writers and reach out to architects and unionists, lawyers and the like 'who could bring a different kind of thinking to bear on this problem'. Certain PEN elder statesmen disagreed, feeling it should remain a PEN enterprise, but Carmel had her way. Two years slipped by before Carmel and Rushdie ever met; until then they talked on the phone, for these were the most dangerous years of all. At the start she thought it would be one or two months' work—a month became ten years.

The Rushdie campaign up till mid-1992 kept a low profile until the last hostage was released in Lebanon: these were the years of 'quiet diplomacy', when British, American and German hostages were being held. Two weeks after the last German hostage was released, 'we were in Denmark,' she said, 'our first trip abroad.'

The strategy was to lobby for Salman as a European citizen. 'It was pretty damn obvious that up to three or four years ago, Britain wasn't doing anything for him. So the strategy was to break this circle of getting nowhere and take him abroad to try and engage other governments in Europe who had better human rights strategies. I never saw it as a British problem,' she said, 'it was always an international problem to me, perhaps because I'm Irish.' The strategy worked brilliantly. Between June 1992 and

December 1993, Salman Rushdie and members of the campaign visited seventeen countries. Their staunchest allies became the European Union and the Nordic countries.

Much of the work of these committees will never be known unless Carmel writes a book one day when time has elapsed and the complete story can be told. The people on the committees she worked with share a special bond: they trust one another implicitly, some of them were journalists who obeyed the edict on confidentiality and never broke the story of a lifetime; she thinks they will remain friends forever.

Gabi Gleichmann was part of the inner circle and Carmel remains very fond of him, 'We all love Gabi!' she declared. He was responsible for Rushdie's visit to Sweden and worked faithfully as a member of the Defence committee. She was never privy to what happened between Gabi and Taslima but knew 'he had great expectations of Taslima', and recalls how deeply distressed he was at the time. 'He had put his life, his work and his reputation on the line for her,' Carmel said, 'and then he was discredited as a result.'

❀

The anti-censorship groups flourish in a world of paradox. Caught up in an atmosphere of intrigue and adventure, the idea of risk taking sounds exciting at first, but much of what they achieve takes years of long, hard, sensitive negotiations at senior diplomatic levels, which they must constantly nurture, by knowing when—and when not—to stoke their public opinion engines. The moves they make must never be seen to jeopardise economic and trade relations.

For security reasons, they are prevented from ever talking publicly about this aspect of their work. Deprived of this outlet, they move nearer to one another for comfort and their stroking and bonding rituals become increasingly important. Together they form a large interconnected club of committed individuals with excellent qualifications who work for very little money and in most cases for nothing at all.

Beyond the smaller freedom of expression groups stand the human rights giants like Amnesty International (AI), who have their own buildings and their own enormous, unwieldy bureaucracies, but are also accountable to their members (more than one million) and known for their painstaking processes of fact checking and intelligence gathering. Everyone I spoke to admired Amnesty's professionalism that seemed above the petty rivalries and character assassinations which often studded the smaller groups, or else AI was better at hiding them.

The cases of Salman Rushdie and Taslima Nasreen have often presented AI with difficulties. While both writers were at risk, they were not prisoners of conscience, which meant that they were strictly outside the terms of reference of AI, which is a prisoner-oriented organisation. AI, however, was comfortable working with PEN's International Writers-in-Prison Committee and both groups, based in London, shared their research and intelligence networks.

Next in line were the writers' organisations. Some are broad based with a conference culture, like PEN, which blazes like a comet once a year and then allows its International London Secretariat to get down to the real business of saving writers. Other writers' organisations, like Reporter sans frontières and the Writers' Parliament, have their own brotherhood—they are largely male, and often behave like adolescents out of a boys' adventure book. The secrecy acts they are bound under actually delight them; they feel they are part of a world of international intrigue.

The Rushdie world was like a village where people lived on top of each other—the curtains might be drawn but everyone knew what was going on. Carmel always kept track of her secrets, which she catalogued away in her incredible memory: certain subjects were out of bounds—anything too close to her beloved Rushdie; but as my interests lay with Taslima, this created no tensions. I was curious, however, about the International Parliament of Writers (IPW), which many of my PEN friends saw as a rival. Rushdie had been IPW's inaugural president; later Wole Soyinka assumed the role. At one stage Taslima had been befriended by some of the leading French personalities from the Parliament. There were those who scoffed at the Parliament of Writers, as a mystical brotherhood of great authors and egos who elected themselves to parliament and whose projects were funded mainly by the European Council. Others valued their projects: symbolic projects like persuading certain capitals of the world to become 'Cities of Asylum' for persecuted writers, just as Berlin had been in 1995 for Taslima.

Miraculously, little of the animosity felt towards IPW's director, Christian Salmon, was ever directed at Rushdie, who, while his life was in danger, was safe from the envy and opprobrium of most of his fellow authors. He was not involved in any ongoing literary feuds except for a heated exchange of letters to the editor between himself and John le Carré in 1997, who exercised his own freedom to dissent from some of Rushdie's actions.

When Carmel's world turned upside down in September 1998, I'd left London for a few days and was in Paris tracking down Taslima's French publisher and the office of Reporter sans frontières. As I watched Carmel on the television screen, in my hotel room, her face looked radiant as she sat next to a shell-shocked Rushdie, while he spoke to the media in, what he called, the 'Final Press Conference of the Rushdie Case'.

'It's all over,' he said. They'd been forced to squeeze into the offices at Article 19; nothing larger could be found at such short notice; many people were still apprehensive of terrorist action and denied them a facility. More than a hundred and twenty journalists and twenty camera crews jostled for position.

Was he a Muslim today, a reporter from *The Independent* asked?

'I'm happy to say that I am not,' he said. In fact one of his few regrets was when he pretended to find religion in early 1990 in an attempt to enlist the help of moderate Islamic scholars in the UK to help resolve the impasse with British Muslims.

But in the main he was conciliatory, while making it clear that he would not apologise, nor was he asking for an apology. 'I'm saying that this is the moment for a fresh start. We just need to turn the page; we don't have to scratch the scab. What I'm saying is end of story, time for another story.' Rushdie wanted to move on with his life and put the last nine years behind him, but many of the journalists persisted on reading between the lines to discover why this change of Iranian heart had come about.

Tim Hodlin, in *The Independent on Sunday*, thought that Rushdie's plight was incidental, but never central, to a renewal of British–Iranian relations, which were economically imperative, he said, because of the enormous natural gas deposits in Iran. His article appeared under the headline 'A Pawn in the Battle for Iran' on 27 September 1998. The genie was back in the bottle, Hodlin agreed, but as in all the old stories, genies may be let out, but they can never be destroyed. In his article he wondered if Rushdie was any safer today. A compromise had been forged over the last few years: the British Government had acceded to Iranian claims that a fatwa cannot be removed once issued by a legitimate authority, as well as accepting that the reward for his death lies outside the remit of the Iranian Government. The fatwa is still in force, the reward is still on offer, but the moderate forces inside the Iranian Government were now publicly renouncing a government-sponsored implementation of the fatwa. Economic benefits to Iran had been the motivating factor, and their desire to rejoin the international community.

The Sunday Telegraph reported a week later that the author was still classified as Risk Factor 2 and still received round-the-clock protection from the Special Branch; he was not out of the woods yet, and senior officers were still worried about 'hardline fanatics', as they called them, and were less inclined to see this as a British political coup.

Could Carmel learn to stroll down a quiet country lane after life on the Rushdie roller coaster? I returned to London to find out and to learn first-hand about what seemed an amazing volte-face from the Iranians. We met a week after the triumphal press conference, at her favourite eating-house, and talked for hours until we were asked to leave, giving us little choice but to move on to an Irish pub. She was as relaxed as I had never seen her before, and had finally done herself out of a job.

'I'll write a book,' she said. 'I kept a journal and there are certain things nobody else knows about.' I hope she does.

The Rushdie connections will not disappear overnight. The European Union will monitor what happens in the future and Carmel appreciates how the Iranian Government needs time to undo the years of propaganda against Rushdie, who was transformed into a devil in the eyes of ordinary Iranians. 'It's like a ship,' she said, 'you can't turn it around quickly; you have to slow down first.'

❀

I'm not sure if Carmel and UK activist Asad Rehman have ever met. During the Rushdie years; I doubt if they'd have marched under the same banner, although their respective organisations, Article 19 and AI, make common cause. Ten years before, when the Rushdie juggernaut began to roll, Asad stood watching closely from the sidelines and it taught him a lesson he never forgot, one he would put to good use when faced with the Taslima case.

Asad Rehman is a man with a constituency and a cause. He is a fast thinker and a fast talker. You learn to keep up with him by finishing off his incomplete sentences in your head. Asad's language is at all times political. He works with the 'black community', he says, 'and with religious communities.' It is hard to imagine him doing anything else with his life.

He is probably in his early thirties but his street-style masks his age. A few amulets are strung around his neck but are of no particular significance he says. Short and stocky, with a round face and a semi-shaven head, he looks like a man who could land a few punches if he found himself cornered, but his preference would always be to talk himself out of any sticky situation. He has a fairly free hand at AI, where he works. Workers like Asad help the organisation distance itself from the White Christian image it has developed over the years.

Asad is an old hand in the race relations arena; he thinks he's seen everything there is to see; watched over the years as people moved from being 'black' to being 'Asian' and then to being defined on national grounds, as Indian, Pakistani or Bangladeshi; now he notices another shift, where people are being defined on religious grounds as Sikh, Hindu or Muslim.

Asad's views are strong and well defined, as one expects from an activist. He has made his peace with religion, and although he comes from the radical Left he is tolerant of believers and comfortable living amongst them. His attitude put him at loggerheads with Taslima when they first met. The author was adamant that those who follow any religion whatsoever are fundamentalists at heart.

For the last fifteen years or more, Asad believed that discussions on Islam have been demonised. Western civilisation saw itself under threat from a dark, barbaric force. 'Muslim' was the new swear word, just as 'Paki' once was, until it was embraced by the community, which used it as an emblem of pride.

Living through the early Rushdie years was painful. The anti-racist movement which he hailed from split: the natural alliance between the liberal forces and the black progressive community seemed at an end. En masse, liberal opinion came out wholeheartedly in support of Rushdie.

Asad disagreed. He belonged to a minority of progressives whose manifesto was, 'While we defend Rushdie's right in the abstract to write what he wants to write, he also has a responsibility.' They were not holding the author responsible because of his Indian-Muslim ancestry. Rushdie was accountable, they insisted, because of his record as an activist.

'Here was somebody who came from the Left, out of the anti-racist movement,' said Asad. 'Rushdie knew what the UK was like; he understood the dynamics of the debate, but he kept silent, maintaining all along that the major issue was his right to freedom of speech. Rushdie should have said something to distance himself from the anti-Muslim feeling that blew up. It fuelled a kind of "liberal racism",' Asad argued.

Rushdie on the other hand, has always maintained that 'If you're going to start being careful, you can't write. Self-censorship is the death of literature,' he once said in an interview with *The Christian Science Monitor*.

Years later, when Taslima Nasreen entered the freedom of speech battleground Asad vowed that history would not repeat itself. This time there must be a progressive Muslim response to Taslima Nasreen's writings, and he promised to bring this about.

❀

The fanfare which always preceded Taslima's entry into the great cities of Europe was muted in London. Not that the author was ignored: she was warmly welcomed in mid-December 1994 at the London HQ of

International PEN; by Amnesty International and by British Humanists and the Rationalist Press; she was written up in *The Guardian* and *The Independent*, and received numerous invitations to give talks in seminars around the country. But the adoring edge so evident in Paris, Lisbon, and other cities was missing. Taslima, happy to leave her Swedish home-base even for a few weeks, scarcely noticed this.

The English press were friendly enough, but at her first press conference in a private house in inner London, the elaborate security measures which her minders engineered were overdone. One by one the journalists arrived, and one by one they left, as quietly as they had entered, but when they discovered they were not getting the exclusive they'd hoped for, not too many printed their stories, or then again, after all these years, maybe they were suffering from Rushdie fatigue.

By coming to London, Nasreen crossed over into Rushdie territory. There was a long history of bitter confrontation between the pro- and anti-Rushdie forces in the UK, especially in the early stages in the late eighties–early nineties. The Muslim groups were not served well by their leaders, many of whom behaved abominably. It became a stand-off between the Muslim immigrant population, labelled across the board as religious fundamentalists, versus the Post-Enlightenment fundamentalists, the self-styled liberal voices. Both sides waged war over 'that man and his book' and made monsters of each other.

To have captured a quarter of the attention that Rushdie had garnered over the years, Taslima would have needed to be the Queen of Sheba. While she was seen as 'exotic' by many of her followers, she couldn't possibly compete with the British author of the hooded eyes, one of the great writers of the twentieth century, winner of the Booker prize in 1981 and the Booker of Booker prizes in 1993 for *Midnight's Children*, the best novel in the prize's twenty-five years' history.

Her reception in 1994 and again on her second a few months later in 1995 was mixed, to say the least, and markedly different to other countries, whose politicians, mayors, and heads of state rolled out the red carpet and lined up to have their photos taken with the attractive author. The UK welcome was polite, but far from ecstatic, and it had nothing to do with the famous British sense of reserve. The British simply knew more; they had experienced more.

To understand why the Taslima phenomenon was looked at in a more balanced way, you had only to look around—the answer was right there before your eyes. A large immigrant Muslim population from South Asia, especially from Bangladesh and Pakistan; a second and third generation of Muslim intelligentsia who were blooded in the anti-racist movement of the seventies and eighties. And something else you couldn't see with the naked eye, but it was there all the same, the UK had experienced five years of testy community relations over the fate of Salman Rushdie and the exercise of freedom of expression. They might be slow to admit it, but lessons were learnt on both sides.

The British-Indian author has always been supportive of Nasreen and in his open letter to her printed in *The New York Times* on 14 July 1994, as part of the famous letter campaign, his good humour and understanding of her situation showed through.

I am sure you have become tired of being called "the female Rushdie'—what a bizarre and comical creature that would be!—when all along you thought you were the female Taslima Nasreen. I am sorry my name has been hung around your neck, but please know that there are many people in many countries working to make sure such sloganizing does not obscure your identity, the unique features of your situation and the importance of fighting to defend you and your rights against those who would cheerfully see you dead.

❖

The reason behind Asad's invitation, on behalf of AI, to Taslima was bedded in his Rushdie experience and had little to do with her needs as an exiled writer or as a human being. He was using her to correct a major tactical error from the past: to make up for the appalling silence on the part of the so-called progressive Muslim voice over the Salman Rushdie controversy.

Asad recalled watching the enormous Hyde Park anti-Rushdie Muslim march in 1989, perplexed by the frustration and hatred he could feel around him. Thirty thousand people marched that day and most of them were young men, but not the kind of youth to be found praying in the mosques. They came mainly from the north of England, and they were out in the streets because at the core of their self-expression and identity there was nothing left for them—no way out—other than to define themselves as 'Muslim'.

'The young saw the furore surrounding the Rushdie affair as another massive racist attack,' Asad explained, 'they were used to being attacked by the Right of politics, but now they believed the Liberals were also joining in. All they had left was Islam and what the mullahs were telling them at public rallies.

'I have a wonderful snapshot,' he laughed, 'it sums up everything. The demonstration was coming past the Houses of Parliament, and on one side of the street you had the Neo-Nazi fascists picketing the demonstration;

on the other side were the hard-core feminists also protesting against the march, with their placards, and then the Muslim marchers coming down the middle, heavily policed by the State.'

Fighting broke out that day. Muslims confronted their old enemies, the Neo-Nazis, but there were also skirmishes with people who had sympathised with Asians in the past. The natural constituency which had fought together over the years when South Asians were being beaten up and murdered by skinheads was now divided.

Two years later Asad organised a 'Black People against the Gulf War' march to counter the 'Bastards of Baghdad' tabloid headlines. 'They threw paper aeroplanes at us as we marched in opposition to the war; so it didn't matter if you were a Muslim or not—you said you were anyway!' Identifying yourself was now a political statement; you were no longer an underground Muslim.

Islamist organisations in the UK were quick to pick up the alienated and disaffected youth, mainly the unemployed, but also the young budding intelligentsia enrolled at university who lacked a sense of worth and felt alienated from what they perceived as a racist British society. *Islamist* is the generic term used by their opponents in the UK to describe Muslims who support religiously based political parties or religious institutions which believe in the supremacy of Shariah or religious law. Some activists use the expression as a euphemism for the Western-derived term *fundamentalist*, which is a contested concept amongst Muslim intellectual opinion.

'In Britain, we let this happen,' Asad said. 'We vacated the space for the religious organisations to move into.

'Our grandparents built religious institutions when they first arrived,' he said, 'as places to meet, not just for religion. The first anti-racist campaigns in this country had a high level of religious involvement. The issues were virginity testing [of female immigrants to ensure bona fide arranged marriages] police violence, immigration, and racial violence.'

'When you wanted to mobilise the community or get numbers for a rally you went to the mosques, or the [Hindu] temples or the [Sikh] gurdwaras.'

'As progressives, most of us came from the mosque communities. We never had a problem standing outside the mosques giving out leaflets on topical issues. We occupied a space, an important space.'

But then, it all started to change and the Left began to move out and away from their communities. 'We had a new attitude,' he explained, 'that religion is personal and should be left to the individual or to the mosque.'

Times had changed since 1980, when a Pakistani man was stabbed to death by four skinheads in the High Street in London's East End for a five-pound bet as to who could be the first to kill a 'Paki'. The Asian communities reacted with massive demonstrations: Hindu, Sikh or Muslim, it made no difference. Photos showed that all the protest banners came from temples, gurdwaras and mosques. Every shop shut in protest; everyone interacted and fought for the common good.

Twenty years later in the same area, 'it's still the Left and the secular community, but the mosques aren't with us any more,' he said. 'We went over to the secularists—we gave the right-wing Islamists the space. We were wrong, I know that now.'

Many of his friends argued against ever joining forces with religious groups—Taslima would have been on their side. They warned him against any alliance with 'believers'. 'It corrupts you,' they said. 'You can't make common cause with these reactionary forces.'

'I argued that they are not reactionary forces: they are forces which contain reactionary and progressive elements, and you have to tap into it and be part of the debate. "We used to," I told them, "Why did we change?"'

The scene, therefore, was set long before the controversy over *The Satanic Verses* began. 'The religious ones made the running; they came down with their pronouncements and there wasn't a progressive interpretation in sight,' Asad finished off, looking grim faced.

While the progressive Left pontificated, looking for a rational position somewhere in the middle, trying to explain to the media that they were neither for nor against Rushdie, the religious Right wasted no time in moving in ahead and the moment was lost; the Left no longer had a role to play, they were too busy trying to reorganise. Asad embarked on a personal journey where he tried to liaise with progressive Muslim scholars who also remained silent during Rushdie's crisis.

Silencing dissent by calling people *kaffirs*, or 'infidels', happens in every Muslim society throughout the world; religious vilification has a long cowardly history. Few people have the inner strength, the resources and the rank to withstand attacks on their spiritual reputation. Many scholars who wanted to speak out in 1989 against the book and effigy burnings instigated by Muslim fanatics and their followers in the Muslim enclaves of the city of Bradford in York, and the intemperate, violent language of the rallies, found themselves under attack from their own congregations and retreated. Nobody was prepared to put forward the view that you can be Muslim and progressive.

Asad, the activist, became worried by what he saw as a rise of ultra-orthodox groups, all busily recruiting young people—some were university students, some were unemployed. On a Friday night, you could visit any one of a number of meetings in East London and each different Islamic society would have at least five hundred regular attendees. 'We progressives,' he admitted, 'couldn't rally five hundred if we spent three weeks trying!'

Why did people attend these meetings? Not because they were reactionary themselves, he decided, nor out of any religious need, but for highly personal reasons, to make sense of who they were and where they were living. Surrounded by what they saw as contempt and hostility, Muslim youth found comfort in what the mullahs were telling them about the glory of their Islamic past.

⊞

When Asad first heard about Taslima Nasreen, he thought his side was being given a second chance. 'We can't let the debate be hijacked again,' he thought. 'Why not set up a platform, invite her to London and get the Islamic scholars to join her on the dais?'

I thought it a doomed position to begin with and told him so. But he answered back like a man used to winning most arguments, that he wanted to explore the whole question of fatwas: Who has the power to make these edicts and what had she done to deserve a fatwa?

The idea of Taslima sitting on the same dais as a group of Islamic scholars debating religious fine points made me smile. I was sure the author would never have put herself in such a position, so it was just as well that Asad failed to pull this experiment off. He made the rounds of Islamic scholarly opinion in London and was told privately by many genuine scholars, 'the "Rushdie affair" was not of our making. We didn't want to make it such a big issue.'

The finger was pointed at political movements happening inside Islam and at certain local leaders who used the increase in racial tension for their own populist ends. Privately they stated that there was no basis in Islam for the fatwa against Nasreen, but one by one they all bowed out, just as they always had in the past when it came time to make public statements.

Asad bounced back with another idea. He would use Taslima in a current discussion on women and Islam. Large public rallies around the country were organised in early 1995: Nottingham, Newcastle, Edinburgh, and then over to Belfast and Dublin. He persuaded many of his old allies from the Left to join him; some of his old feminist friends teased him. 'Good God! You're going to grow a beard now!' It was a standard joke that wearing a beard meant a Muslim was becoming 'religious'. A number of female speakers agreed to join Taslima: Gita Sahgal, Sara Hossain, and a well-known group called 'Women Against Fundamentalism'—an all-women platform where most men feared to tread—under the auspices of AI.

The Special Branch gave Asad instructions about using stewards to check people's bags. Not wanting to fall into the trap of protecting Taslima from the 'mad hordes', he refused to have armed guards; but he heeded their advice not to use public transport, and they were always met by local police in every city.

There was little reaction from local Muslims to Taslima's visit. Most of the demonstrations consisted of a hundred people outside their own mosques on a Friday holding up placards—it all died down very quickly. Before her first visit, New Scotland Yard infiltrated the local Bangladeshi community in London, which includes large numbers of immigrants from Sylhet (generally regarded as a fairly conservative lot), the home district of the old Soldiers of Islam group, which had first made death threats in 1993. The Yard believed that there was no obvious danger.

As Taslima's visit drew nearer, Asad became nervous. People he described as being on the secularist side of the fence in Dhaka began sharing some of their 'Taslima experiences' with him. 'We pleaded with her,' they told him. 'Don't go out on a limb. We've got to fight the Islamists on issues where we are stronger. We'll end up defending you, but we'll lose!' They used harsh words, calling her actions politically criminal. 'She threw oil on the fire, it was madness the way she gave her enemies an easy target.'

But Asad was still determined to show everyone that it was wrong to think that only non-Muslims defended her. 'Islam allows you to dissent!' was his slogan. He was a man who liked his slogans. Asad found the Taslima campaign tough going; it wasn't the Islamists he had difficulty with, it was Taslima the dissident. 'It was really odd,' he mused, 'but I actually found her as dogmatic—as fundamentalist if you like—as the fundamentalists!'

The Taslima–Asad entourage travelled together for about ten days, with Asad's wife as part of the group. Once on board an aeroplane, breakfast was served with a hearty helping of bacon on the side. Asad informed the attendant that he was a Muslim and didn't eat bacon. In other matters he was liberal, but this taboo he could not put aside.

'Taslima looked at me curiously,' he remembered. '"Don't you eat bacon?" and I answered no, that actually I only ate *halaal* food.'

'"So you are a fundamentalist as well!" she said.

The air in the cabin grew a little warmer as he told her his dietary habits had nothing to do with fundamentalism. 'This is your real problem,' he said. 'You are not tolerant. You are saying that no one has a right to believe.' For the ten days they travelled together they argued about religion. 'Be sensitive,' he urged her. 'Let people have their faith.'

Taslima scorned all religions. 'Religion gives birth to fundamentalism as surely as the seed gives birth to the tree,' she said in an interview with Sara

Whyatt from London PEN in 1994. 'We can tear the tree down, but if the seed remains it will produce another tree. While the seed remains, we cannot root out fundamentalism. All believers have narrow minds,' she said.

Taslima and Asad were both dissenters and believers in their own causes, but in everything else they were poles apart. She was a writer living inside her own head, and Asad was the political activist, rigorously schooled in Black activism and Marxist political strategy.

'I argued with her that we must split the Islamists, who were way ahead, doing what the Left had always done: winning the hearts and the minds of people.'

'No!' she replied. 'You cannot make any alliances with them.' To his frustration she much preferred talking to his wife about Indian films, cricket and shopping—anything rather than listen to his political arguments.

Taslima overturned Asad's apple cart by being herself. The romantic notions he'd cherished of Taslima becoming a symbolic bridge for unity were dashed. He'd pictured her standing on the stage declaiming aloud, 'It doesn't matter if I'm Muslim or not, but I have rights which Muslims and non-Muslims need to defend.'

'But a lot of her speeches,' he found, 'contained an anti-Muslim stance, and what she said privately was even worse.' He was horrified.

Two secularists from very different backgrounds: it was easier, I suspected, for Asad to feel empathy for the religious when they were not a threatening power, in a land where a safe place exists for agnostics, and when your secularism is not as recent and as politically immature as Taslima's. He belonged to a minority which had learnt to defend itself and demand its rights. Taslima had more in common with her rationalist friends intent on combating unscientific, non-rational world views through a critique of religion than she did with Black activists and feminists in the UK.

The audiences Taslima faced in the UK were different from her usual foreign audiences. Asad called them 'mixed', which meant there were always people from the Indian subcontinent next to liberal UK sympathisers and admirers. There were also intellectuals living outside Bangladesh, many of whom sympathised with her but were not blind to how she put herself in this predicament.

Taslima felt nervous and vulnerable: these audiences were different to her adoring public in the Nordic countries. Wherever there were Muslims listening to her there was always the likelihood of her being rigorously questioned, even heckled. When I had visited her in Stockholm, in 1997, she told me there'd been problems in the UK. 'At Nottingham University,

I had to stop my lecture,' she said, 'and was taken out of the lecture room by the police because Islamic fundamentalist students created problems and shouted.' In other speeches she said she was attacked.

Asad's version of what took place was very different and stamped him as an experienced campaigner. Many in the audience, he said, were from the Subcontinent and there were some visible Muslim scarves around and a minor protest from a Jordanian Islamic group, an unpopular fringe group, banned in Jordan, but nothing much, he said. The Jordanian group, he mentioned, was as unpopular in the local mosques as a Rushdie or Taslima. The radicals urged their young neophytes to oppose mosque el-ders, to confront them by telling them that they were backward and going nowhere. Other Islamic organisations were not present on that evening, he said.

'We knew there were going to be some Islamists in the audience and for me that wasn't a problem,' he said. 'I wanted to start up a dialogue with them anyway.'

Again his own political needs were to the fore and it was time that I taxed him over this. 'All right you wanted a dialogue with them, but don't you think Taslima was the wrong person to use?'

He pulled a face. 'Yes, I realised that later,' he said. 'I'd made a huge fundamental mistake.' He said this with good humour. I was beginning to admire his willingness to admit to his own frailties—there was a little of Gabi in Asad.

'I wanted to take the running in this case and perhaps I moved too quickly. I took the risk and I think it did pan out for me, in terms of what I wanted out of it.'

'At Nottingham the students didn't disrupt the meeting, really. At one point a few of them stood up as she was speaking and moved towards the stage. I made sure that they would have to pass me if anything went wrong, but they just sat down again. It was a game they were playing: intimidating her by seeming to walk towards her, but anyone involved in politics knows that this is all gamesmanship—people do it all the time. This wasn't dangerous; you know, this wasn't Salman Rushdie up there on the platform facing three thousand Muslims from the local mosque.'

⁂

I thought it unfair to expect Taslima, a woman under intense pressure at the time, to look behind the show of intimidation, and to see it for what it was—a huffing and puffing by the local bully boys of religious politics. A stranger to the culture of local community confrontations, how could she know any better? Had anyone bothered to brief the frightened author?

Perhaps if supporters like Nicholas Walter, founder of the Rationalist Press Association, had been part of her entourage he might have been the one to reassure her.

Walter, an ardent admirer of Taslima's and an authority on the subject of blasphemy, was the man who organised the humanist meetings for the visiting author at Conway Hall whenever she came to London. He'd had his own experiences with militant Muslim students, as he told me in his meticulously phrased English with its odd flourish of polite humour.

Not too long ago Walter, and his colleagues would, on occasion, find themselves invited, as atheist guest speakers, to a particular Muslim forum in London. Two strong young men would lift Nicolas Walter out of his wheelchair and onto the stage with consideration and no show of awkwardness, and reverse the procedure at the end of the evening. 'We expected fanatical, unpleasant people,' he said, 'but in fact they were all absolutely charming and rather like evangelical Christians: extremely polite, clean and no smoking or drinking.'

Later however, Walter learnt that their hosts were known as a very militant group in the throes of taking over as many other Muslim student organisations as possible. Added to his discomfort came the discovery that he and his friends were being used as a kind of circus freaks' attraction. Walter found a leaflet advertising a meeting he was to address which read, "Do you care about God or do you prefer atheism, homosexuality, drug taking and paedophilia." 'I refused to speak,' he said, 'so we lost that connection.'

'But compared to speaking at political meetings of Marxists, Anarchists, and Liberals it was all very nice, I must say. They were lovely people, outstandingly courteous. But I don't know what would have happened, of course, if Taslima had got caught up with them for I gather with their own people they can be very harsh—like the Christian fundamentalists,' he added, 'and of course the Marxists are a bit the same when they impose their own orthodoxy.'

Asad, of course, as a veteran of Muslim community politics, knew how to recognise bluff when he saw it, but not Taslima. 'She was badly frightened by what to me was hardly a major incident,' he said, 'and wanted to leave the hall immediately, so we left, I can't remember if she finished her speech or not.'

'The black feminists were glad that she came; from the Liberals it was, "Yes, Taslima you are a darling, you are so brave"; from my tradition of progressive black activists it was more like, "Hmm, yeah I defend her right to say what she wants, but she doesn't make it bloody easy. You can understand why the Islamists were against her . . . jeez man, why her? Why does it have to be Taslima?" '

The ongoing search for the perfect dissident is like searching for the perfect diamond, unflawed, brilliant; a gem that never shatters.

This was the behind-the-scenes story—officially everyone was pleased. Taslima had her tour and received favourable publicity and the local black and brown women had been given a platform. I think in the end Asad was quite relieved that it was all over.

'I would never invite her back,' he swore to me as I left his office. 'I would never choose to fight a battle on her ground again. Politically she is. . . .' Words failed him for the first time that day and I was impressed by the power of Taslima, after all this time, to stop him in his tracks.

Taslima's friend and publisher Christianne Besse is concerned first and foremost with Taslima as a woman and as a writer—the politics and the causes her author finds herself embroiled in as a symbol of free expression have generated huge publicity but have detracted from her abilities as a writer, of that she is convinced.

I'd been fortunate in catching up with Taslima's French publisher, during my few days in Paris; she suggested that we meet the following month in London for a longer session.

'I am a European!' Christianne Besse told me in her flamboyant way. She made travelling from one capital to the next sound like boarding a local bus, but I could never picture Besse using public transport.

Besse had no time at all for what she called 'the Rushdie clique' ensconced in Paris. Anything that reflected badly on her 'Taslie', as she called her, earned her implacable ill will and it was true that the continual comparisons with Rushdie were in the end not flattering to her protégé. If there was one thing this fiery Frenchwoman loathed it was French intellectuals—in truth she wasn't fond of Frenchmen at all, which seemed an eminently sensible viewpoint for a Frenchwoman who had married an Englishman.

She was more than Taslima's publisher: she displayed a fierce maternalism that protected Taslima from negative forces that gathered, waiting for her to make a mistake. Taslima was still ripe for exploitation, she believed, which at first sounded incongruous coming from a canny publisher like Besse. The publishing industry is not supposed to have a heart. But Besse had a heart and if not quite from the start of her engagement with Taslima, then very shortly thereafter, they developed a rapprochement that helped stretch Nasreen as a writer and gave the lonely author the psychological support she'd left behind in Bangladesh.

Besse is a powerful woman with a definite elan: a cynic with a heart of gold to match her shoulder-length hair. She oozed the dramatic style Taslima admired so much. The Frenchwoman seemed like a kindred spirit to Taslima, imprisoned by Swedish correctness. Taslima would have felt safe with Christianne Besse and drawn to her spontaneity. Of all the Europeans I met along the way, Besse saw a side to Taslima that nobody else glimpsed, or took the trouble to find. When she looked at her author she saw more than the ringing of cash registers. I think she loved her.

'At the end of everything she is a little girl, she is very moving; I thought this from the first time I ever saw her,' she said. 'These people who call her "Taslima the sphinx, or the woman of a hundred masks"—I think this is all bullsheeeet, if you excuse me! She is a girl who by nature and by education has been brought up to hide her feelings; it is not proper for a Muslim girl to show her feelings.'

'When you read her latest book, you will know even more about her.' Taslima's French memoir *My Girlhood*, an account of her early pre-pubescent years, had just been released by Stock, Besse's company.

'She's essentially a girl from the provinces', said Besse, refusing to romanticise Taslima's background, 'a girl from the lower middle class.'

We sat in club chairs, drinking champagne in the lounge of her London hotel, red plush carpets, swathes of cream and gold brocade, attentive waiters. Christianne rarely drank anything else but champagne, French of course.

'Taslima has developed fantastically as a writer,' she declared. 'I discovered this two years ago when I asked her to write for *Le Monde*. She wrote an excellent article translated by a very good translator and that is when I realised what the girl could do. She is a writer!'

We both saw her earlier work *Lajja* as being in the polemical tradition of the pamphleteer. As it was translated and extended into English and other languages, it doubled in size, losing its initial raw charm—it was ruined. 'She was not served well by those dreadful English translations,' said Besse.

Besse maintained that her writer had matured. 'Before, she had not seen the world. Now she is like a sponge; she soaks everything up, she is very intelligent and has time to think.'

Two very different women, yet a strong friendship had been forged. Its beginnings lay in Besse's commercial instincts, her publisher's nose for seeking out good books. New York–based Indian author Amatav Ghosh, a good friend of Besse's, who is godmother to one of his children, first told her about Nasreen the writer. Besse had introduced Ghosh's first two books into France, and as she phrased it, 'We won the Medici prize for *Circle of Reason*.'

Besse wasted no time in sending Taslima a fax when she was still in Dhaka, and when the author made her first Paris visit in April 1994, Besse offered her a two-book deal, for *Lajja* and a second book which four years later had finally been completed. A bizarre set of circumstances took place: the advance for *Lajja* was stolen and Taslima's cheque ended up being cashed in New York by person or persons unknown; a fax Besse sent to Dhaka was altered and she was accused of being an agent of the BJP, the Hindu fundamentalist party which headed a coalition Indian Government in 1994.

She laughed while she sipped her champagne. 'I thought it was very chic,' she said, 'to be accused of being an extremist Hindu agent. 'You know I would have paid for that! Very exotic! *Alors*, I next saw her in Sweden and it was awful! Her hosts organised a big press conference and although she was quite good, she didn't have the kind of English necessary,' she paused searching for the right words, and I offered a phrase, 'To show you are an intellectual?'

'*Exactement*! And I suffered for her each time she was brought into the lion's den; the questions they asked her were unfair, set by Western standards. And then, my dear, when she came to France! Well that was the beginning of the big story and she was in the headlines for weeks!'

The story behind Taslima's sensational second visit to Paris in late 1994 was highly political. She was invited to appear on France's main television cultural show hosted by Bernard Pivot.

'At first the authorities refused her a visa saying they could not assure her safety and then they granted her one for twenty-four hours only, so we all protested massively and then, finally, that old rascal the Home Minister Pasqua decided [for political reasons] alright, if she wants to come then we will have her for ten days at the expense of the French Republic, which meant that the taxpayers were footing the bill. He hoped that this would turn the tide of public opinion against her.'

The conservative Home Minister used the visit as an excuse to introduce a new policy to control immigrants whereby anyone who 'looked Arab' could be stopped in the streets and have their papers checked. Talk circulated about an Algerian network of terrorists linked to Bangladeshi extremists, which anyone with a knowledge of Bangladeshi politics knew was ridiculous.

While Besse never discussed the fallout from the excessive, almost 'royal visit', Antoine de Guademar, a senior journalist, confirmed, when we met in Paris, that Taslima's second Paris visit caused a backlash against the author. He described her fall from popularity as 'a long fall...a cruel fall.' He sympathised because she had been built up to the heavens and then suddenly she was exposed to a barrage of criticism.

The wily politician Pasqua succeeded in turning Taslima's promotional tour into a state visit, with a motorcycle cavalcade with three limousines and Taslima riding inside a bulletproof car, the streets of Paris blocked off to everyone's inconvenience as the cavalcade sped by. Observers said she had more security than President Clinton. Public opinion began to turn when they realised that the public purse was paying for all of this; journalists who'd previously been muted in their criticism became louder. Jean Edern-Hallier, friend to BMU in Germany, wrote against her and Professor Minowski, a well-regarded intellectual, said the Dhaka he knew was not the one she described.

Nevertheless, President Mitterand, Minister of Health Simone Weil, and Jacques Chirac, the Mayor of Paris and later French Prime Minister, all wanted to meet Nasreen and to have their photos taken with her, something they'd never ventured to do with Rushdie. She received a standing ovation from a huge audience of French intellectuals at the Palace of Versailles. Honour after honour was heaped on her head, and some symbolic gifts were presented: a bust of Voltaire and a precious first edition of the French philosopher's treatise on tolerance.

'We reserved a wing of the Ritz for her,' said Besse, 'with forty-five secret service agents guarding her: three teams of fifteen people around the clock. One morning when I arrived they told me she hadn't woken up. I rushed to her room. We had an appointment with Simone Weil. Taslima lay in bed. I shook her. She'd been up till 4:00 AM calling Bangladesh and then was so wound up she couldn't get to sleep and had taken sleeping pills. I got her dressed in her sari and while I was pushing her here and there like a sleepy doll telling her to hurry up, I thought, "What am I doing? Me doing such terrible things to this poor girl who wanted news of her family." She always felt guilty, you know, because she'd left them behind; she was terrified but wouldn't show it.' From that moment on, Besse promised herself that she would look after Taslima.

Taslima and her French publishers both made money out of *Lajja*, which sold better in France than anywhere else outside of the Indian subcontinent. 'Yes, she made a lot of money,' Besse said nodding her head, 'but she is so generous and she has her family around her all the time and I worry about her finances; maybe that is why she trusts me because she knows I try to make the best deals for her.'

Others in the publishing game had tried to exploit the author, mixing culture and politics into something they could use for their own ends, publishing letters without Taslima's permission and claiming 'exclusive' interviews on very shaky ground.

'I hate feminists!' Besse thundered suddenly. Amused heads turned in our direction but we ignored them as we waited for the waiter to bring another bottle of champagne. 'I am much more than a feminist, my dear! French feminism is totally outdated. The real feminists were my grandmother and my poor great grandmother trying to get the vote.'

'What about Simone de Beauvoir,' I countered, offering up my hero to Besse.

'Oh, a bore!' she parried. 'I know everyone will hate me for saying it. . . . Yes a bore, but a necessary one!' Besse considered de Beauvoir's *The Second Sex* a mish mash of intellectual thoughts but paid homage to her four-volume autobiography, which she described as one of the greatest books written. 'When she says at the end "I was cheated", it is true: Life cheats you and you never do all the things you want to do. I love her for that one sentence.'

Besse was not pleased by the latest spate of publicity that her author was attracting. Reuters newsagency broke the news on 15 September 1998 that Taslima had returned to Bangladesh—after protesting for four years that this was too dangerous. Besse, however, instead of welcoming all this new attention, as most publishers would with a new book coming out, believed that inevitably this would mean less, not more, publicity for the new book: the clock would be turned back to the old days of 1994 and her author's writing talent diminished by being turned into a political figure—it had happened before with *Lajja*. For two years they'd ignored her and now the whole circus seemed to be starting up once more.

'Her new book doesn't need this kind of publicity. It needs to be read on its own merits. Not simply because she's in danger again. I don't want the book to be overtaken by the event!'

I reminded her gently that it was Taslima who was so fond of retelling the same old story.

'I have told her to stop it!' Besse rallied. 'I've urged her, "Please talk about your book, your bluurdy book".'

But Taslima had raced off to Dhaka to be with her dying mother and had told neither her publisher nor her New York ally, Meredith Tax, of her intentions.

'The last time I spoke to her, I told her not to return, but her family puts pressure on her,' Besse shrugged helplessly.

Taslima, the rebel, always urging independence, has never found a sub-stitute for her family. Besse had seen with her own eyes how completely abandoned Taslima felt in Sweden, so much so that her father and then her brother joined her, spending six months with her at a time in Sweden and Germany.

'Little by little her memoir will make its way, I am convinced,' said Besse. 'Her old friend from Ananda Bazaar—she always keeps that connection going—Nikhil Sarkar, praised it to the heavens when he read it. It has taken her four years to produce this book, and I think it needed the kind of anguish—that sense of alienation that living in exile causes, for her to finish it.'

Besse understood why she'd returned. 'She felt so guilty, because she didn't recognise her mother's cancer when they were together in Sweden. As a doctor she blamed herself.'

Taslima's family in the past have often played on her feelings of guilt claiming that she put them at risk. She has repaid them many times over. The world was opened wide for Taslima and she, in turn, opened the door of opportunity to her siblings and her favourite nephew. Many Bangladeshi observers think, on balance, that her relatives have done very well with their American visas and opportunities to travel around the world—all paid for by Taslima. Perhaps these informants are a little envious: an opportunity to live overseas is much sought after. Her parents, her eldest brother Noman and his family remained in Bangladesh but her sister Yasmeen and her second brother, and their families, were given political asylum in the USA, after claiming that they were being persecuted because of their sister. The USA handled the matter quietly without any great media reaction or diplomatic repercussions; but they could not do the same for Taslima, whose trial brought by her own Government was still pending.

'For a long time Taslima couldn't let go of what had happened to her,' said Besse. Besse was thrilled that Taslima has at last come into her own as a writer. 'She has also become wise and knows when she is being used.'

In spite of the French circus, Taslima was forgotten after she left Paris in late 1994. Besse had foreseen that this would happen, that people would move on to something new, another star.

'She has no constituency, you see,' she said, leaning forward and staring at me intently. 'Rushdie has this enormous constituency: London, Paris and all around the world. We have this saying in France, "Pass me the rhubarb and I will pass you the senna".'

'You scratch my back and I'll scratch yours?' I asked.

'*Exactement!* You have this little circle of big-name writers and intellectuals in France,' she pouted and interrupted herself to tell me that she still didn't understand what being an intellectual meant although by now she should as she was 'a bit long in the tooth. Perhaps it only means, who is in and who is out at the moment. These men have nothing else to do but sit around talking and moving from one cafe to the next.'

As I left Besse in her glorious five-star hotel with the maroon-uniformed porters and the well-bred concierge manning the front desk and made my way home on the tube to my down-at-the-heels, Indian-run, no-star establishment in Earl's Court, I was struck by Besse's vision of her 'Taslie'. Her vision enabled her to see the Taslima hiding between the public and private persona. It was the difference between who you are and who the world demands you should be.

⊕

The most difficult feat for a veteran campaigner is to do nothing. With Taslima back in Bangladesh, her old friends felt they should be doing something—but what? Should they mount another campaign to save her all over again? Emails flashed around the world: humanist groups, PEN centres, Reporter sans frontières and Christianne Besse, all yearning to help in some way. But this time at London HQ, PEN International was proceeding cautiously and liaising closely with her London-based lawyer Sara Hossain. Anything like the media campaign of 1994 must be avoided. To complete the picture, the author herself was behaving more circumspectly, for the moment.

'Reckless' was a word Sara Whyatt used to describe Taslima, she meant it as a compliment, saying she found it a very attractive trait. Sara had only recently spoken to Taslima on her mobile phone in Dhaka, it was early October 1998 and the papers were saying she was once again in hiding. Taslima told Sara that everything was different. The Dhaka crowds were only in their hundreds this time and not in their thousands, she laughed, and Sara said she seemed in good spirits.

Apparently Taslima had taken advantage of the floods, which had devastated Bangladesh, and just slipped in quietly using her national passport—officially nothing untoward happened: she was a Bangladeshi citizen with the right to return.

The two Saras—Whyatt and Hossain—were working hard to head off any campaigns which might harm her legal case, which was still pending. They were in favour of letters requesting the Home Minister to provide the author with protection and guarantee her safety, but that was all. Everything must remain low-key.

That same evening Christianne Besse called me from Paris. She had just received an Email purportedly from Taslima, forwarded to her from New York by someone claiming to be a confidante of the Bangladeshi author, a man called Warren Allen Smith. She felt she should relay this letter to *Le Monde* although I suggested she wait to have it authenticated.

If the message was genuine what new game Taslima was playing at? Why break her own media embargo? For her letter called on the world to help her and said her life was in danger. Burkhard Mueller-Ullrich was right—there was a new story in the air. Once more the carousel was being wound up and, if you listened closely, you could hear the organ music in the background.

Chapter 9

Passionate Women

One thing is certain: Nasreen cannot go home again.
David Richards, Washington Post, July 7, 1998

The authorities will not let me in, even though I have the right to go there.
Taslima Nasreen, 1998

When I first set out in the summer of 1998, there were three good reasons for me to fly from London to New York: Taslima, Meredith Tax and Minar Mahmood, Taslima's third husband, who was driving a yellow cab in New York. But after hearing that Taslima was no longer in New York, and had in fact returned to Dhaka, leaving me with only two good reasons, I was tempted to pack my bags and go home. However, Meredith Tax held pieces of Taslima's story that nobody else knew about.

I had done my best to snare Meredith at the Helsinki PEN Congress, the previous month, but found her too preoccupied with conference politics. I half suspected that she would check me out thoroughly before agreeing to meet with me—Tax is a careful woman.

PEN cronies warned me. 'Watch out,' they said, before moving on to list all of her good points. They were tight lipped about why I should tread warily, leaving me to imagine that certain PEN identities must have crossed swords with her in the past and come off either second best, bloodied, or both.

And so I arrived in the USA, in October 1998. I approached New York the way most first-time travellers look at Calcutta or Dhaka: I wasn't at all sure how to negotiate my way around this exotic place and in the end came away with some very strange impressions of the 'natives'. A studio loft in Greenwich Village is where I pictured myself, but this was not to

221

be and like many immigrants I ended up spending ten days in a motor inn on Queen's Boulevard, Woodside, a noisy eight-lane highway in Queens, where after sunset the rooms were rented by the hour—not a studio loft in sight, just the fire brigade across the road.

Travel guides rave about New York's multiple personalities: cultured New York; New York the city of writers, New York the financial powerhouse. My New York was seedy—not even a sighting of Bloomingdales or Macys on the horizon. My schedule was tight and funds were low. The closest I ever came to the New York I'd read about in books and seen on the screen was after I exited the subway at Pennsylvania Station and walked the few blocks to Women's WORLD and Meredith in the old furriers' district of Manhattan.

Meredith Tax is the woman Taslima calls on whenever she's in trouble. In my imagination they were always an unlikely pair, for in background, looks and temperament they came from different worlds.

Tax is the New York activist who discovered herself and a sense of community in the women's movement. There is a writer locked away inside Tax, stifled for more than a decade: a heavy price to pay for her commitment to other women and other causes—she is essentially an introverted loner who taught herself, many years ago, to work with others. Taslima is the ambitious, narcissistic protest writer from a provincial town in Bangladesh who was catapulted into fame by a hungry media pack and political events beyond her ken or control—she is a loner who cannot work with others. The centre of Tax's universe is other women's lives and a dedication to collective action; the centre of Taslima's world is herself. Taslima stopped herself from going insane by writing, Meredith found sanity through the women's movement; the unlikely pair are sisters under the skin after all.

'I was a misfit, shy and angry, with my nose forever in a book.' The voice is not Taslima's, but Meredith's, recording her own feelings as a young girl in an essay published in *The Feminist Memoir Project*, 1998. Her immigrant Jewish grandparents came to the United States fleeing pogroms and starvation; her parents moved up the ladder into the suburbs, but Meredith remained an outsider. She had no language for how she felt; she simply knew that the life she was being offered was unbearable. Later, her university studies and her reading and involvement in the anti–Vietnam War movement in the late sixties moulded her and she changed almost overnight from what she called 'an artsy bohemian' into a student of politics. The politics of the socialist left captured her head and heart many years ago and she has remained loyal through all the ups and downs that radical left-wing groups experience in capitalist countries.

Early on in her activist days, she recognised other angry voices—raw female voices—making themselves heard in the women's liberation movement of the seventies. She threw herself into any number of famous groups of the day like the Chicago Women's Liberation Union and co-founded, in the late sixties, the pioneering feminist organisation from Boston 'Bread & Roses', whose glorious name came from the old union women's song.

Looking back at her life, in another autobiographical essay, Meredith asks herself why she simply didn't go on with her writing. Book contracts were in the offing, she'd written a US feminist history *The Rising of the Women* and two novels. Marilyn French reviewed her last novel, *Passionate Women*, written in 1985 and wrote: 'In everything she does, Meredith Tax remains true to certain principles which shine through her work. I have the greatest respect for her.' The young Meredith could easily be a character from French's modern classic *The Women's Room*.

The women's movement made Tax understand who she was and gave her a sense of community. She loved the movement so much, she couldn't bear to see it fail to reach its potential. So she paid her dues: she worked in factories, joined different left-wing radical groups, married, divorced, was a single mother, remarried and divorced.

By 1986 Meredith was a member of the American PEN Centre and was beginning to focus on the international human rights arena; she and her friend Grace Paley faced down a malevolent Norman Mailer who chaired the 1986 PEN Congress in New York. Two hundred women, including Betty Frieden and Canadian author and eventual Booker Prize winner Margaret Atwood, helped push forward the concept of a women's committee against some amazing opposition, the same event where Salman Rushdie spoke out from the floor in support. The women lost, but lobbied hard over the next four years. 1991 saw victory and a proud Meredith presented the resolution at a congress where even British PEN, who'd held out for years, were finally won over. Two years earlier, the opposition was so strong that Meredith's faction couldn't risk bringing it to a vote, she reminisced in a hard-hitting article written for *The Women's Review of Books* in 1992.

'I love women,' said the French delegate, Gallic to the bitter end, 'they are my muse, but why should they have a committee?'

⁂

Taslima's single-mindedness and refusal to recant reminded Meredith of the union women and early suffragettes of America: defiant women standing on boxes, exhorting crowds in the street to support their general strikes; she sees in Taslima the same kind of defiance she has always admired since she was a young girl reading *Hedda Gabler, Saint Joan* and *Little Women*. Hidden in the text of Meredith's writing is a romantic which never revealed itself in our quick impromptu meetings in her office. I observed Meredith the feminist, Meredith the campaigner, strategist and historian, but never the romantic.

Meredith realised, half way through the Taslima campaign, that an alternative structure to PEN was needed for women writers, and together with Grace Paley and a number of other women sharing the same ideals set up Women's WORLD (Women's World Organisation for Rights, Literature and Development) which transported Meredith into the multi-ethnic world of women writers and gender-based censorship: she saw the restrictions placed on women writers as a human rights issue with its own distinct patterns that made it different to political censorship.

❈

Taslima Nasreen loves secrets: keeping people filed away in separate compartments, using them whenever she needs to, gives her a feeling of power, and Taslima is still the needy woman she always was. Wherever she goes, people of strong empathy are drawn to her.

Taslima's vulnerability found solace in Tax's strong sense of moral obligation. As an addendum, the American's political savvy warned her that if Taslima was not protected, the cause of persecuted women writers would be set back. Her passion was a powerful antidote to the cynicism of other freedom of expression activists who, by 1996, were starting to grow weary of Taslima's antics. A long list of writers were at risk from around the world who also needed their attention and scant resources, and Taslima had received a lion's share of both over the years. But Meredith has never abandoned Taslima and always rallies to her side whenever a crisis is imminent.

Taslima suspects most people she meets, often with good cause, but her relationship with Meredith is resilient: occasionally it stretches out of shape but soon springs back into its original form and the relationship moves on again. Placing herself in Meredith's hands is eminently sensible. Her American ally has connections, will try to rescue her from any number of bureaucratic dilemmas she finds herself in, and, most important, Meredith never stays mad with her for too long. Others who have quarrelled with Tax and lived to walk away are amazed because from their own experience, 'Meredith stays mad for a long time.'

Taslima's foibles have driven weaker mortals to distraction: her laziness, lack of accountability, and incompetence when it comes to handling visas, book deals, speaking engagements or hundreds of other matters—small and large—requiring patience or at least a willingness to follow up, can push you to the brink. She is also notorious for forgetting—or not bothering—to inform people working on her behalf, if she has other irons in the fire, or if she's changed her mind from one day to the next. Her self-involvement and rudeness astound many. Others are drawn to her childlike behaviour and reach out to protect her. If they are determined to keep Taslima an infant, then it suits her purposes as well.

The vast majority of activists tolerate Taslima's idiosyncrasies because of what she symbolises, but with Tax the attachment goes deeper. When she looks at Taslima, she sees herself as a young angry woman.

A young woman is walking down a city street. She is excruciatingly aware of her appearance and of the reaction to it (imagined or real) of every person she meets. She walks through a group of construction workers who are eating lunch in a line along the pavement. Her stomach tightens with terror and revulsion; her face becomes contorted into a grimace of self-control and fake unawareness ... No matter what they say to her it will be unbearable. (Meredith Tax, extract from essay 'Women and Her Mind: The Story of Daily Life', New England Press 1970)

> You're a girl and you better not forget that when
> you step over the threshold of your house men will
> look askance at you. When you keep on walking down
> the lane men will follow you and whistle....
> (Taslima Nasreen from her poem 'Character')

In Sweden, London, Dhaka or New York, people sum up Taslima's behaviour by smiling helplessly and telling you, 'She is difficult.'

Meredith Tax is no fool; she understands that Taslima is better at burning bridges than building them, but she tolerates Taslima's peculiar brand of folly because the American's sense of mission overpowers everything else.

Taslima is a difficult woman, but she is only behaving as she has always behaved. In her Dhaka days she was adept at manipulating the deeply entrenched client–patron custom, making it serve her own ends: she was never the grateful client, and people were angered because this is not how the game is played in the Subcontinent. Right from the outset, she refused to play pupil to any male guru.

Now that she finds herself in the West, Taslima has seen no need to change her ways and one is inclined to agree with her. There is always Meredith, or Sara, or Eugene on the human rights side of the fence; there is always Christian John in Germany and others from the humanist belt who reject religion, substituting instead a belief in science and a rational way of life. These allies don't expect Taslima to be grateful—helping Taslima is a part of their charter, she represents the cause. And now, after six years in the West, Taslima knows her own worth.

Almost anyone else would have jettisoned Taslima long ago; she can wear you down and tear your heart out, but Meredith is tough, a veteran campaigner who allows Taslima to drop in an out of her life whenever she pleases. Although her demands on Meredith have lessened, there was a period when the two women were almost in daily contact with each other, at the peak of the Taslima affair in 1994. At the time, most of this was concealed—it was better so—for everyone involved.

❈

It all began in late 1993 when Tax held the chair of the International PEN Women Writers' Committee, a novice committee, still proving itself to PEN's old guard. The case fell into her lap almost by accident. On September 25, 1993, she received a fax from the London Writers'-in-Prison Committee enclosing a small Associated Press clip from a London paper. London asked Tax to verify the reports which were starting to trickle in. Farid Hossain's piece, written in Dhaka at around this time, had obviously reached the outside world and, of course, at around the same time, the venerable President of India PEN, Ananda Shankar Roy, was also spreading the word to his brother centres and the BBC.

The Taslima affair was the right case at the right time and Tax has never pretended otherwise, or hidden the fact that it gave her committee the kind of high profile case they needed to test themselves on and show the critics what they could do. Tax set out on her 'journey', bringing to bear the resources of the international women's movement who moved her from one woman to another, by telephone or fax, until she came within reach of Taslima: within three days she'd tracked Taslima down.

Dr Hameeda Hossain, President of Ain O Salish Kendra, a Bangladeshi legal rights organisation, threw in her lot with Meredith. Hameeda Hossain is also the wife and mother of the two Hossain lawyers, Dr Kamal and Sara Hossain, who would, within a few months, start representing Taslima. Meredith Tax contacted Taslima for the first time on October 5, 1993. The author wasted no time in accepting the American's offer of help and they began communicating regularly. The more she heard about Taslima, the more Meredith came to identify with her and so her agenda became more personal.

'If I had been born in Bangladesh I would have been in the same kind of trouble,' Meredith said to me as we sat talking in her well-secured, small office at Women's WORLD where e-mails and faxes streamed in from all corners of the world. 'There are certain kinds of people who are always in trouble no matter where they are, because of what they say and what they write. We have to defend each other.'

At the same time Tax began putting together her intelligence network by drawing in a number of US-based Bangladeshi journalists, feminists and development workers who briefed her on the Taslima situation and women's rights in Bangladesh—they continued to be her sounding board and occasionally acted as couriers during 1993 and 1994 when it was suspected that certain phones in Dhaka were being tapped.

PEN's campaign began in earnest in late 1993 with the goal of getting Taslima's passport returned to her and fighting the ban on her book *Lajja*. Tax was able to call on the London Writers-in-Prison staff to advise her how to deal with diplomats and foreign missions. Her strong card was her experience at building coalitions, coordinating action, arranging demonstrations and liaising with the media—Tax was settling in for a long campaign.

Early in the piece, like any good feminist, Tax became worried that her writer did not have the Bangladesh women's movement behind her. Taslima's Indian interviews might be increasing her book sales in India, but progressive circles inside Bangladesh found themselves on the defence and blamed Taslima.

'You don't have to answer every question the media ask,' she told Taslima by fax. 'Reporters want a sensational story because that sells papers, but it is not necessarily best for you.' She needed to be more selective and less trusting, Tax advised.

In her reply, Taslima promised to be more careful. 'You are one hundred per cent correct,' she told Meredith. 'Western publicity is my best protection.' It was a promise she did not keep; it was not in her nature to shirk the media spotlight.

In November 1993, Meredith organised an op ed (the opinion piece printed opposite the editorial) for Taslima to write for *The New York Times* which drew the foreign writer to the attention of readers in the United States for the first time. But she was still relatively unknown, as American translator, Carolyne Wright, learnt. Wright tried unsuccessfully to have Taslima's poems published in *The New Yorker*; they were turned down, but picked up the following year when Taslima's name was a cause célèbre.

✥

There are many different ways of silencing writers: torture, incarceration, execution—not to overlook the less-expensive, more popular method these days of sending writers into exile. Banning books is just one more extreme style of censorship, but sometimes more ingenious methods are brought into play.

Halfway through the Taslima campaign, a children's book Tax had once written called *Families* was targeted in a campaign orchestrated by the Christian Coalition in Fairfax County, Virginia, in January 1994. These good people felt her book glorified divorce and objected to its inclusion of lesbian couples. The book had been in print for fourteen years but, finally, the publishers put it out of print on the grounds that it was not selling. Whether they chose this course rather than become embroiled in a controversy is speculative, but they certainly did nothing to take advantage of the publicity the debate was generating. Here was Tax calling on a foreign government to lift the ban on Taslima's book, while Christian fundamentalists in her own country were objecting to her 'undermining of traditional family values' and ensuring her book was removed from the required reading lists.

Finally, the Bangladeshi Government became so embarrassed by the bad press that they returned Taslima's passport in April 1994, but her book continued to be proscribed. Meredith was told by Bangladeshi officials in the United States that as the author had resigned from medical service she need only apply for a new passport and that would be the end of the matter. For reasons which are still unclear, the Bangladeshi Embassy continued to send signals through PEN using them as intermediaries, instead of normal diplomatic channels.

As Taslima was completely unknown outside the Indian subcontinent, without the international agitation spearheaded by the influential American PEN Centre and the women's movement, foreign observers, and most Bangladeshis, think it unlikely that the Government would have given in so easily.

Taslima's lawyers beg to differ. Sara Hossain in London just prior to my New York visit wasted no time telling me that the lawyers were prepared to go to court if the passport was not returned by a set deadline, meaning that a legal remedy would have carried the day, anyhow. The Government would not have wanted to face the embarrassment of being taken to court and would have returned the passport—eventually. Otherwise, the argument goes, the media, both local and overseas, would have had a field day. It is an interesting point, but circumstances rendered it hypothetical. However, it illustrates once more that the story of international intervention has always taken the spotlight while the legal efforts of her lawyers and the rule of law have disappeared into the background, scarcely noticed at all.

As both the legal and human rights fraternities were to learn, however, this was just the beginning. In time, Taslima's passport episode would seem like a dream of happier days.

At midnight on June 16, 1994, Meredith received a desperate-sounding fax from Taslima calling for help, followed by plaintive telephone calls in the dead of night with a little voice whispering, 'Help me, help me,' and then hanging up.

Edited versions of Taslima's midnight faxes soon featured in papers around the world.

> I am in grave danger. At any time
> fundamentalists will kill me . . .
> I wanted shelter in any embassy.
> But they did not give shelter . . .
> I am not safe inside the jail even.
> Mullahs are everywhere . . . try to give
> me political asylum in your country.
> If I stay here they must kill me.
> Meredith, please save me.
> (it was dated 13 June 1994)

As an insider who knew better, Meredith has consistently played down the exaggerated aspects of Taslima's departure by emphasising, as she did at a press conference in 1995, that 'she [Taslima] did not flee the country or *officially* [my emphasis] ask for political asylum, but merely went abroad while her trial was continued. She did so with the consent of her Government and plans to return to Bangladesh when it is safe to do so.'

❀

Taslima continued to turn to Meredith while she was in Stockholm under Gabi's benign watch. From correspondence it was clear that Meredith and Gabi did not always see eye-to-eye when it came to questions like campaign journalism, publishing deals and literary agents.

Meredith tried her best to prepare Taslima for her new life, 'older-sister's advice,' she called it in a letter faxed to Taslima, August 14, 1994, four days after Taslima first arrived in Sweden.

> . . . you may have to be abroad a long time . . .
> You have two choices now . . . If you adapt,
> you will "make a virtue of necessity," learn all
> about the world, travel everywhere, meet people
> and see things you never dreamed existed. . . .
> learn English as well as possible, and live a
> cosmopolitan life. Or you can choose to live as a
> writer-in-exile, homesick, regretful . . . living

mainly among Bengalis, making exile a destiny or a
curse. I think you have it in you to make the first
choice. . . . you are alive, Taslima, and that is what counts.
You have survived. Make it mean something. Survive
to bear witness. You have a wider canvas now. Use it
all . . . Let exile open you up, shake off your old self
like a snake casts its skin, feed on the new and
grow . . .

❁

There is a prize that up till now has eluded Taslima: even with Meredith's connections it remains out of reach. Although there have been some
misunderstandings with various American embassies in Europe, Taslima has
been permitted to freely enter the United States on an extended tourist visa
on many occasions. But, this is not the visa she wants. In 1995 she began
enlisting Meredith's help to secure her the 'Rolls Royce of Visas', the O
visa. The US Government grants these to 'authors who have risen to the
very top of the field . . . writers of extraordinary ability.'

After assessing Taslima's application, US authorities found that the documents supporting her petition failed to discuss her published works. The
conclusion was that 'the beneficiary's fame and recognition is based on the
beneficiary's protest against the [sic] religion and as an advocate for women's
rights. The issue here is not on the beneficiary's protest or belief . . . the
issue is on the beneficiary's status as a writer.'

Even with the help of a sympathetic Congressman, the rules were not
bent and without this special visa or a Green Card, Taslima could not work
in the United States. There were many invitations she wanted to accept,
writer residencies at colleges around the country, but this was impossible
on a tourist visa. At the time this was a major setback for the writer, who
was not allowed to accept a salary, or any kind of moneys, when she was in
the United States.

❁

The exact size of the Bangladeshi community in the United States is unknown because of the large number of illegal immigrants; a conservative
estimate in 1998 places it at about 120,000, with more than 50,000 in the
greater metropolitan area of New York City. Most are highly educated:
dentists, doctors, engineers and computer experts, with a sprinkling of less-
educated people working in restaurants or driving taxis. There are about

six weekly Bengali newspapers in New York that exist through ads and subscriptions.

Bangladeshis are a resilient people shrugging off natural calamities, making sacrifices and always on the alert for that lucky break. Life is a lottery for immigrants, with a deeper meaning for the lucky winners of one of 55,000 places drawn each year in the USA's lottery visa system. When it first began in the nineties, Bangladeshi entries scored 5,000 out of 20,000 visas for the entire world: the sheer volume of applications ensured that. Even today they continue to win a disproportionate number of places. Each year, as the visa deadline draws near, great excitement sweeps the country and a small industry springs into place, with secretaries typing out thousands of applications and post offices struggling to cope with the mail because many aspirants enter hundreds of applications. Ten thousand dollars (US) is the going rate for anyone wanting to buy the promise of a better life from a countryman willing to pocket the dollars and, in return, surrender his dream along with his visa.

Leaving Bangladesh does not mean turning your back on domestic politics. Political parties have their branches in the United States, the UK and elsewhere. Official names are not always used and there are front organisations set up by the religiously based Jamaat Party, an organisation which formed the hub of the anti-Taslima forces in her home country. Younger men under forty join the parties; men who belonged in their young days to the student wings of parties back home continue their wheeling and dealing, still participating in home politics with a fullness and zeal which they'll never taste in the United States at least for two or three generations, perhaps in another century. They fly the flag, raise funds and watch one another closely. There is always one young man or another rushing out to La Guardia or Kennedy Airport to meet, or be part of an entourage for, a party bigwig; some important party figure is always arriving, making speeches, collecting money and departing.

In 1994 Bengali American papers covered the Taslima story and reflected the opinions circulating in Bangladesh at the time: some were noncommittal, some critical and some in favour of her book. Most non-Muslims from the Subcontinent took Taslima's side. But even her Bangladeshi supporters in the United States were annoyed with Taslima after an interview published in *The Washington Post* on 7 July 1998.

'I do not always feel safe [in the US]. There are a lot of Muslim fundamentalists here,' she said. 'Sometimes when I come home at night from Manhattan in a taxi, the driver recognises me and starts to ask me questions. . . . I say "Stop the taxi right away." I get out and take another taxi.'

Expatriate Deshis in New York thought the writer was up to her old tricks of exaggerating her situation to keep herself in the news. And of course they sent word back to Bangladesh.

∰

I needed help in tracking down Taslima's third husband, Minar Mahmood. Naim reached out from Dhaka and enlisted the services of an old friend who acted as my guide in Queens and Manhattan. Manjur Islam was a young professional who once used to gad about Dhaka with Taslima and her second husband, Naim. The young man disliked Taslima intensely.

'I know her,' he said, 'she doesn't fool me. There are strong personal feelings that I can't control.'

I later regretted that we argued as much as we did over Taslima for I could not fault him as a host or as a fellow sleuth. Manjur tracked down the elusive Minar Mahmood, leading me from one Bangladeshi taxi haunt to the next. They were small, spotlessly clean cafes in Manhattan where the drivers met, read Bangla papers, exchanged gossip and ate their spicy food. Minar agreed to talk to me only because he trusted Manjur, and my Pakistani-Muslim ancestry made him feel comfortable, he said. American journalists had pursued him in 1994, but Minar had remained silent.

Minar Mahmood was handsome, dashing and full of life, who probably reminded Taslima of Rudra, once his close friend. Their pals in Dhaka thought the newspaper editor and the doctor-poet made an ideal pair, and he was certainly more of a match for her than either of her previous men. Minar's career had never been smooth sailing: his existence as a newspaper editor had been ruined twice over in Bangladesh when he ran foul of government. His views were seen as too radical, too critical and although there is no official censorship in Bangladesh there are other methods of forcing journalists into line (self-censorship)—being beaten up by *goondahs* in the pay of political parties, or depriving owners of government advertising, or government-controlled newsprint. Under President Ershad's regime he found himself gaoled for three months in 1991, an unheard-of sentence for an editor, but as he said, his mother was widowed and he had no family connections to protect him.

Minar was quite the raconteur and regaled me with one story after the other about his early courtship of Taslima, although he neglected mentioning that he'd divorced his first wife in order to marry Taslima in 1991. On one occasion he found himself on the wrong side of Taslima's father, who was making an unannounced visit to his daughter's quarters in Dhaka and flew into a rage when he found a strange man visiting her. Dr Ali packed up his daughter and all her belongings, including her young maid, and dragged them back to Mymensingh, where he locked Taslima in her room for two days before she managed to escape with her maid and run back to Minar. His mother would not tolerate Taslima staying at their house in an 'unmarried condition' and insisted they marry, which they did in 1991—they divorced six months later.

The tensions between Taslima and her father were unresolved for many years and only ended in 1994 after she became disgraced at home and famous abroad. Her second husband Naim had long ago noticed the bizarre way Taslima spoke to her father. During their three-year relationship, never once did she address Dr Ali as 'father' in Naim's presence—an impossible way of behaving to your father in a Muslim society. It would take a will of iron to keep this up, but as the stories from her childhood revealed, Taslima had many reasons for punishing her father.

Minar's newspaper career and his marriage ran aground at the same time; this time he fell foul of the BNP Government. He could not give Taslima the life she wanted and he was too busy trying to keep his fledgling newspaper afloat. But there were other signs.

Once he offered to help her establish her own medical clinic, so that she could resign from government service, which she hated; this would make her independent, he thought. Her reaction was swift and unpleasant. Taslima accused him of trying to make money out of her. Minar, in turn, didn't like the people she was mixing with: 'sycophants,' he called them. She took to coming home late from parties and he worried about her safety. Stories drifted back to Minar that she would buy people beer, telling them as a joke, 'Drink up, it's not my money, it's Minar's.' 'That hurt,' he said.

After his second newspaper venture failed, Minar immigrated to the USA in 1993, where he now drives a taxi. The qualifications and skills of a journalist who writes in Bengali do not travel well: doctors, engineers or scientists have portable qualifications that have a chance of being transposed in their adopted country; they may need a bridging course or additional training, but many of the text books they have studied were written in English, which is also accepted as the pre-eminent language of science around the world. Journalists and other writers have it much tougher. For Minar, English was a second language, but he still writes a column for a local Deshi paper about what he sees and hears from the driver's seat of a yellow cab and contains his bitterness. There is never any malice directed towards Taslima Nasreen for the changes in his circumstances, just a warm glow of nostalgia.

Minar Mahmood was the last of Nasreen's husband-mentors; those days are long gone. At last she is independent and controls her own sexuality, reproduction, her movements and personal space along with her resources.

In the West she may have platonic relationships with men; or live with a man outside of marriage and not be called a whore; she can live alone if she wishes without people dragging her name into the gutter.

Yet, wherever Taslima goes, she remains controversial: her international audience demands nothing less than perfection from its heroes, especially those who spruik human rights on the celebrity circuit for a living—stumble along the way and you pay the price of being shunted to the sidelines, as happened to Taslima in Sweden and Germany.

As an observer I've always stood outside the fellowship of fans who worship dissidents. The imperfections and the flaws in human nature, the contradictions and the inconsistencies, are to me the stuff of life and books. Name any of the seven deadly sins and there is always some dissident in some corner of the world who show themselves as flawed as the rest of humanity. Dissidents are not gods, but they are capable of heroic efforts and that is why we look up to them. The critical stance they take on issues of conscience that too many of us turn away from, out of cynicism or apathy, is why we need them in our lives. The written word takes on the weight of public opinion and powerful institutions—the dissident is a minority of one, their only weapon is their 'voice'.

I listened to Minar's story with a sinking feeling, knowing I'd heard the same words once before. I remembered Naim insisting, one afternoon in his Dhaka office, that I hear him out when all I wanted to do was turn away and block my ears. Now, in New York, it was Minar's turn to rekindle a disappointment that I couldn't quite control.

Nasreen's behaviour, Minar said, caused him to struggle with his own feelings: 'love and repulsion,' he said—'in the end love won out'.

Both men disapproved of the way Nasreen, as they always called her, treated her child servant: she would often scold and hit the little maid; wake the child up late at night to serve them food and massage her limbs. Minar once arrived at her flat to find the door open; the child, 'who looked like a little doll,' he recalls, had run away to Mymensingh and it took them two days to discover that the girl had reached home safely. The maid came from Nasreen's hometown and was small for her age, which Naim guessed to be between ten and thirteen, although Minar thought her younger. Undernourished mothers give birth to undernourished babies, and the child, brought up in poverty, may not have looked her age. Neither man remembers the child's name but she was a young pre-pubescent girl, at an age when they are seen to be more pliable and less likely to be 'spoilt', and in her treatment Nasreen was no better or worse than the average middle-class housewife. The child could be woken up at midnight with a smack to rouse her, and never seemed to have a day off. Like many servants she was locked in to prevent her from running away and becoming lost. Minar remembered the poor-quality food the child ate, 'rubbish food,' he called it compared to the delicacies Nasreen's mother brought with her when she visited her daughter.

Naim was not telling his stories out of malice, he said, but simply to illustrate that the Nasreen he knew was 'just like any other girl in Bangladesh', a local woman who behaved 'typically' for someone from her background. At the time I thought there were other stories he might have chosen to make his point, but I never questioned his motives. I don't believe that Naim or Minar were trying to influence me against Taslima, for by turning a blind eye, neither man appeared in a good light. Naim in Dhaka, and Minar in New York, doing their best to explain the simplicity and the complexities of their former love.

Naim wanted me to understand that her conduct did not make her a monster, and he is right. Taslima was behaving like many other women in her position. She is inordinately fond of children, openly affectionate to her nephews and nieces; there are many photos of Taslima nursing babies and smiling down at infants. She would never dream of waking up a 'child' to massage her feet or wait on her late at night, but many women and men in Bangladesh from her class are socialised not to think of servants—child servants—as 'children'. Nasreen, unorthodox in so many of her ways, was apparently unable to shed this cultural trait. This kind of indifference and much worse she witnessed as she grew up in Mymensingh. It is also an attitude that cannot be attributed to a colonial heritage, as middle-class Deshis argue. There are times when you can't blame the British for everything! Taslima at first carried this behaviour with her into exile: in Sweden she was unpopular with her security guards, who refused to carry her parcels and be treated like servants; some people felt that she used Gabi as her 'boy' to do her errands, and her strange abrupt behaviour in Sweden and Germany, her habit of not saying hello, or goodbye, is not typically Bangladeshi but pure Taslima at her narcissistic best. Paradoxically, Taslima was both flawed and shaped by the society she criticised.

The one story I'd kept at arm's length because I didn't want to believe it seemed true after all, and I couldn't overlook its message. I wanted the author and dissident, who wrote about child abuse and women's slavery and those who prowled on the weak, to look more kindly at the individual human beings she met along the way—outside the pages of a book.

✤

Taslima Nasreen has paid a heavy price for her personal freedom, but she has said publicly time and again that she will never say *tauba* (I repent):

although she wants to return home and public repentance would pave the way and stop the mullah-minded in their tracks.

Fortunately, for Taslima, she has many new friends who applaud the defiance she acts out through her public persona and in her writing. There is none more loyal than Warren Allen Smith, an incredibly fit man in his mid-seventies and a devoted humanist. Whenever his hero's name is mentioned, his eyes light up, his nostrils flare and he turns into a Taslima dragon slayer of the first order.

Warren Allen Smith is a very funny New Yorker who, if he wasn't a professional humanist, would have made a great columnist in the style of Hedda Hopper or Louella Parsons. He leads you along a track strewn with witticisms, famous names and innuendoes which he scatters with all the charismatic exuberance of a Broadway star. He is an entertainer and was once in the recording industry as he never fails to mention, and in the end you forgive him his outrageous self-promotion—that's showbiz and you're in New York! Smith is a self-confessed 'roue and Sybarite', which he emphasises (dare I say religiously?) in all of his voluminous biographical data. On the night that I visited him in his Greenwich Village co-op apartment, he mentioned three times in so many minutes that he had been on Omaha Beach. As an Australian, it took me a few minutes to determine the significance of this World War II disclosure.

Two years have passed since our meeting but I still stay in touch with his exploits by browsing the Warren Allen Smith web page, where one day in mid-2000, I read that he's completed an enormous reference work of twelve hundred pages, *Who's Who in Hell*, a well-received biographical dictionary of tens of thousands of living and dead free thinkers, secular humanists, Unitarian Universalists and other famous folk who hewed to no religious creed, as the review in *Publisher's Weekly* tells us. Of course amongst the living and the dead, amongst the movie stars and the philosophers, there's an entry on Taslima Nasreen.

Smith of New York, as he sometimes liked to be called, has been a loyal friend to Taslima over the years: when she flew to New York in 1998 to meet her parents and organise their medical treatment, he helped find her an apartment, buy furniture, order papers, install a telephone, and only a few months prior had agreed to Taslima's request that he sponsor her sister and brother for American citizenship. Nothing is too much trouble for Warren: Taslima's mother could not endure the hospital's aggressive treatment for cancer of the colon and begged to return home after three weeks, but she wanted to see the ocean before she left and so Warren took the family, with both parents in wheelchairs, to Coney Island, where they watched the cold waves of the Atlantic Ocean.

Warren was the only person outside of her family circle who knew that Taslima was thinking of returning to Bangladesh. They spoke the night before she left with her family. Sensing something was in the air, he asked her bluntly what she was up to. Taslima was evasive, although Warren suspected that she might already have bought the ticket.

'I'll tell you later,' was the only answer she would give. Taslima knew her mother was dying; she would go with her and because they would all disapprove and try to dissuade her, she would tell no one in advance, not even Meredith.

After her arrival in Dhaka on 18 September 1998, Smith became so worried about her safety that he mounted a new campaign to help Taslima, drawing in more than two hundred addresses with help from international groups like the Council of Secular Humanism. Taslima's campaign this time round would be led by the humanist, rationalist and atheist brigades; it would be Internet driven by Web pages and e-mail messages, with Smith assuming the role of Web master.

Reading the Taslima Web page, carefully guarded and updated by Warren, I couldn't help but wonder after my return to Australia in late 1998, and in the years to follow, what impact letters from the American Atheist Association would have on the Prime Minister, Sheikh Hasina, at the time, who headed a pro-secularist government but is a believing Muslim who made her pilgrimage to Mecca before being elected to government in 1996.

The Smith campaign gave rise to an interesting situation, with the potential for an ideological tug of war over the author. From my vantage point I could see that for the first time the humanists were emerging from the wings and taking centre stage.

Working on one side were Sara Hossain, London PEN and Meredith Tax, representing the freedom of expression organisations, acting with purposeful restraint, wanting at all costs to avoid the hype and hysteria that paradoxically marred and 'made' the first international campaign of '93–'94 and conscious that any use of the media was a double-edged sword. Legal matters as usual were sensitive. Taslima's old case was still pending and a new suit had been filed against her by a private citizen merely to harass the author.

On the other side the humanists, as a subculture, entered the drama later, post-1994, and had not learnt the lessons that too much media hype would elicit a backlash in Bangladesh, and that to ignore local Bangladeshi politics was to do so at your own, or Taslima's, peril. The humanists played the old refrain that Taslima was in terrible danger again, with Warren in the foreground, calling for donations on her behalf. He admitted to me, sheepishly, that he'd done this without Taslima's permission—he knew she'd be furious, but he couldn't stop himself because he knew her finances were low. Such moneys, he said would be used solely by Taslima as she alone determined what would best further her causes.

Despite Warren's best efforts, American papers were slow to cover the story this time round. He was angry that *The New York Times* had written not one word about Taslima's latest trouble, but were full of Rushdie stories about how the Iranian Government had lifted his death sentence. Warren refused to be stalled by those with more experience. He saw himself as Taslima's voice reaching out to the world from Dhaka. It was Warren who forwarded Taslima's e-mails out of Dhaka to Christianne Besse, in Paris. If you wanted news of Taslima, tune in to Warren Allen Smith. He even went on the BBC, much to the horror of certain PEN veterans.

The question remains, was Warren Taslima's mouthpiece? Or was he initiating the campaign himself? A little of both, I suspected, but he was irrepressible. At a time when her old-time allies were advising her to stay out of the world press, Smith was doing his best to strike up the band.

⁂

The two friends first met at an international humanists' conference in Mexico City in 1996. 'We had a rapport right from the beginning,' Warren said. Soon after Taslima wrote to him asking for his help with a speech she was writing. As Warren explained, 'Her English needed a little panache.'

Since then he'd been doing all of her speeches, starting with the one she gave at the European Union, one in South Africa, Scotland, but not the Prague paper, he said. He even visited Taslima and Gunnar in Stockholm in 1996 and they all had a great time. 'She is so down to earth and so playful,' he said making her sound like a frolicsome puppy.

'I didn't change her speeches,' he emphasised, 'All I did was polish the syntax. She'd give it to me in English; sometimes she gets faxes in New York from someone in India. Doesn't she write in Sanskrit [sic] or something and somebody else translates it [into English]?' he asked me off-handedly.

Once more it became apparent that the friendly hand of Ananda Bazar continued to reach out and assist their author with her speeches for important occasions; there is overwhelming evidence, going back to her days in Germany in 1995. It has always been easy to distinguish Taslima's voice in most of the speeches she gives, but there are times when the pronouncements are so scholarly and the allusions so beyond her cultural context and educational background that it leaps from the pages—then it is clear that they are more than mere translations. A Taslima who speaks of Disraeli and nineteenth-century Britain is not using her authentic voice. It is difficult to assess how much of her original voice is left in these speeches, but when the stories are about the suffering of women in Bangladesh, it is her voice. The embellishments attempting to turn her into a scholar-philosopher like Salman Rushdie come from outside.

In the end I decided that this was of little consequence. Most politicians and celebrities have professional speechwriters and wordsmiths labouring on their behalf. Although it might at first sound odd for a writer to have her speeches written for her, one needs to remember that Taslima is a Bengali-language writer – as she once told me in Sweden with a dignified, calm firmness that put me in my place, 'I will write in my language, not English.'

Still it is hard to escape the irony of using an Indian publishing house to help produce a speech about the oppression of Bangladeshi women which Taslima presented to the European Union as an expert witness in mid-1995. Word soon leaked out in Calcutta, and from there to Bangladesh, that Nikhil Sarkar was [allegedly] writing most of Taslima's overseas speeches. This gave her critics more ammunition: 'So she has her speeches written by a man,' they sneered, forgetting that Taslima is not a puppet. The passion, the anger are always Taslima's, the local references and the women's stories come alive in her writing.

Warren excelled at giving Taslima's speeches a dramatic edge, to help her create what he called 'an empathy with her audience'; one line he remembered fondly in a Canadian speech she gave in July 1998. 'When she said, "I am considered a dangerous woman," I suggested that she play it as an actress would. "Take out your pocket book," I told her, ask the audience, "Do you think I am a dangerous woman?" Then reach into your bag and give them five seconds to wonder what you're going to do, and slowly take out a pen and say, "This is why I'm a dangerous woman!" I know the Ottawa papers caught that,' he laughed.

A year later a copy of the speech given in Ottawa crossed my desk. The references to English poet Mathew Arnold and his essay on 'Culture and Anarchy' sounded like the voice of Warren Allen Smith. In this address, given in late July 1998, Taslima asked her audience: 'Will you come forward with a rope and hang me because of what I am saying, which is what will happen if I return tomorrow to the public square in Dacca [sic], the capital city of Bangladesh?'

Just how many of her Canadian audience, I wondered, would remember her declaration when she returned to Dhaka, a month later, and was not hanged in the public square, receiving instead the protection of the law she was entitled to as a citizen?

Shortly after the Canadian speech, Taslima was once more on Bangladeshi soil. 'Martyrdom on behalf of real culture is not too great a price to pay,' she had told her Canadian fans. Who wrote these melodramatic lines? Warren or Taslima? Or was it a collaboration of two kindred spirits? I suspected the latter and thought of French writer Phillippe Sollers, who'd tried to warn Taslima against 'the morbid lure of martyrdom for humanity'. There was no need for her to repay her benefactors with 'humanist declarations' he said quoting his favourite Voltaire, 'Please, no martyrs,' the philosopher had once implored in a letter.

Nevertheless it was the heroic Taslima that Warren and most of her supporters really adored. 'I call her the contemporary Antigone! She is the most inspiring person I have ever met,' he enthused.

It had been a long evening of hyperbole, and before I could stop myself I blurted out, 'Did the American feminist movement pass you by Warren?' I bit my tongue but Warren is good humoured enough to overlook a boorish guest.

'I never quite understood what the feminists were doing, I guess' he said.

Taslima's New York friend is more than twice her age, but Warren Allen Smith is young at heart and a man who knows how to have fun and where the 'in' places are. Taslima often needs to set aside her public persona and enjoy herself—playing Antigone, all your life, can be tiring. With Warren, she has the luxury of being herself, for he makes no demands. Their friendship is helped by his lack of interest in politics and his naive understanding of South Asian societies, so that he is inclined to believe whatever he is told and thus arguments are avoided.

He believes that Bangladesh is divided into 'good Muslims' who supported Taslima and 'bad Muslims' who didn't; the latter will always be a problem, not only for Taslima but, for the whole world, he told me before we parted. For Warren it is as simple as that.

Chapter 10

Missing Pieces

If one tells the truth, one is sure sooner or later to be found out.

Oscar Wilde

'By Allah,' the king thought to himself, 'I won't slay her until I hear some of her wondrous tales.'

Richard F. Burton. *The Thousand and One Nights.*

L eaving all the Taslima cities behind me I returned to Australia, but the feeling that something was still missing persisted. Local newspaper accounts and a few Bangladeshi friends had hinted of behind-the-scene dealings in August 1994; the main religious party had mildly protested the Government's apparent involvement . . . but very little else was ever said and it troubled me. Driven to locate those missing parts before I could end my story, I needed to turn the clock back once more to Dhaka, July 1994, when it all began.

The news that Taslima was in hiding to avoid the Government's warrant of arrest was disconcerting to her supporters overseas. They had worked non-stop for the last six months, to win her passport back—and for the life of them—could not understand why, when she had the chance of remaining abroad, she had returned from Paris to Dhaka in May of 1994, to the home capital that she spent all of her time telling them was a death trap. Her allies had expected her to travel and see something of the world, to stay away for as long as necessary for the furore to die down, and at the time there was no warrant out for her arrest, no charges had been laid against her. She might well have toured Europe and the United States; the Swedes were offering her a writer's residency. If things were really so grim, why did she return?

Only one answer seems possible: When Taslima left for the Paris conference in late April 1994, her life was not in danger and she understood this.

Witnesses attest to her good spirits and excitement that the Western media
was so taken by her story. Clearly she had been playing to the cameras up
till then, with the help of her friends in India, and there was no reason for
her not to return to Dhaka. By mid-1994, however, the tempo and tensions
surrounding the anti-Taslima protests had heightened.

❈

What exactly happened between June 4 when the Government's warrant
went out for the author's arrest and the moment of her court appearance
sixty days later? At some point in my journey I had crossed over and
become obsessed with finding answers. I was not so much turning away
from Taslima, but shifting my focus to the events which had determined
her fate: circumstances which explain why she now lives in the West.

The official story leapt from June 4, when Taslima went underground,
to August 4 when she reappeared in court. It seemed to happen almost
overnight, but in reality it was a long-drawn-out process with two scenarios
unfolding.

The first scenario was Taslima in hiding: her own private drama where
she was moved from house to house at night, never staying in one place for
too long, her nerves unravelling under the stress of not knowing what the
future held—an extremely frightened woman whose imagination ran riot.

Yet, as always, it was the politics behind the drama which drew me like
a magnet: the negotiations played out behind the scenes involving Taslima's
lawyers, the BNP Government, and the 'Taslima-friendly zones' which had
sprung up around the world.

What deals were struck behind closed doors? Earlier visits to Dhaka in
'97 and '98 failed to yield the insider information and level of detail I was
after. Nobody seemed to have the entire story or was prepared to break
ranks, and Taslima's lawyers were bound by sub judice and client privilege,
although in retrospect I was far too reverential to their law degrees and
reputations. I half suspected that the Hossains were unsure about what kind
of a book I was writing: whether or not it would serve their client's purpose
or their own. It was difficult for them to influence me without being
seen to influence me. And why should they risk compromising themselves
and their client's case to satisfy my need to know, which was starting to
weigh even me down? Nearly five years had passed; it was now March
1999. The Taslima court case was still pending, but surely over the passage
of time attitudes were less partisan and one or two closed doors might
open?

The idea of returning for one last attempt at finding the missing pieces
took hold in February 1999. I rationalised my decision, telling myself I'd

be killing two birds with one stone: fill in those maddening 'gaps' while discovering all I could about Taslima's reception four months earlier when she'd flown home with her parents from New York to Dhaka keeping everyone, except Warren Allen Smith, in the dark. Talking to local people would let me know if the Taslima Web page, courtesy of WA Smith, was dealing in half-truths. Smith's account seemed intent on turning the clock back to the days of 1994. But in September 1998, when the author slipped into the country, the mood of Bangladesh had shifted.

The airport authorities did nothing to stop Taslima from entering the country in September that year. There were no instructions from the Government: nobody had expected her, so she was able to sneak into Dhaka without officialdom noticing. It was a clever move, a touch of the Taslima boldness of old. The worst flood damage the country had ever experienced in a hundred years preoccupied everyone. Many of the *madrassahs*, those old hotbeds of fanaticism, were either closed or under water. So for the first seventy-two hours, Dhaka received their errant author with an almost deafening silence.

After a few days the news was out and some of her old enemies made the time to organise an obligatory demonstration or two, to protest her return. But the level of anti-Taslima agitation remained low compared to 1994. Newspaper and verbatim accounts, including Taslima's telephone conversation with Sara Whyatt in London, confirm this. Farid Hossain, in his Associated Press article, talked of 'dozens [not thousands] of Islamic extremists' out in the streets yelling 'Hang the *murtaad*!' although, as he pointed out, the charges Nasreen faced for allegedly insulting the Qur'an carry a maximum penalty, under the law, of two years. Still such inconsistencies never stand in the way of a lively demonstration in Dhaka.

Nasreen told her old journalist friend Farid Hossain that she wanted her freedom back. 'This is my country and I've every right to freely live here.'

The local press mainly ignored her: one paper printed a small front-page article and photo; while the largest pro-Islamist paper failed to cover the story. Twenty-three mullahs from the smaller Islamist parties signed a petition demanding her trial. Apparently, there was not much news and not much of a protest. Read the Warren Allan Smith Web page and you feasted your eyes on a different version. Once more she was in hiding in fear of her life, calling on outside help, a very worried woman who seemed to finally realise that she could never lead a normal life in Bangladesh again. The latter statement had the ring of truth. Many of the other allegations had that familiar tone of half-truth, half-exaggeration which has always coloured the Taslima narratives. What received almost no coverage at the time was the police protection Taslima was receiving.

The Indian press was more attentive, especially *The Statesman* in Calcutta, which wrote a number of articles defending Nasreen, arguing that it was 'time to wrap up the Taslima case. Respect is due to her not witch hunt,' said the paper sounding as if it wanted to make amends for the controversial interview of four years ago, which had precipitated her fall from grace. Generally, the voices were muted, this time round, except for Taslima's outside appeals to the BBC, and the coverage in French and Indian papers.

In an e-mail message sent on 30 September 1998 to her old allies in the West, she claimed that 'if I am arrested, I will be put in prison. If the Government fail to arrest and hang me, then the fundamentalists have declared that they must kill me. Every day thousands are out in the streets,' she said. She ended her plea for help by calling on the democratic governments of the world to lobby the Bangladeshi Government to ensure her security and drop the case against her.

Central to the Taslima mythology was always the assertion that she could not return to Bangladesh, yet her safe return showed the weakness in this claim, especially after she was given protection by the police and the Supreme Court. PEN activists working behind the scenes in Sweden were required to do some swift lobbying at the time with their Government, for Taslima had been given political asylum, the implication being that she could not enjoy a normal relationship with her own Government—if she did, technically she was not a political refugee.

Without mounting a campaign, Amnesty and PEN quietly urged the Government to protect their writer friend. A French television crew made its way to Dhaka in early October, but it was minimal media attention compared to the past and the language had completely changed. The word *fatwa* was no longer being used except by Taslima, the Indian Rationalist Association and a few Indian papers; otherwise the expression *death threats* was substituted. The only references to Rushdie were made by Taslima herself in several 'exclusive' telephone interviews.

'The difference between me and Salman Rushdie is that I am living in the country where thousands of people want to kill me,' she said. 'It is really, really dangerous.'

A prisoner of her own mythology, the author never tired of comparing herself to Rushdie. Taslima's name and misadventures might have slipped out of sight, but who could forget Rushdie and his Iranian fatwa. Her status was chained to his misfortune and so she allowed herself to become a professional victim. Sheherezade needed 1,001 tales to survive; Taslima seemed to have only the one story.

The European Parliament rallied in early December 1998 in a carelessly worded resolution riddled with factual errors that described Taslima as seeking refuge in the EU in order to escape arrest for blasphemy. Not long after, a leader of a visiting EP delegation said, 'We are keeping an eye on the matter and we believe that nothing would be done that endangers the safety and security of the writer.'

The Awami League Government, in power since 1996, handled matters sensibly, keeping a firm lid on demonstrations and issuing press releases, making it clear that anyone who broke the law would be punished; Taslima was given police protection, but the Government refused to drop the case brought by their predecessors. Neither did they instigate proceedings against those men who had broken the law by threatening her in 1994.

The Home Minister played down her return by saying that the writer was always at liberty to come home as she was on indefinite bail from the High Court of Bangladesh. She would receive security, if she wanted it, he said in his press statement, like any other citizen of the country. His colleague, the Foreign Minister, told the press that coming home to see your mother was one thing, but using the opportunity to make appeals to the international community, in an attempt to rekindle a new campaign, was quite another, especially while taking advantage of legal protection in your own country. 'The law will take its own course and Taslima is not above the law—she will, however, get protection according to the law.'

Reading between the lines, the warning was clear: 'Not again, Taslima, not again!'

Prime Minister Sheikh Hasina played an adroit political role by chiding both sides for having 'crossed the line.' Nobody should threaten anyone else and nobody should ignore religious sentiment. Neither the mullah-minded nor the civil libertarians were likely to have been appeased by Sheikh Hasina's comments, although it was seen as a breakthrough by Taslima's foreign supporters, who were puzzled, nevertheless, by the Prime Minister's statement where she announced: 'Her writings are vulgar, not feminist. I being a woman can't read her books.' The Prime Minister advised Nasreen to surrender to the courts. 'She should go to the court. There is a rule of law in this country,' Hasina said.

The Statesman in India was less tolerant. 'The impression is of a petulant schoolteacher trying to separate two warring factions of her pupils. Sheikh Hasina will have to do better than that.'

It was an open secret in Dhaka that Hasina the politician disliked Nasreen the writer. Years before, while in Opposition, a reluctant Hasina had been persuaded to assist Taslima, who was being harassed by the Bangladesh Doctors' Association and found herself transferred to one remote hospital

after the other by a BNP administration more than willing to sign the Association's transfer orders. Before agreeing to help, Hasina made it plain that
she strongly disapproved of Nasreen's public comments on Islam. Taslima
tried to explain that she was only criticising the mullahs, but Sheikh Hasina
would have none of that, and accused her of criticising the basic principles
of Islam. Perhaps in the end she relented because Nasreen had written a
poem 'Joi Bangla' about Hasina's dead father, Sheikh Mujib, which the
BNP Government would not have liked.

❁

Taslima's Islamist enemies have long memories and they have the resources
and the will to continue harassing her. After her return, the extremists
soon devised a new stratagem by rekindling an old complaint from 1994, a
different charge to the Government's first case; she and her lawyers knew
nothing about the complaint at the time it was issued. The case was weak, a
frivolous complaint that should have been thrown out at the Lower Court
level, but was meant to flush the author out of hiding and force her into
court: it was harassment, plain and simple. The order by the Dhaka District
Magistrate's Court to reissue the old warrant for her arrest and revive the case
came ten days after Nasreen returned to Bangladesh. The legal manoeuvres
started up once again. A man described as a 'devout Muslim', in the court
records, complained about certain remarks made in a book of essays written
in 1991.

The largest anti-Taslima demonstration took place on 4 October 1998,
against the Awami League Government, when a group of activists from
Islami Okiyya Jote, the alliance of smaller mullah-based parties, led by my
old mullah 'friend', was stopped by the police from presenting the Home
Minister with a petition. The protest was directed at the police, blaming
the Awami Home Minister for not having Taslima arrested, which the
demonstrators claimed was deliberate. Police used tear gas shells and *lathi*
(baton)-charged the protesters, who retaliated by throwing brickbats and
crude exploding bombs. At this stage it degenerated into a battleground,
with one killed and fifty injured. Reports of crowd sizes swung from 'hundreds' in one account to 'two thousand' in another.

Had the Government been serious about arresting Taslima, she could
readily have been served with a warrant. Although she stayed away from the
public eye, unofficially in hiding, her whereabouts must have been known
to senior officials as she was receiving police protection. This time round,
her main opponents were from the smaller Islamic parties, while Jamaati,
the largest and most disciplined of the religiously based parties, kept a low
profile, even forcing a branch chairman into line when he offered a reward

to anyone delivering Taslima [alive] to the authorities. It was a strong public rebuke that did not go unnoticed by the Taslima watchers.

On 22 November, Taslima made a surprise appearance at the Supreme Court—just as she had four years earlier—where she again surrendered before the Court and faced the arrest warrants for the new case brought against her. The Judge kept her appearance from the public and the media to avoid any 'unpleasant scenes.' After a half-hour hearing, her lawyer's plea for anticipatory bail was granted, but no trial date was set.

In reaching this decision the Supreme Court overturned the Lower Court decision not to grant bail, removing any danger of the author's property being confiscated. It was a significant legal move: her lawyers were permitted, from then on, to represent her in absentia, the judges accepting the argument that it was dangerous for her to appear in open court. In 1994 and again in 1998, the Supreme Court's decisions gave the author protection under the law.

The Times in London summed up the mood of the country over the latest Taslima crisis in its 'World in Brief' report from Delhi. 'The popular mood in Bangladesh cares little for the somewhat contrived controversy,' it wrote on 22 November 1998.

Taslima left Dhaka and started out in search of yet another new beginning in Sweden, in January 1999. I found myself once more bringing up the rear, but trailing in the wake of Taslima was by now a habit.

❈

All was not well in Dhaka in March 1999 when I returned. Law and order had deteriorated in the last two years and the former BNP Government, now in opposition, was making the Awami Government's political life hell—it was a simple reversal of roles: partisan politics and political violence once more to the fore. The opposition was looking for an issue to hang Awami with—Taslima was a political liability and they would use it if they could; therefore the Awami Government needed to be vigilant. Awami was not about to inherit an international embarrassment of BNP's making, and wished Taslima would go away.

In 1999 I began to appreciate fully that the author could not lead a normal life in Bangladesh. In spite of the police protection and the 'less strident' demonstrations, only her most stubborn critics believed that she was not at risk. Usually they were the same local figures, the feminists and other activists, insisting, as they had years before, that the calls of 'Hang her!' were more symbolic than real, a part of the nation's political culture. But Bangladeshi political culture had changed over the last decade and, as I observed, all was not well in Dhaka.

There was talk of terrorism from outside: unverified reports of money and arms smuggled in from Afghanistan, hidden away behind the gates of remote *madrassahs*, it was rumoured. The country's much beloved national poet, Shamsur Rahman, had survived an attempt on his life on 18 January 1999 from an axe-wielding assassin. His wife wrestled the weapon from the attacker, sustaining injuries to herself.

Two years before the attack, I'd visited the elderly poet in his home. Thick glasses and a mane of grey hair did nothing to detract from his charm; his way of listening lulled you into believing you were the only person in the room. He had always defended Taslima even though he had mixed feelings about *Lajja*, which he considered a good subject, but lacking balance. 'She is a courageous writer,' he said. 'She overdoes it, but I like her boldness.'

Even before the attempt on his life, he'd talked about the danger in being publicly identified with liberal causes. 'A writer has no protection excepting his books; if someone wants to kill me they will do so without reading my books. This Government [Awami League] may not do anything against me because they know I am not a bad man, but the mullahs don't like me; they don't like me at all, just as they don't like my old friends professors Kabir Chowdhury and Ahmed Sharif. One bullet is enough to kill a man.'

In the twilight of their years, the three men were still seen as dangerous enemies by the mullahs and their fanatical followers, who hated 'the three musketeers', as they were called by their admirers. Now in their seventies, age did not silence them and they continued to speak out against religious fanaticism—all three had publicly supported Taslima's freedom as a writer.

Yet if a man like Shamsur Rahman was not safe in his own home, then, I suspected, neither was Taslima.

Wild rumours circulated that a hit list of prominent writers (some accounts said thirty, others only three) had been compiled and that Nasreen's name was on the list, according to testimony obtained through 'interrogation' of the prisoners. Hundreds of organisations came out in the streets, marching together with thousands of individuals; the mayor of Dhaka, university teachers, religious scholars, citizens in all the major towns signed petitions and waved their banners in street processions demanding justice and protection for Shamsur Rahman.

The massive show of public support for the seventy-four-year-old poet affected me strangely—not because I didn't agree with it. He was a lion-hearted warrior, part of the country's history. It was Taslima I pitied. I couldn't help but compare Rahman's testimonial and the denunciations hurled at his attackers, with the puerile support shown to her in 1994, and again on her return in 1998.

She was not totally alone as a letter published on 3 October by a dozen prominent activists showed, but it was a human rights and a political statement lacking personal warmth, and it showed they supported her more out of principle it seemed, and perhaps also because of their respect for the Hossain family.

People felt differently about Taslima; she rarely drew their sympathy at a personal level. However, Taslima was now more than a name on a page to me and I could feel her pain. The mood of the country's intelligentsia had not softened and she was still susceptible to the ill will swirling around her, with little sign of a truce between Nasreen and the men and women who were her natural allies but seemed happy enough to forget her.

'Nobody talks about Nasreen any more,' was the response when I raised her name. 'We only think of her when you visit and ask us about her.' The kind of rejection this implies must hurt the writer. If she is ever to return permanently the secular side of politics and Nasreen must learn to coexist.

Following her mother's funeral, Taslima quietly exited the country and returned to Sweden on 25 January 1999. She was wise to leave just before the general strikes, or *hartals*, were about to paralyse the country—these strikes were not about Taslima; the opposition was trying to force the sitting Government into an early election. The Awami Government was relieved to see her go. It was winter and, as everyone knows, winter is the season of *hartals*, the season of weddings, and the season of foreign consultants and visiting authors.

The hidden story that I was so intent on unveiling emerged slowly and stubbornly. I was never blessed, or cursed, with a definitive account of what happened during those last sixty days: no single informant ever came to my rescue. Brooding over what I didn't know, and reinterpreting facts, sometimes out of sheer habit, became a way of life, like counting religious beads. Remembering how someone had smiled at a certain point in a conversation, or shook their head, or if I was in luck, passed me on to someone else who could tell me what they could not—all of this kept me going.

Taslima, as we know, was a scapegoat for both the power-hungry mullah elements and the Government, whose houses were beginning to shake by mid-1994. If there had been no Taslima then someone else would have served as a diversion. An interesting aspect surrounding Taslima's case goes back to the controversial Calcutta newspaper interview. There has never been an official inquiry of what purportedly happened, or was said, in a country outside of Bangladesh. Her lawyers have always argued that the case was improperly admitted under the Criminal Procedure Code by the BNP Government, who carried out no investigation prior to issuing the warrant for her arrest.

The Bangladesh Embassy in Calcutta most likely forwarded the Calcutta article featuring Taslima's interview to Dhaka, where it appeared in the government-trust–owned newspaper which ran a banner headline of *The Statesman* piece, which originally was a small article and never a front-page story in India. The article was then picked up by *The Inquilab*, essentially a reactionary publication, trumpeting the cause of religion, known for its anti-Indian stand.

The Inquilab translated the article from English into Bangla and ran it as a banner headline for several days. Through sheer repetition of the alleged blasphemy, it created a situation. By taking the original article out of context and ignoring the other issues in the article, the article became a flashpoint. This went on for nearly a month, and other papers joined the hunt as well. Taslima's denial in Bangladeshi papers was also covered, but did little to ease the situation. To many her explanation sounded as bad as, if not worse than, the original alleged statement, where she was supposed to have called for a revision of the Qur'an.

By now the religious demonstrators had proven that they had control of the streets even though the pro-secularists were out in equal numbers taking them on in counter rallies. And still the BNP Government turned a blind eye, making no move to curtail the demonstrations. BNP used what might have remained, without their collusion, a fringe exercise, as negligible in the end as the Soldiers of Islam 'fatwa', which dribbled into nothing and was really quite unimportant.

The Government chose instead to bolster their electoral fortunes. The Home Affairs Minister, it seemed, was not only pro-Jamaat, but also had links with many of the smaller mullah-led groups in Dhaka and held an important Cabinet position, with primary responsibility for maintaining internal security, including the police and paramilitary forces. He was the man suspected by many of being behind, or at least condoning, the orchestrated attacks against NGOs in early 1994. The police made no arrests nor undertook any investigations into the attacks on NGOs, the punishments handed out to women in remote villages, or the death threats to Taslima.

The Government's grand scheme to exploit Taslima failed. By July 1994, they knew they had blundered but seemed powerless to pull back. Nasreen was becoming a rallying point and the mobs were becoming dangerous. The BNP Government could only control the mobs by using force, which meant injuring, even killing, some of their allies. This would have been an act of political suicide. Taslima, who had no political support, was lost.

In the words of Gabi Gleichmann, the Government had, so to say, 'the choice between plague and cholera. If the charges against Nasreen were dropped, the fundamentalists would paralyse the country. Should she be punished, the country ran the risk of losing economic aid from the West.' The best solution for everyone concerned was for her to leave the country. Eventually a political arrangement was worked out between the Government and the international forces, with her lawyers brokering the deal.

'Without international intervention the Government's strategy would have worked,' says Syed Muhammad Ullah quite emphatically. A senior journalist and former editor, he now lives in New York, but continues monitoring Bangladeshi politics. I had come to rely on his political savvy and the fact that he was unafraid to speak out, although I suspected that residing most of the time in New York with his family aided his candour. He is sure that Taslima would have languished in gaol for many years, either in protective custody or as a convicted criminal. 'Everyone would have accepted the Government's version,' Ullah argues, 'and no doubt a verdict in their favour would have been handed down.'

❀

The rule of law is a fragile concept which needs protecting in the evolving democracy of Bangladesh. A senior political correspondent smiled at me when I pressed him on this subject. 'In countries like Pakistan and Bangladesh you have the rule of law and you don't have the rule of law,' he said enigmatically. 'To a great extent, the Government in power determines the course of a case.'

My informant cited two well-known cases, claiming they were not prosecuted vigorously. 'The Government can always select the officer they want to prosecute a case,' he said, 'there are enough Assistant Attorney Generals in the wings.'

His comment threw light on Taslima's case. The Attorney General who led the Government's case against Taslima on the day of her bail hearing was a respected human rights advocate. Jamaati and the smaller Islamist groups would have understood the message at two levels. Firstly, Taslima was being prosecuted by a team led by the Attorney General, a famous human rights activist totally opposed to a blasphemy law who made no secret of his opinion, which the media was quick to report. Secondly the Supreme Court was seen to have jurisdiction over the Taslima case, turning it into a different 'game' altogether.

Human Rights and the law do not always stroll hand in hand in many parts of the world, especially at the Lower Court levels. The US Department of State's report on the state of human rights practices in Bangladesh for

1998 describes how the law operates. Reading between the lines is difficult because, while it is meant to be informative, it is also couched not to give offence. 'The judiciary displays a high degree of independence at appellate levels; however, lower judicial officers fall under the executive, and are reluctant to challenge Government decisions.'

The higher levels of the judiciary were seen to be 'significantly independent' and often ruled against the Government in cases—even politically controversial cases. Yet what was the significance of the phrase 'significantly independent'?

Most corruption takes place in the Lower Courts, where magistrates preside. Bribes in the form of 'fees' are also expected to be paid. These courts are part of the administration, often more than willing to carry out the wishes of their political masters. Taslima's family usually experienced difficulties when it came to filing complaints against the men publicly threatening her with violence. Magistrates seemed to take little or no action until a complaint was filed against the author, when they moved even without investigating whether there was a case to answer or not.

To bring my quest to an end, I needed answers not found in foreign embassy reports nor inside the heads of well-meaning people wanting me to see a blemish-free Bangladeshi legal system. At last I began asking the right people the right questions so that piece by piece the story came together.

I learnt that when a new Government is elected, it often moves at a snail's pace with sensitive cases brought by its predecessors—the cases seem more dead than alive! They simply sleep on the case.

'The courts will not bring the cases themselves,' confirmed one informant. 'They will not remind the Prosecution, and if the Prosecution does not remind the court, then the court will not ask them about the case.'

It is not unknown for files to simply disappear, in the fullness of time; many friends and colleagues have borne witness. And Taslima's file? Would it one day 'disappear' by some sleight of hand?

Many high-ranking individuals took a hand in resolving the Taslima affair, some more visible than others who were forced to remain in the wings according to diplomatic conventions. Overall it was an impressive ensemble. Patience, influence, desperation all played a part. The negotiations were happening out of sight: that was the way it had to be played out to the end. Different, competing power plays were being juggled and it was difficult— some thought it impossible—to reach a consensus which would satisfy the different interests involved. But in the end, political, diplomatic and legal sleight of hand resolved the problems.

Dr Kamal Hossain was no ordinary lawyer. Formerly a popular, high ranking member of Awami, in 1993 he fell out with the party he'd been a member of for nearly a quarter of a century. The new political party he set up was the Gano Forum. Hossain had written the country's first constitution and served in a number of portfolios, including Foreign Affairs: he understood the law and he understood diplomacy. He was a man well thought of by the foreign enclaves in Dhaka and in Washington and London.

Hossain and his colleagues were not blind to what was at stake here: everyone wanted something. On the Bangladeshi side stood a BNP Government with its back to the wall; its on-again, off-again ally Jamaat, applying pressure with its new 'unofficial' electoral ally, Awami League, watching and waiting in the wings. The Awami League was successful in keeping a distance from Taslima; they could not risk being called anti-Islamic. Officially, they remained silent. Crouched in the middle of all of this, a very frightened Taslima listened, and sometimes ignored her Bangladeshi lawyers. If it hadn't been so very serious it would have resembled a farce.

To understand the tangle of organisations, interests and individuals, I divided the affair into three blocs, or zones, made up of different cliques all involved in a game of international cum literary politics.

Inside the 'Dhaka zone' you found the BNP senior politicians and party machine 'heavies'—'the boys' who run everything and always decide, in the end, what is feasible and what is not; then came Taslima's legal defence team (and perhaps representatives from the Attorney General's office) and finally, what we can loosely call certain missions from inside the Dhaka-based Foreign Diplomatic Corp. The American Ambassador, the Swedish Ambassador and possibly the French and German were the most involved. The evidence strongly suggests that all the embassies whose countries belonged to the European Union converged as well. All these different interest groups were meeting in different forums at different times, with the senior members of the Taslima legal team trying to stay on top of everything.

Each player inside the Dhaka bloc had to see to their own constituencies: deals could not be made if certain conflicts were not resolved. The BNP Government needed to consult with the right wing faction leaders of its own party, with the influential Jamaat Party leaders, and I imagine Awami were kept in the picture by Dr Kamal Hossain, or members of his legal team with Awami affiliations. The foreign missions in turn were reporting to their own ministers at home. Oh yes! And there was Taslima.

It was political horse-trading at its best. A typical scene emerged where certain points would be agreed to after a long discussion by the key negotiators, but there would be a recalcitrant party, often the Home Affairs Minister, who reportedly held out to the last and needed to be persuaded—multiply this by the number of different interests involved and you began to appreciate just how problematic it all was.

At the end of a hard day of negotiating, the foreign Ambassadors would drop by informally to have a word with the Foreign Minister, letting him know in a friendly way, of course, how the eyes of the world were watching Bangladesh, and how public opinion in the donor countries was starting to question the huge amounts of foreign aid going to a country seen in danger of falling to the Islamists, a country they were beginning to think of as having a poor human rights record.

The second bloc, the 'Taslima War Zone' was New York–based; it included American PEN and Meredith Tax, as Chair of PEN's International Women Writers' Committee and other interested parties who stepped in and out of this informal circle, with Washington staying abreast of news through its Dhaka Embassy. The NGO end was held together by Meredith Tax, who shared her information with bloc number three and had a finger on the pulse of what was happening inside Dhaka—she was too close, some PEN people in London thought.

The Third Bloc was more of a European alliance in style and politics, and involved Gabi Gleichmann as Swedish PEN, the Swedish and Norwegian governments, and a keenly interested European Parliament. Reporters sans frontières and certain individuals with links to the French-based Parliament of Writers were also part of this informal coalition.

The Dhaka players supporting Taslima held a handful of slippery cards: one by one they laid them slowly and carefully on top of each other to build a house of cards. Sometimes on bad days, when the other combatants acted impatiently, or the Government dug in its heels, the house of cards came tumbling down and then the process would have to start over again.

Taslima's side knew there were four options available to them: the Government could be persuaded to drop the case—highly unlikely; she could be brought to trial and found not guilty—untested, but also unlikely; they could turn a blind eye and allow her to leave the country illegally by crossing the border into India, where she could seek political asylum in Calcutta at the American Embassy—a solution more likely favoured by the Government, but not by her lawyers.

Or they could negotiate a legal solution enabling her to leave the country as a law-abiding citizen. This solution won out in the end, but when tensions heightened in June, the option of crossing the border into India and seeking political asylum was entertained for a short period and appears to have been the option favoured by the US and European blocs. Evidence suggests they were quietly urged along this road by Bangladeshi missions abroad. The 'crossing-the-border-to-India plan', with or without asylum at the end of the road, was appealing for the Bangladeshi Government as well—anything to get rid of the woman! Who could blame them if the fugitive ran away? The plan also had the merit of increasing the latent anti-India feeling in Bangladesh.

Taslima had her own plans, of course, and from her hiding place, as early as mid-June, was telephoning the American Embassy in Dhaka for asylum inside their walls. At the same time she was sending her dramatic midnight faxes to Meredith in New York and to friends in London, Sweden and France. After checking with Washington, the answer rocketed back. Unequivocally no! The idea was dismissed, although it continued to emerge in different guises until mid-July. The Americans remained firm: as long as Taslima remained in Dhaka, asylum was impossible. While it might have been feasible to have come to her aid before, when the religious zealots were baying for her blood, now that her own Government had issued a warrant for her arrest—well, that was a different ball game—and they gave the appearance of washing their hands of the matter.

A wild story of a mob marching on the American Embassy came over the news wires in the West. The real story revealed that a crowd of demonstrators headed in that direction but were stopped by the police long before they ever neared the embassy, which is built like Fort Knox. Any such possibility horrified the Americans, although in this example of media hype, one man's riot is another man's demonstration.

An alternative asylum idea was suggested through another third party and it involved crossing the border from Bangladesh into India. There is always a small steady stream of figures moving furtively across the border at different points, mostly at night. Smugglers know this, sex traffickers know this, everyone living near the border knows how it's done. Taslima could disguise herself, cross at a safe place, make her way to Calcutta and knock on the door of the American Embassy there, or even make straight for the airport and buy a ticket for New York. She should make sure to take her passport with her.

Running away was a plan of last resort, for by fleeing Taslima would have become a fugitive and made everything worse, not only for herself, but for many of the people assisting her. These and other faxed messages were conveyed in cryptic written form to her friends and occasionally delivered verbally to Taslima by supporters acting as couriers. It was feared that telephones in Dhaka were being bugged and so on occasions faxes to Dhaka were sent via neighbouring countries. The negotiators faced long, difficult days ahead. They had no idea that their client was acting independently and actively seeking political asylum with the United States from inside Dhaka.

The case against Taslima was never going to disappear into a puff of smoke. Amongst her cadre of lawyers in Dhaka, opinion was divided: some thought she should stay and stand trial; others thought there had to be another legal solution ensuring both her safety and the sovereignty of the country—something that the Bearded Ones might be forced to tolerate. But as long as the author remained in Dhaka, the agitation showed no sign of dying down.

Of course the asylum story was bound to leak out, and on 26 June the news broke in Dhaka that the author was actively seeking political asylum abroad, giving Meredith Tax instant notoriety, making Taslima even more unpopular and stalling negotiations. The lawyers hardly needed this extra burden and the playmakers were cautioned to be more circumspect.

Different schools of thought were beginning to emerge from the three Taslima zones. The local legal experts knew how matters stood around the bargaining table and how their countrymen hated the thought of foreign nations interfering in their internal matters and showing all the signs of bullying them.

Some Westerners at first believed that the more press coverage, the better, especially activists like Gabi and the French coterie who began their letter campaign in mid-July without informing the other circles. But no damage was caused, for the letter campaign was not picked up by the local press and it certainly turned Taslima into a household name in most of Europe.

In the end the Dhaka bloc focussed its energies on finding a legal solution, while New York, London and the Europeans concentrated on locating a safe country for Taslima. This led to the 'Swedish Plan', or an earlier prototype. Taslima would receive an invitation from Swedish PEN while she was awaiting trial and should accept it even it if meant 'turning herself in'.

Follow this advice and her safety would be guaranteed, she would not remain in custody and would be turned over to the Swedes. Implicit in this plan was the underlying threat that if things went wrong, then the donor states would rethink their aid policies and Bangladesh could expect retribution. Once Taslima was in Sweden she could move to the United States. The Government should remember that the world was watching, they were told. There were obvious gaps in the plan but at least it seemed legal. According to confidential documents, the idea was to 'focus world attention on the front door to facilitate entry through the back'. This was how matters stood in late June 1994.

Dhaka responded swiftly. Her advisers were optimistic but counselled patience to avoid increasing the hysteria of the mobs and their masters.

By now the stage was crowded and the actors were jostling each other. There were simply too many players involved, each convinced that they had the solution, each party desperate to get Taslima out of an insupportable situation. Signals were getting switched in the middle of the night and the Dhaka lawyers were becoming angered by the extra cards threatening to bring the whole edifice down. Bangladeshi missions in New York and in London were also starting to run interference and began suggesting options to end the impasse in a strange game where messages were being relayed through PEN.

By mid-July the message was clear: 'Dr Kamal's efforts and that of the diplomatic community are exclusively directed at working out a legal solution' that excluded fleeing to India by land and the door was closed once and forever on the political asylum scheme. Even entertaining the idea of leaving the country clandestinely was enough to incense her lawyers, who were so close to working out a compromise. Their interests lay in finding a judicial situation and here they were supported by the foreign diplomats in Dhaka; they wanted to hear nothing more about illegal measures or any other foolish adventures.

By late July every piece seemed in place. Only one recalcitrant player remained: the Home Minister, the man suspected of uniting the Islamic fundamentalist forces, and in the end he either fell into the spirit of things, for the good of his country's international image, or washed his hands of the whole business—or had he done some horse-trading himself?

On Taslima's side, all the conditions were met: she would fly to Europe via Bangkok; New Delhi must be avoided at all costs. She could not set down, even in transit, on Indian soil, which would feed the fiction of 'Taslima the Indian agent'. Her destination was kept secret, but they all guessed it was Sweden, and Gabi was certainly geared up to receive his guest.

Finally after a nail-biting last twenty-four hours, the agreements were honoured on both sides and Taslima quietly left her country not to return until four years later, which she was able to do legally, because she was not a fugitive.

※

And so in 1994, THE GRAND *TAMASHA*—the great spectacle— vanished into thin air as suddenly as it began. Did a political Sorcerer from the tribe of dragon magicians clap his hands and call out to the crowds: 'Enough! Go home! You have done your duty, my brothers! The *tamasha* is over—for now. We have won as much as we can. Let us bide our time.'

Perhaps the Sorcerer and his apprentices judged the moment because, as we know, the theatre was never about moral outrage, it was always about politics. Almost overnight the streets of Dhaka returned to normal, or as normal as the mega city of ten million ever gets. Both sides were resting now; the djinns were in hiding.

There was even cause for thinking that, on this occasion at least, Law outwitted Magic.

Magic and the Law—An Epilogue

Supreme Court, Dhaka
March 2000

Barristers in wigs and swirling black gowns stalk by like Shakespearian actors performing on stage. Along the verandahs of the court building, they promenade: dandies in black jackets, waistcoats and grey striped trousers. Most members of the legal profession are enjoying themselves in a show of camaraderie, but others scurry past with frowns and worried clients in their wake. Young, old, portly or thin, bearded, moustachioed—but rarely clean-shaven—the legal fraternity of the Supreme Court, represented by the cream of Bangladeshi barristers, passes before me like a hierarchy of jurisprudence.

Kamal Hossain strides by, deep in conversation with junior colleagues following in his footsteps. A few minutes later Amrul Islam, elegant as always, leads a small procession of lawyers hanging on his every word. There are more than sixty thousand lawyers in Bangladesh, but only the more senior and expert are ever allowed to tread the centre stage of the Supreme Court.

Today, another member of Taslima's legal team will petition the learned judges to dismiss a second case against his client lodged in 1998. Taslima is not required to be present. Two years ago, the Supreme Court decreed that she could be represented in absentia.

Her advocate, Idrisur Rahman, who is handling the case today, makes arrangements for me to return the next morning and watch the proceedings, which I will understand because they are in English, the language of the Supreme Court. My young legal guide, Fayazuddin Ahmad, tells me that those in the know are confident that this particular case—not to be confused with the Government's old case of 1994—will be quashed. Idrisur Rahman

259

smiles and tells me that I have arrived in Dhaka at exactly the right moment. My head is swirling; I can't believe my luck.

My euphoria is short-lived. After waiting three hours, nothing happens; it is the same the following day, when advocate Rahman arrives late. By the third day I have received a sombre lesson about the meaning of court delays, Bangladeshi style. My head is still spinning but for different reasons. It dawns on me that this petition for dismissal will not be granted today, nor for many days to come, I fear.

The entire Bangladeshi system of jurisprudence is bogged down in a backlog of cases, 600,000 in 1998 was par for the course, with approximately 37,000 persons or 71 per cent of the prison population either awaiting trial, or under trial. Lengthy adjournments are normal practice.

Nevertheless, on day three, I am optimistic that Taslima's petition will at least be heard. Fayaz suggests I remove my sunglasses and dispose of my briefcase, which is unsettling the courtroom guards, who are watching my every move. I sit in the austere, dimly lit courtroom, listening to the two Justices as a long line of advocates pleads one by one for a continuance, or bail, or some other legal decision. Fans crank slowly overhead. A courtroom clerk invites me to sit in the more comfortable area reserved for counsel. The men with whom I have been sharing a wooden bench at the back of the courtroom—at a respectful distance—are visibly relieved.

Petition follows petition.... The judges are in good form and twenty lawyers have been processed before it is 'our turn', but there is only forty-five minutes left before the session closes for the day.

The Courtroom bench officers have copies of Nasreen's book, *Selected Columns*, a prize-winning book first published in 1991. The learned judges hold copies in their hands. Surely this frivolous complaint will be thrown out, I tell myself. Sitting below the two chief justices, the bench officers are laughing to themselves as they read Nasreen's book. They nudge one another and compare excerpts, looking for the racy bits. One of the bench clerks has brought his young son to sit beside him today; the child sits staring down at us with huge round eyes, taking nothing in.

The leading Justice slowly turns the pages that the complainant, described as 'a peace-loving, simple and honest person and a Muslim by faith,' finds so offensive. His religious sentiments have been seriously wounded, the devout one claims. The remarks he finds so objectionable are related to the Islamic Laws of Succession; the taking of a second wife and the insulting way that Muslims have been described in the said book. The pages and sections are listed and everyone busies themselves reading, while the guards rub their eyes, yawn and eventually nod off.

The lead judge reads Nasreen's biography aloud; he is smiling benignly as he reads the front flap of the book to the court; he reads the petition aloud and then continues to entertain us with the preface and first chapter. He makes comments about similar incidents he's heard of. It is all rather friendly and cosy. There is no feeling of urgency. I sense that the case is not being 'taken' to the judges, who sit looking down at their audience, nodding and reading to each other. The clock ticks on. Other lawyers still waiting to be heard are not amused.

As the judge continues to recite passages, the Government prosecutor turns away to hide his laughter. He tries to catch the eye of a female colleague on the opposite side of the court. Taslima's description of how men often pay an extra twenty taka to have a woman cut their hair in some local barbershops has tickled his fancy. 'The extra twenty taka is for 'the female touch,' she writes.

Everyone, except Taslima's lawyer, is having trouble keeping a straight face; giggles break out. To my eyes at least, the judges seem to be playing with the case for the moment. Their religious feelings show no sign of injury and there is only one serious man in the court, and he is Taslima's advocate!

The courtroom interlude is a comedy of manners underscoring the coy behaviour and attitudes of a traditional society like Bangladesh where maintaining a silence over anything remotely sexual is like keeping the faith. Yet beneath the surface I catch a glimpse of something else. Silencing a writer, especially a woman writer, can be accomplished by simply laughing at her words. The laughter is an unconscious act but an insidious part of a male-dominated culture and a way of censoring women and keeping them in their place. And that is what I witnessed that day: a group of educated, liberally inclined men ridiculing, with their gentle laughter, a prize-winning bestseller. I could not imagine them treating any male writer of Taslima's stature in this way. I think Taslima would have preferred the angry shouts of Muslim fanatics who at least take her words seriously   I know I would have.

What has happened in chambers that I am not privy to? I know this is an important case, for if the High Court finally gives a ruling; it will set a direction and become a precedent in the law books. Is the delay a political manoeuvre, or part of the 'pending culture', or an amalgam of both?

Nothing is decided that day. It is deferred for eight months hence and then will be deferred once more to take its place alongside case number one, brought by the Government in 1994, which set the whole 'Taslima affair' in motion.

❈

Politics and the law will decide the future of Taslima Nasreen—but when? Until then Taslima must live with a curious impasse that is moving as slowly as the proverbial tortoise. The judiciary wants a political solution: the Government should drop the charges, they argue. Their defence is based on this premise; their arguments are convincingly worded to this end.

However, the Government, whether Awami League this year or BNP the next—it makes little difference to her case—has dug in its heels and is insisting on a judicial solution. Taslima continues to be a political liability and the Awami League Government, in power in 2000, cannot afford to— nor does it want to—intervene: it plays a strictly neutral game, as it has always done, right from the beginning of the Taslima trouble. Awami has always been strongly supported by the intelligentsia, whose anger may have abated towards Taslima, but who now seem apathetic, even indifferent. She is a writer without a constituency in her own country. As a party which has lived in the political wilderness for twenty-one years, Awami guards against being labelled 'anti-Islamic' by its political opponents. The next election (which they will lose in 2001) is less than two years away.

The lack of political will aggravates the legal stalemate. The Supreme Court wants the case dealt with by the Lower Court; her lawyers want the Higher Court to intervene. Backwards and forwards it goes, with Taslima trapped in the middle.

There will be no show trial for Taslima, as many of her supporters first wanted. When she left Bangladesh for the West, that chapter was closed. If she had remained, some of her activist critics are fond of saying, they would have supported her and she would have won. At the time could she have trusted them to do that, I wonder? Besides having had my taste of the 'pending culture', I think her case could have remained trapped between courts. With Taslima remaining in Bangladesh, the political crisis would have worsened and the calls for a blasphemy act would have reached a crescendo.

Yet in spite of the stonewalling, the rule of law continues to protect the defendant. Still as far as quashing the charges against her, the Supreme Court persistently refers this back to the Lower Courts. This deadlock between politics and the law and between the Supreme Court and the Lower Criminal Court shows no sign of shifting.

The game continues without the presence of the defendant, who con- tinues her life on the international carousel: from Sweden to France, then back to Sweden, with intermittent trips to India and the USA.

Perth, Australia, February 2001

❀

Five years later and little has changed: she continues to write and the Bangladesh Government continues to proscribe her books, turning them into best-sellers on the black market. I, in turn, continue to view Taslima as a complex and contradictory woman for reasons unrelated to her mythology. The escape story the media indulges is the invented drama of how she came to leave Bangladesh. Yet there is another escape story worth the telling: how a young woman turned her back on the unwritten laws, and reinvented herself. Certainly it didn't happen overnight and she needed help, but the single-mindedness applied in acting out her needs, and carving a niche for herself in the world of writers, would be applauded in many societies, but is not admired in her homeland, where women rarely act out their dreams in public, nor display Taslima's self-absorption.

She says that living outside her country mutes her anger; but she seems to have found a surrogate now that she is a member of the worldwide anti-Islamist movement. All the adulation she receives outside Bangladesh maintains her reputation as a free speech icon on the international humanist circuit. I am not sure if Taslima will ever return permanently to Bangladesh—or if she even wants to! People ask (as they do of Daud Haider), 'Why on earth would she want to come back? Doesn't she have everything?' Only Taslima can answer that. There are cynics who even label her an economic migrant. The overwhelming feeling is, 'Enough of Taslima! Let her stay in India with her friends.'

Only outside the borders of Bangladesh is Nasreen recognised as a protest writer, and just as the Swedes and the Germans expected Taslima to be the perfect dissident, so have her own people expected her to be the perfect Bengali woman and the perfect protest writer—morally and ideologically sound in the Bengali way. They fail to see that she has made an existence for herself out of the most desperate parts of her life. Her most recent memoirs where she reveals the sexual escapades and extramarital secrets of Dhaka's top intellectuals, some of whom she had affairs with—all of whom supported her when she began her career fourteen years ago—has widened the gap. The woman who always told her Bangladeshi friends that she lacked the skills to stand on a dais making speeches now spends much of her time doing just that.

'They hurt me; I hurt them,' she once answered in response to a question from Australian television interviewer Kerry O'Brien on the ABC *Lateline* show, who asked whether one could combat intolerance with intolerance. The interview revealed a self-involved woman who genuinely has enormous difficulties in understanding any other person's point of view; it lies beyond stubbornness.

Caught between two different worlds, Taslima needs the treasures of the West: the recognition, the resources, the support and sanctuary it offers her, but can't survive as a writer in a non-Bengali environment. Neither does Taslima belong to the new wave of writers from the Indian subcontinent who write in English and whose work is avidly read around the world; she is a Bengali writer whose work must be translated if it is to reach an international audience; her good fortune remains that Bengali is a major language in India. Her mother tongue is called Bangla in Bangladesh.

✿

Two deliberate tactics were employed by the Indian and Western media in 1994 to promote Taslima. One compared Taslima with Salman Rushdie, and the other compared Bangladesh to Iran. There were dozens of women writers the freedom of expression activists could have chosen, to raise on high, but they chose Nasreen, partly because they could distil her experience into a Rushdie-like analogy and because she told them what they wanted to hear, by feeding a latent anti-Islamic prejudice. In a strange way Taslima Nasreen has been punished by two conflicting myths: the first turned her into a saint, the other demonised her—the madonna and the whore all over again.

In media jargon, a story strong enough to run for a long time is said to have legs. Nasreen's story originally had more legs than a centipede: fanatics, fatwas, death threats, banned books, freedom of expression. . . . A market existed for Taslima and she was created for that market by a media frustrated by the Rushdie–Iran impasse. The religious militants obliged by putting on a huge *tamasha* for one and all: a show with marching crowds and snake charmers happy to join in the circus with their pets coiled around their necks. The Western media saw the demonstrations through the eyes of their camera lens—Bangladeshis saw the demonstrations through different eyes.

Taslima the martyr and Nasreen the author have always been good box office for campaigners. The mythmakers of 1994 inflated Nasreen's image at the cost of deflating every other voice engaged in the same battle and, inside Bangladesh, this still rankles, for Taslima shares the stage with no one, not even famous human rights activists of the past and the present—men and women—who still do daily battle against obscurantist forces.

The first Taslima campaign was Indian and commercially motivated; the second campaign was global and ideologically motivated by mainly European activists with strong media links, 'enchanted by the goodness of their motives'; the third campaign is managed by humanists and atheists who have adopted Taslima and at whose forums she receives standing ovations. These days, however, she must work a lot harder, for the media has moved on to fresh game.

The Taslima affair gave rise to a form of counter fundamentalism as intellectually and as morally questionable as the fatwa variety. At the time it was short-lived, but while it lasted, every word that fell from Taslima's lips was accepted without question. As happened with Rushdie in the UK, attempting to find the middle ground in a situation of two extremes was always a doomed position from the start.

Belief and expression flow easily along comfortable streams in the West: debates are rational affairs, emotions are kept in check, lives are not at risk. The ground realities are different in the Indian subcontinent. Writers cannot cut themselves off from the consequences of what they write. You cannot ridicule and criticise religion without expecting a reaction. Taslima has the right to express herself; she has always excelled at eliciting reactions even more aggressive than her own words, so she has known what to expect. Yet Taslima, under the law of the land, has been charged, while the men threatening her life have walked away scot-free. Given her unpopularity and the mystique of the religious card in Bangladesh politics, I think these double standards are unlikely to change in the future.

What does life hold for her? The ideal situation for Taslima is to live in Calcutta surrounded by her friends and fans; her books continue to sell very well in India, and in the last seven years she has written one novel and four memoirs of a planned seven-part autobiography. Both her parents are now dead and other relatives have emigrated to the USA. As a writer she needs a sense of place and her own language to continue writing, and the Indian city of Calcutta, in the State of West Bengal, is where she wants to live.

While her love affair with Calcutta is constant—it is the circle she has always yearned to be part of and the recognition she receives there, she will never find in Bangladesh; it seems an on-again, off-again affair with the Central Government in New Delhi (the Hindu-based BJP is no longer in power). Both Federal and State Governments worry about communal tensions between Hindus and Muslims and her anti-Islam themes; in 2003 a ban was placed on one of her memoirs by the West Bengal State Government, only to be lifted by the Calcutta High Court in September 2005.

There are occasions when the Federal Indian Government has its own political problems, so there are times when Taslima is made welcome and granted a visa and there are times when the door is closed, which happened in early 2005 when she applied for citizenship, or a long-term residential permit visa, and was refused on both counts. In September 2005 the government partially relented and she received a twelve-month tourist visa.

Taslima was again in trouble and her old support base was fragmenting—well might Indian writers laugh when she outed their brother writers across the border, but they squirmed when her writerly attention turned to their own sexual peccadillos. Most of these men have strong connections with Ananda Bazar and Taslima now has a new Indian publisher.

Internationally Taslima remains a relevant voice in a post–September 11 world where many see Islam and terrorism as synonomous. In 2004 she

made first-round nominations among one hundred and ninety-nine nomi-
nees for the Nobel Peace Prize. In the same year she received an UNESCO
prize for her promotion of tolerance and non-violence; this news was received in Bangladesh with stunned disbelief by progressive men and women,
followed by some minor protests from a few mullah-led groups.

Perhaps one day there will be a movement to bring Taslima home and the
government of the day will listen to the voices; this is all in my imagination
for there are no signs of this at present. Moving too close to India without
reaching a truce with the progressive elements in Bangladesh is a dangerous
card to play, it leaves her permanently estranged from her countrymen.

There are times in Bangladesh when I am embarrassed to mention the
author's name. My journalist friends, my feminist contacts, and the NGO
workers that I know are so committed to keeping their country secular and
democratic, so focussed on a hundred and one urgent issues and projects for
illiterate and impoverished men and women—how can Taslima be anything
but irrelevant to their concerns? *The Daily Star* paper reports in 1999 that
'the race is on now to save between 18 and 24 million people who face
death by arsenic poisoning' [from tube wells]. In the same year a World
Bank survey covering 10 per cent of the country's 4 million wells found
40 per cent of the wells contaminated with arsenic. Taslima is the forgotten
woman and I am not surprised.

In 2002 a local magistrate in Gopalganj sentenced Taslima in absentia to one
year's imprisonment for wounding yet another 'devout Muslim's religious
feelings.' She knew nothing of the case, was unrepresented and sentenced
in absentia—it no doubt served some local fanatic's agenda but was another
way of keeping her away. I doubt Taslima will lose much sleep over her nonsensical sentence from the hinterlands of Bangladesh, but it again illustrates
that, outside Dhaka, the rule of law is fragile.

My local friends tell me that in the end it all comes down again to a
question of political will. If the 'Party Big Boys', as they are called, wanted
to ensure Taslima's safety beyond police protection, which is often more
symbolic than effective, they have only to declare a 'Hands off Taslima'
edict and this would be obeyed by the *goondahs* paid to do the party's
dirty work—enforcement tactics. If the party power brokers of the elected
government of either party, who decide what is politically viable and what
is not, decide in her favour, then she will be safe. For the moment, at least,
Taslima Nasreen is a political nuisance it can do without.

So it seems that the politicians and her own people don't know what to do
with Taslima Nasreen, and India is not always comfortable with her literary

gaze either. Don't expect Taslima to blink: she knows how to confront and to expose; there are no signs that she is interested in learning how to co-exist.

❈

In early March 2006 Taslima joins with her old allies Salman Rushdie, French philosopher Henri-Bernard Levy and a cast of other exiled/expatriate writers who sign a manifesto calling for resistance to religious totalitarianism. 'After having overcome fascism, Nazism, and Stalinism, the world now faces a new global threat: Islamism,' they write. They are responding to the 2006 Danish cartoon mocking the Prophet Muhammad and the violent overreactions which it aroused in some Muslim societies.

The reaction in Bangladesh was level headed: parliamentary speeches calling for an apology and emotional rhetoric from local mullahs but the government ensured that protests were kept peaceful.

I hear little of Taslima these days and what information I glean comes from the Internet. My friends in Dhaka never mention her name and seem surprised that I still think of her—twelve years on she remains more a part of my life than theirs.

'It's time for you to move on,' they tell me. 'Time to close the book on Taslima.'

Melbourne, Australia, April 2006

Index

About the Author

HANIFA DEEN is Senior Research Fellow at the Centre for Muslim Minorities at Monash University. An award-winning Australian author of Pakistani-Muslim ancestry who writes narrative nonfiction and lives in Melbourne, Deen has held a number of high-profile positions in a career spanning twenty-three years in human rights, ethnic affairs, and immigration, including: Hearing Commissioner with the Human Rights and Equal Opportunity Commission of Australia; Deputy Commissioner of Multicultural Affairs Western Australia; and a Director of Special Broadcasting Services (SBS) Corporation. She now works full-time as a writer, which she sees as the perfect medium for a woman with an irreverent tongue, a maverick-Muslim perspective on life, and a passion to subvert stereotypes wherever they lurk.